# Corporate Governance

Corporate governance is an active area of research and public debate. The recent generalization of "shareholder value" ideas and institutional investment, the establishment of codes of best practice for boards of directors, and the controversy about whether market-oriented, bank-oriented, or relations-based systems are better for economic performance provide cogent examples. The outcome of the debate is important for industrialized nations, developing countries, and transition economies. The volume takes stock of the most recent research in the topic, criticizes the standard agency view, and presents new ideas and analysis about the role of competition, the political economy of corporate governance, the effects of different systems on growth and performance, the governance system by venture capital in Silicon Valley, and human capital and control in the new corporation.

Xavier Vives is Director and Research Professor of Economics, Institut d'Anàlisi Econòmica (CSIC), Barcelona, and Research Fellow of the Centre for Economic Policy Research (CEPR). He has taught at Harvard University, New York University, Universitat Autònoma de Barcelona, Universitat Pompeu Fabra, the University of California at Berkeley, and the University of Pennsylvania, and he has been Director of the Industrial Organization Program of CEPR (1991–1997). Professor Vives's fields of interest are industrial organization, information and uncertainty, and banking and financial economics. He has published in the main international journals and edited several books. Professor Vives is the author of *Oligopoly Pricing: Old Ideas and New Tools* (MIT Press, 2000), co-editor of *Capital Markets and Financial Intermediation* (Cambridge University Press, 1993), and now serves as editor of the *European Economic Review*, co-editor of the *Journal of Economics and Management Strategy*, and associate editor of the *Rand Journal of Economics* and the *Journal of Financial Markets*. He is a Fellow of the Econometric Society and has received several prizes, including the Premio Juan Carlos I in 1988 for research in social science and the Societat Catalana de Economia Prize in 1996.

T0312114

# Corporate Governance

Theoretical and Empirical Perspectives

*Edited by*

## XAVIER VIVES

Institut d'Anàlisi Econòmica, CSIC, Barcelona

CAMBRIDGE
UNIVERSITY PRESS

CAMBRIDGE UNIVERSITY PRESS
Cambridge, New York, Melbourne, Madrid, Cape Town, Singapore, São Paulo

Cambridge University Press
The Edinburgh Building, Cambridge CB2 2RU, UK

Published in the United States of America by Cambridge University Press, New York

www.cambridge.org
Information on this title: www.cambridge.org/9780521781640

First published 2000
This digitally printed first paperback version 2006

*A catalogue record for this publication is available from the British Library*

*Library of Congress Cataloguing in Publication data*
Corporate governance : theoretical and empirical perspectives / edited by Xavier Vives.
p.   cm.
Includes index.
ISBN 0-521-78164-7
1. Corporate governance.   I. Vives, Xavier.
HD2741.C779      2000
658.4 – dc21                                                              99-059175

ISBN-13  978-0-521-78164-0 hardback
ISBN-10  0-521-78164-7 hardback

ISBN-13  978-0-521-03203-2 paperback
ISBN-10  0-521-03203-2 paperback

The Institut Català de Finances, founded in 1985, is a public credit
institution which is owned 100% by the Generalitat de Catalunya. To
date it has granted close to 1,000 million euro in loans and guarantees
for investment projects, mostly to small and medium-sized
enterprises in the industrial and service sectors.

# Contents

CONTENTS

# Preface

Corporate governance is an active area of research and public debate. The recent generalization of "shareholder value" ideas and institutional investment, the establishment of codes of best practice for boards of directors and the controversy about whether market-oriented or bank-oriented or relations-based systems are best for economic performance are examples of the interest in the topic. The outcome of the debate is important as well for developing countries and transition economies.

The present volume contains papers presented at a conference on "New Ideas in Corporate Governance," held in Barcelona in October 1998, organized by the Institut d'Anàlisi Econòmica (CSIC) and sponsored by the Institut Català de Finances (Generalitat de Catalunya).

The aim of the volume is to present new developments, theoretical and empirical, in the study of corporate governance. The volume opens with an introduction to the topic, taking stock of received knowledge, summarizing the contribution of the different chapters, and offering a point of view about the relevance of corporate governance. The following chapters deal with the role of competition and its interaction with corporate governance, the political economy of corporate governance, the effects of different corporate governance systems on growth and performance, the governance system by venture capital in Silicon Valley, and human capital and control in the new corporation.

I am grateful to the Institut Català de Finances for making this project possible, in particular to its director Ernest Sena, and also to Gemma Gimeno, and to Angela Hernández for efficient secretarial assistance.

# Contributors

Franklin Allen
Department of Finance, The
   Wharton School
University of Pennsylvania

Masahiko Aoki
Department of Economics
Stanford University

Marco Betch
ECARE
Free University of Brussels

Wendy Carlin
Department of Economics
University College London

Douglas Gale
Department of Economics
New York University

Miguel A. García-Cestona
Department of Economics
Universitat Autònoma de
   Barcelona

Martin Hellwig
Department of Political
   Economics
University of Mannheim

Carmen Matutes
Institute of Economic Analysis
CSIC, Barcelona

Colin Mayer
Said Business School of
   Management Studies
University of Oxford

Jorge Padilla
Center for Monetary and
   Financial Studies
CEMFI, Madrid

Raghuram G. Rajan
Graduate School of Business
University of Chicago

Joan Enric Ricart
IESE, Barcelona

Vicente Salas
Department of Economics
University of Zaragoza

Monika Schnitzer
Department of Economics
University of Munich

Andrei Shleifer
Department of Economics
Harvard University

Xavier Vives
Institute of Economic Analysis
CSIC, Barcelona

Luigi Zingales
Graduate School of Business
University of Chicago

# CHAPTER 1

# Corporate Governance: Does It Matter?

## XAVIER VIVES

## I. Introduction

The influential work of Berle and Means (1932) suggested that the modern corporation was run by professional managers who were unaccountable to dispersed shareholders. This pointed to a narrow view of corporate governance (CG): how to ensure that managers follow the interests of shareholders. This view fits in the principal–agent paradigm. The principals (shareholders) have to solve an adverse selection problem: select good managers. They also have to solve a moral hazard problem: check that the managers put forth appropriate effort and make decisions aligned with the interests of shareholders (for example, taking the right amount of risk and not pursuing their own private benefits). "Somewhat more generally we can define corporate governance as the set of methods to ensure that investors (suppliers of finance, shareholders, or creditors) get a return on their money." (Shleifer and Vishny 1997)

More recently a broader definition of corporate governance, related to the concept of the stakeholder society, is gaining ground (see, for example, Kay 1996). A firm has many stakeholders other than its shareholders: employees, customers, suppliers, and neighbors, whose welfare must be taken into account. Corporate governance would refer then to the design of institutions to make managers internalize the welfare of stakeholders in the firm (Tirole 1999).

The interest in the topic is not only academic. There is a lively debate about how to improve corporate governance practices, with codes of best practice for boards of directors (Calpers in the United States, Cadbury in the United Kingdom, Vienot in France, Olivencia in Spain), for example, and about which system of CG is better, market oriented versus bank oriented or relations based being the principal models. The outcome of the debate is important as well for developing countries and transition economies. The topic is charged furthermore from the busi-

I am grateful to Ramon Caminal and Masako Ueda for providing useful comments on this chapter.

1

ness ethics point of view and has close connections with political economy issues.

As we will see in this book, there is limited evidence of the effectiveness of internal and external mechanisms of governance, managers seem to get their way most of the time, nonprofit institutions fare well in competition with for-profit firms, and other factors, like competition in the product market, seem to be more important for economic performance. According to this view different systems of CG are more or less on an equal footing in terms of economic efficiency. All this points to a puzzle in which the main question is: Does corporate governance matter?

In this chapter I start in Section 2 by reviewing briefly the main features of the existing CG systems. In Section 3 I consider the standard agency approach to CG from the theoretical and empirical perspectives. After taking stock of the received knowledge, the new ideas contributed by the authors in the volume are reviewed. Section 4 presents a criticism of the standard view by Allen and Gale (Chapter 2) on the role of competition, and by Hellwig (Chapter 3) on the political economy of CG. Section 5 introduces new results by Carlin and Mayer (Chapter 4) on the effect of CG on economic performance, Aoki (Chapter 5) on the role of venture capital as CG mechanism, and Rajan and Zingales (Chapter 6) on CG in the new corporation. The concluding remarks contain a personal assessment of corporate governance systems and the necessary development of a research agenda.

## II. An Overview of Corporate Governance Systems

In a broad (and somewhat impressionistic) sense we can distinguish between market-oriented (mostly the US and the UK) versus bank-oriented or relations-based systems (continental Europe with Germany as main model and Japan). In the latter system firms and banks enter into long-term relationships as opposed to the arm's-length finance associated to market-oriented regimes.

In the United Kingdom and the United States large companies are listed in stock markets and have their ownership dispersed among institutional and individual investors (ownership concentration is modest), there is a market for corporate control (in which the threat of a hostile takeover is important), and banks play a limited role. (In the United States the Glass–Steagall Act, repealed in November 1999, kept banks out of CG – they could not own equity – but in the United Kingdom banks could have gotten involved and they chose not to do so.) Furthermore, there are limitations on cross holdings so that competition in the product market is not restricted. In theory corporate governance works balancing internal controls (such as the board of directors) with external ones (such as hostile takeovers).

In continental Europe, and for that matter outside the Anglo-Saxon world, most companies are private, the ownership of listed companies is highly concentrated, and family ownership is very important, hostile takeovers are rare, and pyramidal control schemes are common (La Porta, López-de-Silanes, and Shleifer 1999).[1] Bank ownership of equity is important only in some countries.[2]

In Germany there is concentrated ownership, large commercial banks control companies through proxy votes, and there are family owners for smaller companies. The *hausbank* of a firm plays a monitoring role and organizes proxy votes. Furthermore, there is a two-tiered system of company board for public corporations over 500 employees, which is consistent with the stakeholder society idea. There is a supervisory board (in a codetermination regime with a 50 percent worker representation, the other 50 percent being other major stakeholders including suppliers and customers) and a management board. In France there is a choice between the Anglo-Saxon and the German system of boards (the first, which predominates, with mostly outside directors – typically nominated by incumbent management). In any case workers are observers in the board. There is also a tradition of government intervention coupled with cross-shareholdings (with a system of *noyeau dur* or core investors) and revolving door for bureaucrats.[3]

In Japan the main bank system is in place. A long-term relationship between the bank and the client firm is established, the bank holds both debt and equity of the firm, and intervenes when the firm is in financial distress. Shareholders have more rights in theory than in the Anglo-Saxon world, but in practice the chief executive officer is in control. Boards are large and have a very limited number of outside directors.

It is important to emphasize that, although in all developed countries the level of legal protection to investors is high, there are important differences between civil and common law systems (La Porta et al. 1998).

Legal protection measures the quality of corporate governance in at least three ways:

[1] La Porta et al. (1999) examine ownership and control in the 20 largest publicly traded firms in the richest 27 countries. Controlling shareholders typically use pyramidal schemes and management participation to obtain power over and above their cash flow rights.

[2] Bank control through equity is important in Belgium, Germany, Sweden, Portugal, Greece, and Spain.

[3] See OECD (1995). However, according to La Porta et al. (1999) cross-share holdings in the control chain are significant only in Germany, Austria, and Sweden.

i The rights of shareholders (the right to vote on important matters, such as mergers or the election of board of directors, and protective measures such as vote by mail, suppression of nonvoting shares, and the protection of minority interests). Managers have a fiduciary duty to shareholders in Organization for Economic Cooperation and Development (OECD) countries (with the United States being tough on managers in the interpretation of the duty).

ii The rights of creditors, in terms of repossession of assets or collateral, priority in getting their money back, and limiting or eliminating the intervention of managers in a reorganization.

iii The level and quality of law enforcement and the standards of accounting.

La Porta et al. (1998) argue that common law countries dominate in all aspects French civil law countries in terms of the legal protection of investors (with German and Scandinavian civil law countries faring in between). The quality of law enforcement is highest in Scandinavia and German civil law countries and lowest in French civil law countries. The authors also find that the concentration of ownership in large public companies is inversely related to investor protection. Furthermore, in countries with low investor protection, capital markets are smaller and narrower (La Porta et al. 1997).

## III. The Agency Approach to Corporate Governance: Where Do We Stand?

A standard approach is to view CG as helping to overcome the incentive problems between an entrepreneur or manager and outside financiers. The basic agency problem is between a principal or principals (investors or financiers or, more generally, stakeholders) and the agent (manager or entrepreneur) due the presence of moral hazard or adverse selection.

Let us concentrate on the relationship between the owners and the manager. The contract between shareholders and the manager leaves the latter a lot of discretion because the manager has the knowledge and the ability to run the company. The consequence is that the manager may engage in all kinds of behavior that are detrimental to the firm: pure theft (for example, by setting up a company and using transfer pricing to appropriate funds); enjoying private benefits of control (perks, pet projects, empire building, and favoring friends and family); entrenchment (to protect the private benefits of control); exerting insufficient effort;

and taking biased decisions (too much or too little risk taking, for example).

There is some evidence pointing to the severity of the agency problem. Jensen (1986) found that in the oil industry free cash flow was reinvested in the presence of poor investment opportunities instead of returning it to investors. The returns of a bidder for a firm are often negative when the acquisition is announced (and more if the motive of the manager is diversification or growth, see Morck et al. 1990). Managers tend to resist takeovers to protect private benefits of control. Control is valued: the shares with superior voting rights trade at a premium. In general, owner-controlled firms tend to do better than manager-controlled firms (Short 1994).

The result of the agency problem is that investors will be reluctant to put funds. It is well established that because of the agency problem external finance is more costly than internal funds (Myers and Majluf 1984). A positive net present value project may not be funded when the entrepreneur does not have enough inside capital (internal funds) or the agency problem is severe (for example, private benefits of control are high).[4] CG attempts to solve or alleviate the problem. The methods are the provision of incentives, the exercise of monitoring or control, and legal protection. We have already discussed the effect of the latter.

*Provision of Incentives*
Incentives can be monetary or based on career concerns and have to be based on an observable measure of performance (better if it is verifiable in court). This performance measure can be absolute or relative to the performance of rivals or the market.

*Monetary* incentives (executive compensation) may be based on accounting data (bonuses for targets on sales, cost reduction, profits, . . . ) or on market data (share ownership, stock options).[5]

Rewards and punishments with regard to the *career* of the manager are decisions about promotion, tenure, or threat of dismissal. The optimal contract will take into account, among other things, the risk aversion of the manager and the effect of his or her decisions on the firm.

However, there are problems associated with the implementation of incentive contracts, because they can be manipulated by the management. Examples include manipulating accounting data or controlling the release of information to favor stock option payments, or capturing the board of directors or the accounting procedure. Furthermore, limited

---

[4] Tirole (1999) provides a simple moral hazard model to illustrate this point.
[5] Diamond and Verrecchia (1982) and Hölmstrom and Tirole (1993) study-reward schemes dependent on the share price.

liability of stock owners may induce excessive risk taking (from the point of view of other stakeholders).

In practice, the literature has found a small sensitivity of executive compensation to the share price (Jensen and Murphy 1990), although this may be optimal due to risk aversion (Haubrich 1994). New studies find a stronger relationship between CEO compensation and performance (Hall and Liebman 1998). There are large differences in executive pay in different countries (higher in the US than in Europe, where it is in turn higher than in Japan), but the sensitivity of pay and dismissal to performance is similar in the three geographic areas (Kaplan 1994a,b).[6] There is little relative performance evaluation (Hall and Liebman 1998) and little "bonding" of managers (for example, in terms of pension plans contingent on performance). However, perhaps relative performance evaluation is important in hiring and firing decisions.

## Monitoring and Control

Monitoring and control take basically two forms: passive (or "exit") and active (or "voice").

*Passive* control aims at measuring better the manager's performance (rather than trying to increase the value of the projects of the firm). The basic idea is that better information reduces the agency problem by reducing the incentive cost (the compensation to the manager for performance) (Tirole 1999). Informative signals can come from the stock market. For example, an institutional investor or pension fund disinvests ("exits") if performance is poor. There is presently a debate about the role of institutional investors, their degree of activism, and whether investment managers are short-termist and take biased decisions.[7] Another form of exit is the nonrenewal of a short-term loan to the firm by a financial institution.

*Active* control is made with the board of directors, by a large shareholder, a large creditor, or the market for corporate control.

## Board of Directors

The evidence points at boards of directors dominated by management. However, having a moderate number of inside directors tends to improve profitability (Bhagat and Black 1998) and if the board is dominated by outside directors it may remove top management after poor performance. In general there is mixed evidence on the effectiveness of

---

[6] However, turnover and compensation in Japan are more sensitive to negative earnings.
[7] See Gompers and Metrick (1998) for an analysis of institutional ownership.

boards of directors because of passiveness. In spite of having different CG systems, the turnover in boards after bad performance is similar in Japan, Germany, and the United States.[8]

Institutional investors are being more active, putting pressure on poor management, imposing changes like reduction in pay for managers, reducing the size of the board, and teaming up with others to change management.

*Large Shareholders*
Concentration of ownership improves the control of managers (by overcoming free ride problems in corporate control (Jensen and Meckling 1976; Grossman and Hart 1980, 1988; Shleifer and Vishny 1986), but it creates private benefits of control and a large shareholder may hurt the interests of small shareholders or debtholders. Controlling shareholders must retain important cash flow rights to have an incentive to monitor management and maximize profits. Otherwise (for example, if control is exerted with a pyramid scheme where control is decoupled from cash flow rights), controlling shareholders will be concerned with appropriating private benefits of control instead. Furthermore, the expropriation of other stakeholders creates adverse incentive effects (such as less investment in firm-specific capital and reduced incentives of the manager to invest and take initiative (Burkart, Gromb, and Panunzi 1997;[9] Rajan 1992). Other factors related to ownership concentration are the trade-off between liquidity and control (Bolton and von Thadden 1988); risk-taking incentives biased toward too much risk; and collusion with managers to expropriate minority interests.

On the positive side, the evidence of La Porta et al. (1999) suggests that in large firms (except the United States perhaps) the problem of separation of ownership and control is not the classical Berle and Means problem (of dispersed shareholders not being able to control management) but the potential expropriation of minority interests by large controlling shareholders. Indeed, those authors find the following: (1) Even the largest firms have, in general, owners (outside the United States), which are typically families or the State. (2) Controlling shareholders have control rights well in excess of cash flow rights because of pyramid schemes or because they manage the firms they control. (3) Significant

---

[8] In Japan, after poor performance, firms are most likely to receive new directors with links to their main bank (Kaplan 1994a).

[9] Too much control may be bad because if management does not get enough rents it will not perform. The problem is that it is not possible to commit to compensate the manager. In this case the discretion of the manager may be good because then he or she has an incentive to acquire and use information.

bank ownership is infrequent. (4) There is little separation between ownership and control in family-controlled firms.

On the normative side, the evidence on the effect of large shareholders is mixed. On the one hand, large shareholders seem to improve performance in Germany (Franks and Mayer 1997) and Japan, where the main bank system eases liquidity constraints and reduces agency costs (Hoshi, Kashyap, and Scharfstein 1990, 1991; Aoki and Patrick 1994). However, the evidence is disputed (Hayashi 1997) and bank control raises the cost of finance and extracts rents from the firm (Weinstein and Yafeh 1998). Similarly, when Japanese firms were allowed to borrow in the capital market, their net worth increased (Hoshi et al. 1993). Evidence in favor of the monitoring role of banks is weak. In Japan banks intervene only when the firm is in distress and bank-dependent firms suffer more when the stock market declines (Kang and Stulz 1997). In Germany banks exert modest control via proxy votes and presence in supervisory boards, and German banks tend to control themselves. The effectiveness of bank involvement seems to have been overemphasized (Edwards and Fischer 1994, Wenger and Kaserer 1998). Finally, managerial ownership of equity beyond a certain level is bad for performance (Nickell, Nicolitsas, and Dryden 1997).

*Large Creditors*
Debt is another instrument to discipline managers and reduce agency costs. The failure to repay implies the transfer of control from the manager to the creditor.[10] Debt holders are tough on managers after default (Dewatripont and Tirole 1994) because they are conservative (they have a concave objective). In contrast, in good times control should go to shareholders, who like risk (they have a convex objective). According to Jensen's (1986) free cash flow theory, debt increases the probability of default and the manager works hard to avoid it. Leveraged buyouts (LBO) where managers purchase firms and finance it with debt may have similar effects. Proposed as mechanisms that ensure (some) repayment of the debt are reputation (Diamond 1989) and the threat of liquidation in the event of default (Hart 1995).

There are problems associated with the use of debt. Among them are debt overhang, where the manager does not choose a good project because most returns will go to debt holders (Myers 1977), and excessive incentive to take risk (Jensen and Meckling 1976). Furthermore, a bank with monopoly power may extract rents from firms with high loan rates.

---

[10] This can be modeled assuming costly state verification or incomplete contracts.

The evidence shows that public debt is not used much, whereas bank debt is used more. LBOs (which should be seen as a temporary financing tool) reduce agency costs that take the form of excessive size and diversification (conglomerates). There is also some evidence that debt improves productivity (Nickell et al. 1997).

*Market for Corporate Control*

The instruments of the market for corporate control are proxy contests, friendly mergers, and hostile takeovers. Takeovers may be complementary with internal control mechanisms (board dismissals) to discipline management (Hirshleifer and Thakor 1998). Hostile takeovers are important in the United States and the United Kingdom (although they first appeared only in 1956) but not elsewhere (see Prowse 1995; Franks and Mayer 1992, 1993). Even in the United States there have been only three waves of takeover activity, starting in the 1960s. Takeovers peaked in the late '80s, then they were replaced by downsizing and restructuring. Recently there is a comeback of merger and acquisitions and takeover activity.

There are several problems associated with takeovers as a control mechanism: free riding makes them expensive (Grossman and Hart 1980); there may be excessive bidder competition to obtain private benefits of control; managers may get entrenched with antitakeover tactics; takeovers need a liquid capital market (junk bonds helped in this respect); and finally, they may be blocked by political concerns promoting national champions in Europe or by antitakeover laws in the United States.

The evidence of the effect of takeovers is mixed. Takeover targets typically are poor performers (Morck, Shleifer, and Vishny 1988, 1989). Takeovers tend to increase the combined value of target and acquirer. However, while the target's shareholders gain, the raider's shareholders do not (Jensen and Ruback 1983), and some of the gains come from the employees. Furthermore, there is scant evidence that operating performance increases after a takeover (Ravenscraft and Scherer 1987).

## IV. Criticism of the Standard View

The standard view of CG helping to solve agency concerns that arise because of the need of outside finance is not without problems.

We have already seen that a clear relation between different CG systems and economic performance does not emerge from the empirical studies and that theory provides effects of CG instruments that go in different directions. There is no strong evidence that CG mechanisms (be they internal, monitoring, or external, market based) are effective.[11]

Other factors that the theory must confront are the following:

a  Internal finance is very important. Even a large stock market capitalization in an economy may be just an indication of high retained earnings (see Chapter 3 of this book, by Hellwig).
b  The corporate finance problem may be more of misallocation than scarcity of funds to be conveyed from households to firms. That is, funds should be distributed from firms with excess cash to those with excess investment opportunities (Hellwig, Chapter 3). Inefficient cross subsidization of divisions in conglomerate firms would be an example of the problem (Rajan, Servaes, and Zingales 1999).
c  Nonprofit firms, despite their weak governance mechanisms, compete successfully with for-profit firms (Allen and Gale, Chapter 2). Examples in the United States are health care and universities (most of which are nonprofit); and in the financial sector mutual savings and loans (formally controlled by depositors or by a mixture of depositors, founding institutions, and local government).[12]

Let us consider in turn the role of competition as a substitute for corporate governance mechanisms (Allen and Gale, Chapter 2) and the hypothesis that CG is explained best by political economy considerations as the outcome of the interests of insiders to the firm (Hellwig, Chapter 3).

### 4.1. The Role of Competition

It has been argued that competition in the product market may act as a substitute for CG mechanisms or, at least, that in competitive markets CG loses importance in terms of enhancing economic efficiency.

There is by now a literature that supports the role of competition in enhancing efficiency. The role of competition is to provide information (on the cost structure of firms, for example) and enlarged opportunities of comparison, and therefore stronger incentives. For example, the increase in the proportion of entrepreneurial firms in a market may reduce managerial slack (Hart 1983) although certain conditions must be fulfilled (Scharfstein 1988; Hermalin 1992). In an intertemporal

---

[11] This message is emphasized by Allen and Gale in Chapter 2 of this book.

[12] A potential explanation of the good performance of nonprofit institutions is that weak control leaves stakeholders with substantial rents and, in consequence, they have incentives to invest in the institution.

framework the effect of competition on managerial effort is positive if productivity shocks across competitors are more correlated than managers' abilities (Meyer and Vickers 1985). A source of ambiguity on the effect of competition on managers' effort to reduce costs is that enhanced competition tends to reduce profits (which is bad to induce effort) but increases margin pressure (which is good to induce effort) (Willig 1987). However, when competition increases the probability of liquidation, the manager works hard to avoid it (and the profit reduction effect is important only if the manager is paid more than his reservation wage (Schmidt 1997).[13]

Allen and Gale (Chapter 2) acknowledge the role of competition and question the agency approach (particularly in its moral hazard aspect rather than in its adverse selection aspect). The authors favor an evolutionary argument according to which competition eliminates inefficient firms: if managers waste resources, the firm will not be able to survive in the long run and all stakeholders will suffer. Badly run firms will not survive and the market will be taken over by efficient firms. This argument goes back at least to Alchian (1950) and Stigler (1958).[14] The explanation of Allen and Gale (Chapter 2) for the comparable performance of different CG systems as well as for-profit and nonprofit firms is the disciplining effect of product market competition.

Evidence on the positive effects of competition for technical efficiency, productivity, and productivity growth and innovative activity is accumulating (Nickell 1996 and Nickell et al. 1997; Blundell, Griffith, and Van Reenen 1995; Caves and Barton 1990; Graham, Kaplan, and Sibley 1983; Porter 1990). There is also evidence on the substitutability between CG and competition. Nickell et al. (1997), with data from the United Kingdom, find that dominant or large external shareholder control, financial pressure (debt), and competition contribute to increased productivity growth and that the first two effects can substitute for the latter. That is, competitive pressure is important for efficiency when corporate governance is weak. Similarly, Aghion and Howitt (1996) find a stronger

---

[13] Aghion, Dewatripont, and Rey (1998) show that the effect of competition on the incentives for cost reduction may depend on the level of outside finance needed by the firm. If the need is low (high), then more competition may lead to less (more) effort. The nature of strategic interaction changes from one regime to the other. Hermalin (1994) shows that asymmetric equilibria in terms of organizational form (incentive structure) among firms competing in a market may arise due to nonconvexities introduced by the agency problem between a firm and its manager. That is, a best response to rival firms providing strong incentives to their managers may be to provide weak incentives to their own manager.

[14] The traditional argument by Friedman (1953) and Machlup (1967) is that competition among firms will select profit maximizers.

positive effect of competition on growth in firms with weak shareholder control. Finally, in assessing the relative efficiency of private versus public firms, what seems to matter most is whether firms operate in a competitive environment (more than the form of property).

## 4.2. The Political Economy of Corporate Governance

According to Hellwig (Chapter 3), the view of CG as an ex ante efficient, incentive-compatible contract is problematic because managers (or insiders in general) have the incentive and the ability to manipulate the game form. In consequence, the applied mechanism design as well as the incomplete contracts approaches are not without problems.

Insiders try to immunize themselves from the interference of outsiders to preserve their autonomy. They have available many instruments to accomplish this: nonvoting shares, name shares, limitations on voting rights, pyramid schemes, cross holdings, changes in corporate charters, and antitakeover measures. In practice it is as if insiders had the residual right to rewrite contracts and the rules of the game. In many instances there is an insider team. For example, in Germany, the bank and the managers exchange proxy votes (no interference with management) for service fees for the bank. In this view the agency problem comes from the anticipation of excessive retention by management (à la Jensen). The situation is maintained with the capture or the exchange of favors between insiders and the political establishment.

The view of Hellwig (Chapter 3) is that in the United States this network of insiders is challenged only by periodic waves of takeovers (which are helped by independent of investment banks with no conflict of interest) and it is limited by an environment with more legal protection for the investor.

## V. New Ideas and Results

### 5.1. Corporate Governance, Growth, and Performance

There are not many studies that relate CG to economic performance. There is evidence though about the relationship of financial development and growth. King and Levine (1993a–c) show that stock market liquidity and banking sector development are correlated with economic growth. However, it is difficult to control for factors that affect growth. Comparing growth rates of different industries across countries, Rajan and Zingales (1998) find that industries dependent on external finance (selected according to U.S. data) grow faster in countries that have a highly developed financial system (in terms of, among other things, accounting standards).

Carlin and Mayer (Chapter 4 of this book) provide evidence of the links between financial and CG systems and performance. The authors relate variables of country structure (size of the banking sector, size of securities markets, degree of concentration of ownership, accounting standards) and industry characteristics (degree of external financing from banks and equity, skill of workers) with activity levels of industries (growth rates, shares of value added devoted to fixed capital formation, and research and development). They find that industrial activity (particularly R&D) is related to the characteristics of industries and the financial and CG structure. In particular:

i    the growth of equity financed and skill-intensive industries is positively associated with market-based systems, and the effect comes from R&D expenditure;

ii    there is a positive (negative) relation in less (more) developed countries between activity in bank-dependent industries and the bank-oriented system of the country;

iii    there is a negative (positive) relation in less (more) developed countries between activity in equity financed and skill-intensive industries and concentrated ownership (that is, concentration of ownership may help alleviate agency problems in developed countries in certain types of industries).

The results are broadly consistent with the idea of Gerschenkron (1962) about the stages of development from bank-oriented to market-oriented systems and with more recent ideas that stock markets are good at financing new risky activities (because they aggregate information) and banks good at monitoring mature activities (Allen 1993).

The authors take their results to mean that there is not an appropriate financial and CG system that is universally appropriate across countries and industries.

### 5.2. The Role of Venture Capital

Venture capitalists retain a control block of shares in entrepreneurial firms and perform a governance role. Two characteristics of venture capital financing are duplication (the venture capitalist finances several entrepreneurs with overlapping activities) and staged capital commitment (only a fraction of capital is committed at the beginning). A cluster of innovating firms develop related products – modules – which need to fit together in the industry or in the design of larger companies. The process works as follows. First, there is project selection and effort expenditure by entrepreneurs. Selected projects obtain start-up financing. Second, the entrepreneurs tentatively specify product design attributes and exchange information to settle on a standard with the help of the venture capitalist. Third, final project selection follows (projects not selected do not get refinancing). Interestingly, this is helped by labor mobility because good engineers tend to leave bad projects, signaling the lack of prospects of the latter. Finally, the distribution of the value is realized (according to the ex ante agreement). Venture capitalists obtain funds typically from institutional investors, and reputational incentives keep venture capitalists in check.

According to the analysis of Silicon Valley by Aoki (Chapter 5 of this book), venture capital performs two main roles apart from its financing character. First, it mediates information sharing about emerging product specifications among independent start-ups and helps the emergence of de facto standards. Second, it introduces governance through tournament. The tournament design may be optimal despite the duplication of investment and monitoring if the R&D effort elasticity of entrepreneurs is small (that is, total value created is high relative to marginal value). In this case competition among entrepreneurs elicits high levels of effort that compensate for the duplication costs.

### 5.3. Human Capital and Control in the New Corporation

We are witnessing a transformation in which the importance of physical assets as a source of rents (and therefore control) is weakening while human capital is becoming more important. This is visible in the financial sector where the share of high skill workers is increasing dramatically.[15]

Traditional CG instruments deal with ways to ensure that financiers get a return on their investment. In this scheme shareholders should have residual rights of control since otherwise the investment would evaporate. The passivity of outside investors is seen as a failure of CG.

According to Rajan and Zingales (1999), in the new corporation power may derive not only from the ownership of physical assets (a de jure mechanism) but also from control of "access" (a de facto mechanism), which encourages specialization. For example, an individual may

---

[15] General evidence of changes in relative wages between skilled and unskilled is presented in Katz and Murphy (1992).

have control over the human capital of others because he controls a key input, which need not be capital. Others are specialized to him or to an asset he owns. In a world of incomplete contracts the allocation of power matters. The role of CG is then to allocate power to the stakeholders of the firm in order to maximize creation of surplus.

In this perspective, why do outside investors need to be protected with residual rights of control? A potential problem is that (concentrated) ownership may discourage effort by other agents and may distort the investment of the owner. It may be better then to assign ownership to a third party with no control rights. This may explain why passive financiers may be owners.

The CG of the new corporation involves

i    flat hierarchies (the decreased importance of physical assets reduces the need of layers of intermediate management – for protection purposes – and increases its cost – because managers have become too important to the firm and have "hold-up" power);

ii    the generalized award of long-term stock options to employees (this ensures employees a share in the product without giving them control and reduces incentive to leave);

iii    venture capital financing for new projects (where the outside financier is given some control in the organization because the ownership of physical assets does not give control).

## VI. Conclusion

The picture that emerges of the role and effectiveness of CG is mixed from both the theoretical and the empirical perspective. One could be tempted to conclude that CG does not matter much and that other factors, such as product market competition, drive economic performance. In this sense differences in the CG systems would not be significant and would just indicate an adaptation to the different environments.

Perhaps it could be even concluded that "shareholder value" should be replaced by the "stakeholder society" idea. Management would be entrusted then with the internalization of the welfare of all stakeholders in the firm and this could be monitored by boards with shared control among stakeholders.

However, to take such a stance would be hasty. First of all, in trying to implement the stakeholder society, managers will lose focus and will be able to rationalize any action on the supposed benefits for some of the stakeholders. The outcome most likely will be a higher autonomy for the manager with more freedom to pursue private benefits of control. Second, the sharing of control may result in a loss of decisiveness (Tirole 1999). In practice, managers would consider the welfare of stakeholders that have power, forming with them an alliance of insiders that would tend to expropriate other stakeholders. At the same time managers would try to influence regulation to promote ideas of a stakeholder society to gain more autonomy.

Furthermore, even taking for granted that competition is the main driving force toward efficiency, it does not follow that CG does not matter. Indeed, different systems of CG have different impacts on the degree of competition in the economy. In relation- or bank-based systems external control is weak and webs of cross participations may weaken product market competition. Furthermore, access to market finance is more difficult for new entrants, stifling competition additionally. Finally, in those systems the capacity of coalitions of insiders to influence and capture politicians and bureaucrats is large.

In fact, a hypothesis is that CG systems are explained basically with political economy considerations. In the United States, according to Roe (1994), managers influence policies to encourage dispersion of ownership in order to gain autonomy. We could think similarly (Hellwig, Chapter 3) that in continental Europe insiders or control families influence policies in order to protect their position. The inverse relationship between investor protection and ownership concentration (La Porta et al. 1999) may be the outcome of the work of different insiders in control in different countries rather than a consequence of exogenous legal systems.

Be that as it may, if the final test is the degree of competition in an economy, then market-based systems with arm's-length finance stand to end up ahead. This is consistent with the evidence presented for developed economies, in particular in relation to sectors with high R&D intensity, and with the flourishing venture capital, which is crucial in the financing of new technologies in market-based systems. These positive aspects should weigh more than potential concerns about short-termism of institutional investors and detected problems with the takeover mechanism.

There are many issues and puzzles that new research should illuminate. Among them are the role of boards of directors, the degree of activism of institutional investors and their potential short-term bias, the political economy of CG, and the effects of competition when faced with different types of managerial failure.

16

## References

Aghion, P., M. Dewatripont, and P. Rey. (1998). "Agency Costs, Firm Behavior and the Nature of Competition." Document de Travail No. 77, Institut d'Economie Industrielle, Toulouse.

Aghion, P., and P. Howitt. (1996). "The Observational Implications of Schumpeterian Growth Theory." In S. Durlauf, J. Helliwell, and B. Raj (Eds.), *Long-Run Economic Growth. Studies in Empirical Economics. Empirical Economics*, vol. 21. Heidelberg: Physica, pp. 13–25.

Alchian, A. (1950). "Uncertainty, Evolution, and Economic Theory." *Journal of Political Economy*, 58: 211–21.

Allen, F. (1993). "Stock Markets and Resource Allocation." In C. Mayer and X. Vives (Eds.), *Capital Markets and Financial Intermediation*. Cambridge: Cambridge University Press.

Aoki, M., and H. Patrick. (1994). *The Japanese Main Bank System: Its Relevance for Developing and Transforming Economies*. New York: Oxford University Press.

Berle, A., Jr., and G. Means. (1932). *The Modern Corporation and Private Property*. Chicago: Commerce Clearing House.

Bhagat, S., and B. Black. (1998). "The Uncertain Relationship between Board Composition and Firm Performance." In K. Hopt, M. Roe, and E. Wymersch (Eds.), *Corporate Governance: The State of the Art and Emerging Research*. New York: Oxford University Press.

Blundell, R., F. Griffith, and J. Van Reenen. (1995). "Dynamic Count Data Models of Technological Innovation." *Economic Journal*, 105: 333–44.

Bolton, P., and E.-L. von Thadden. (1988). "Blocks, Liquidity, and Corporate Control." *Journal of Finance*, 53: 1–25,

Burkart, M., D. Gromb, and F. Panunzi. (1997). "Large Shareholders, Monitoring, and the Value of the Firm." *Quarterly Journal of Economics*, 112: 693–728.

Caves, R., and D. Barton. (1990). *Efficiency in U.S. Manufacturing Industries*. Cambridge, Mass.: MIT Press.

Dewatripont, M., and J. Tirole. (1994). "A Theory of Debt and Equity: Diversity of Securities and Manager–Shareholder Congruence." *Quarterly Journal of Economics*, 109: 1027–54.

Diamond, D. (1989). "Reputation Acquisition in Debt Markets." *Journal of Political Economy*, 97: 828–62.

Diamond, D., and R. Verrecchia. (1982). "Optimal Managerial Contracts and Equilibrium Security Prices." *Journal of Finance*, 37: 275–87.

Edwards, J., and K. Fischer. (1994). *Banks, Finance and Investment in West Germany since 1970*. Cambridge: Cambridge University Press.

Franks, J., and C. Mayer. (1992). "Corporate Control: A Synthesis of the International Evidence." IFA Working Paper No. 165–92, London Business School, London.

"German Capital Markets, Corporate Control and the Obstacles to Hostile

Takeovers: Lessons from Three Case Studies." Working Paper, London Business School, London.

"Ownership, Control and the Performance of German Corporations." Working Paper, London Business School, London.

Friedman, M. (1953). *Essays in Positive Economics*. Chicago: University of Chicago Press.

Gerschenkron, A. (1962). *Economic Backwardness in Historical Perspective*. Cambridge Mass.: Harvard University Press.

Gompers, P., and A. Metrick. (1998). "Institutional Investors and Equity Prices." NBER Working Paper No. W6723.

Graham, D., D. Kaplan, and D. Sibley. (1983). "Efficiency and Competition in the Airline Industry." *Bell Journal of Economics*, 14: 118–38.

Grossman, S., and O. Hart. (1980). "Takeover Bids, the Free-Rider Problem, and the Theory of the Corporation." *Bell Journal of Economics*, 11: 42–62.

(1988). "One Share–One Vote and the Market for Corporate Control." *Journal of Financial Economics*, 20: 175–202.

Hall, B., and J. Liebman. (1998). "Are CEOs Really Paid Like Bureaucrats? *Quarterly Journal of Economics*, 113: 653–91.

Hart, O. (1983). "The Market Mechanism as an Incentive Scheme." *Bell Journal of Economics*, 14: 366–82.

(1995). *Firms, Contracts, and Financial Structure*. London: Oxford University Press.

Haubrich, J. (1994). "Risk Aversion, Performance Pay, and the Principal-Agent Problem." *Journal of Political Economy*, 102: 258–76.

Hayashi, F. (1997). "The Main Bank System and Corporate Investment: An Empirical Reassessment." NBER Working Paper 6172, Cambridge, Mass.

Hermalin, B. E. (1992). "The Effects of Competition on Executive Behavior." *Rand Journal of Economics*, 23(3): 350–65.

(1994). "Heterogeneity in Organizational Form: Why Otherwise Identical Firms Choose Different Incentives for Their Managers." *Rand Journal of Economics*, 25: 518–37.

Hirshleifer, D., and A. Thakor. (1998). "Corporate Control through Board Dismissals and Takeovers." *Journal of Economics and Management Strategy*, 7: 489–520.

Holmstrom, B., and J. Tirole. (1993). "Market Liquidity and Performance Monitoring." *Journal of Political Economy*, 101: 678–709.

Hoshi, T., A. Kashyap, and D. Scharfstein. (1990). "Bank Monitoring and Investment: Evidence from the Changing Structure of Japanese Corporate Banking Relationship." In R. G. Hubbard (Ed.), *Asymmetric Information: Corporate Finance and Investment*. Chicago: University of Chicago Press.

(1991). "Corporate Structure, Liquidity and Investment: Evidence from Japanese Industrial Groups." *Quarterly Journal of Economics*, 106: 33–60.

(1993). "The Choice between Public and Private Debt: An Analysis of Post-Deregulation Corporate Financing in Japan." NBER Working Paper No. 4421.

Jensen, M. (1986). "Agency Costs of Free Cash Flow, Corporate Finance and Takeovers." *American Economic Review*, 76: 323–29.

Jensen, M., and W. Meckling. (1976). "Theory of the Firm: Managerial Behavior, Agency Costs, and Ownership Structure." *Journal of Financial Economics*, 3: 305–60.

Jensen, M., and K. Murphy. (1990). "Performance Pay and Top-Management Incentives." *Journal of Political Economy*, 98: 225–63.

Jensen, M., and R. Ruback. (1983). "The Market for Corporate Control: The Scientific Evidence." *Journal of Financial Economics*, 11: 5–50.

Kang, J.-K., and R. Stulz. (1997). "Why Is There a Home Bias? An Analysis of Foreign Portfolio Equity Ownership in Japan." *Journal of Financial-Economics*, 46: 3–28.

Kaplan, S. (1994a). "Top Executive Rewards and Firm Performance: A Comparison of Japan and the United States." *Journal of Political Economy*, 102: 510–46.

(1994b). "Top Executive Rewards and Firm Performance in Germany." *Journal of Law, Economics and Organization*, 10: 142–59.

Katz, L., and K. Murphy. (1992). "Changes in Relative Wages, 1963–1987: Supply and Demand Factors." *Quarterly Journal of Economics*, 107: 35–78.

Kay, J. (1996). *The Business of Economics*. Part III. Oxford: Oxford University Press.

King, R., and R. Levine. (1993a). "Financial Intermediation and Economic Development." In C. Mayer and X. Vives (Eds.), *Capital Markets and Financial Intermediation*. Cambridge: Cambridge University Press.

(1993b). "Finance and Growth: Schumpeter Might Be Right." *Quarterly Journal of Economics*, 108: 717–37.

(1993c). "Finance, Entrepreneurship and Growth: Theory and Evidence." *Journal of Monetary Economics*, 32: 513–42.

La Porta, R., F. López-de-Silanes, A. Shleifer, and R. W. Vishny. (1997). "Legal Determinants of External Finance." *Journal of Finance*, 52(3): 1131–50.

La Porta, R., F. López-de-Silanes, and A. Shleifer. (1998). "Law and Finance." *Journal of Political Economy*, 106: 1113–55.

(1999). "Corporate Ownership around the World." *Journal of Finance*, 54: 471–517.

Machlup, F. (1967). "Theories of the Firm. Marginalist, Behavioral, Managerial." *American Economic Review*, 57: 1–33.

Meyer, M., and J. Vickers. (1985). "Performance Comparisons and Dynamic Incentives." *Journal of Political Economy*, 105: 547–81.

Morck, R., A. Shleifer, and R. Vishny. (1988). "Characteristics of Targets of Hostile and Friendly Takeovers." In A. Auerbach (Ed.), *Corporate Takeovers: Causes and Consequences*. Chicago: University of Chicago Press.

(1989). "Alternative Mechanisms of Corporate Control." *American Economic Review*, 79: 842–52.

(1990). "Do Managerial Objectives Drive Bad Acquisitions?" *Journal of Finance*, 45: 31–48.

Myers, S. (1977). "Determinants of Corporate Borrowing." *Journal of Financial Economics*, 5: 147–75.

Myers, S., and N. Majluf. (1984). "Corporate Financing and Investment Decisions When Firms Have Information That Investors Do Not Have." *Journal of Financial Economics*, 13: 187–221.

Nickell, S. (1996). "Competition and Corporate Governance." *Journal of Political Economy*, 104: 724–46.

Nickell, S., D. Nicolitsas, and N. Dryden. (1997). "What Makes Firms Perform Well?" *European Economic Review*, 41: 783–96.

OECD (1995). "Corporate Governance Environments in OECD Countries." February 1.

Porter, M. (1990). *The Competitive Advantage of Nations*. London: Macmillan.

Prowse, S. (1995). "Corporate Governance in an International Perspective: A Survey of Corporate Control Mechanism Among Large Firms in the U.S., U.K., Japan and Germany." *Financial Markets, Institutions and Instruments*, 4: 1–63.

Rajan, R. (1992). "Insiders and Outsiders: The Choice between Relationship and Arm's-Length Debt." *Journal of Finance*, 47: 1367–400.

Rajan, R., and L. Zingales. (1998). "Financial Dependence and Growth." *American Economic Review*, 88: 559–86.

Rajan, R., H. Servaes, and L. Zingales. (1999). "The Cost of Diversity: The Diversification Discount and Inefficient Investment." Mimeo.

Ravenscraft, D., and F. Scherer. (1987). *Mergers, Selloffs and Economic Efficiency*. Washington, D.C.: Brookings Institution.

Roe, M. (1994). *Strong Managers, Weak Owners: The Political Roots of Corporate Finance*. Princeton, N.J.: Princeton University Press.

Schaferstein, D. (1988). "Product Market Competition and Managerial Slack." *Rand Journal of Economics*, 19: 147–55.

Schmidt, K. (1997). "Managerial Incentives and Product Market Competition." *Review of Economic Studies*, 64: 91–213.

Shleifer, A., and R. Vishny. (1986). "Large Shareholders and Corporate Control." *Journal of Political Economy*, 94: 461–88.

(1997a). "A Survey of Corporate Governance." *Journal of Finance*, 52: 737–83.

(1997). "Large Shareholders and Corporate Control." *Journal of Political Economy*, 94: 461–88.

Short, H. (1994). "Ownership, Control, Financial Structure and the Performance of Firms." *Journal of Economic Surveys*, 8: 203–49.

Stigler, G. (1958). "The Economies of Scale." *Journal of Law and Economics*, 1: 54–71.

Tirole, J. (1999). "Corporate Governance." Mimeo.

Weinstein, D., and Y. Yafeh. (1998). "On the Costs of a Bank-Centered Financial System: Evidence from the Changing Main Bank Relations in Japan." *Journal of Finance*, 53: 635–72.

Wenger, E., and C. Kaserer. (1998). "The German System of Corporate Governance – A Model Which Should Not Be Imitated." In S. Black and M.

Moersch (Eds.), *Competition and Convergence in Financial Markets – The German and Anglo-American Models.* Amsterdam: North-Holland Elsevier Science, pp. 41–78.

Willig, R. (1987). "Corporate Governance and Market Structure." In Razin and Sadka (Eds.), *Economic Policy in Theory and Practice.* London: Macmillan.

CHAPTER 2

# Corporate Governance and Competition

## FRANKLIN ALLEN AND DOUGLAS GALE

### I. Introduction

In most countries, managers of corporations are legally responsible to the shareholders. In their seminal contribution on the separation of ownership and control, Berle and Means (1932) argue that in practice managers do not pursue the interests of shareholders. Instead they pursue their own interests, which results in waste and inefficiency. The contrast between the legal rights of shareholders and the de facto control of managers highlighted by Berle and Means led to the development of the agency approach to corporate governance (see, among others, Coase 1937; Jensen and Meckling 1976; Fama and Jensen 1983a,b; and Hart 1995). An excellent survey is contained in Shleifer and Vishny (1997).

The agency theory of corporate governance focuses on the question:

> *"How can shareholders ensure that managers pursue the*
> *shareholders' interests."*

We argue that this focus is much too narrow. A comparison of governance mechanisms in different countries and in different sectors of the economy suggests that an alternative approach is called for.

In Section 2, we review the actual operation of corporate governance in the United States, United Kingdom, Germany, France, and Japan. In the United States and United Kingdom, the mechanisms for ensuring that managers operate in the interests of shareholders are the strongest. The main internal governance system is the board of directors; the main external governance system is the market for corporate control. The effectiveness of both mechanisms has been widely questioned. There seems to be some evidence, particularly in recent years, that boards of directors are dominated by management and by the chief executive

This paper was presented at a conference on Corporate Governance in Barcelona, Spain, in October 1998. We thank the discussants, Monika Schnitzer and Jorge Padilla, other participants, and Xavier Vives for helpful comments and suggestions. We are grateful to the Wharton Financial Institutions Center and the National Science Foundation for financial support.

officer in particular. Although stock market prices of acquirers and acquirees rise in aggregate when mergers and takeovers are announced, there is mixed evidence from studies of the ex post profitability of acquisitions based on accounting data regarding the effectiveness of takeovers in improving corporate performance.

The Japanese system of corporate governance lies at the other end of the spectrum from the United States and United Kingdom. The expressed goal of managers in Japan is to pursue employment stability for workers rather than dividends for shareholders. The standard corporate governance mechanisms (the board of directors and the market for corporate control) exist in Japan, but their operation in practice has not successfully promoted the objective of implementing value creation for shareholders. The board of directors is typically a large, unwieldy group dominated by insiders. The prevalence of cross holdings of shares in Japan means that, even though there are no legal impediments, hostile takeovers do not occur in practice. It has been argued widely that the main bank system is a substitute for the standard Anglo-American corporate governance systems. This system involves a large bank, which is a major provider of funds to the firm, being responsible for monitoring its activities and ensuring the funds borrowed are efficiently invested. However, in practice the main bank intervenes only in times of financial crisis. Apart from this, corporations are effectively autonomous and there is little if any pressure for performance through standard governance mechanisms.

Germany and France occupy an intermediate position between Japan, on the one hand, and the United States and United Kingdom, on the other. In Germany and France, the interests of shareholders are supposed to be pursued by management, but not exclusively. The interests of other stakeholders, in particular employees, are also important. In Germany, the system of codetermination formalizes this balance of interests, and both the shareholders and the employees are represented on the supervisory board. In France, the attendance of employee representatives at board meetings as observers and extensive government ownership of industry has had a similar effect. In both countries, complex patterns of share ownership by holding companies and cross shareholdings severely limit the market for corporate control, as they do in Japan. Although hostile takeovers are legally permissible, they are very rare. Monitoring by financial institutions also appears to be limited. As in Japan, the explicit governance mechanisms to ensure corporate performance are weak.

Corporations represent only one type of economic organization. Non-profit organizations, which represent a significant portion of economic

24

activity in all the countries considered, provide a particularly interesting example. They are the organizations that perhaps have the least outside discipline on their governance. Despite this lack of outside discipline, in many cases nonprofit organizations compete directly and successfully with for-profit corporations.

In a broad-brush view, corporations in all the countries considered perform well and each country has examples of global leaders. The fact that the effectiveness of corporate governance mechanisms in ensuring corporate performance in Japan, Germany, and France in particular is limited, together with the range of successful nonprofit organizations in the United States and United Kingdom, suggests that other factors are important. In Sections 3–5, we examine the role of competition in product markets as an alternative mechanism for ensuring corporate performance. The traditional view discussed in Section 3 is that competition from profit-maximizing firms will reduce managerial slack by forcing managerial firms to match the performance of entrepreneurial (profit-maximizing) firms. In Section 4 we shift the focus away from moral hazard (managerial slack) toward the question of which managerial team is most effective at using resources. In this view, competition serves to reveal managerial quality (through relative performance) and eliminate ineffective managements. It is not necessary to take over the inefficient firm in order to replace the management; its market can be taken over instead. In this way, competition provides a substitute for explicit governance mechanisms such as the market for corporate control. Section 5 provides a formal model of how competition works in this way.

## II. Different Concepts of the Firm

This section starts with a discussion of the legal definitions of the firm in the five countries. We then look at regulatory restrictions on share ownership and the resulting differences across countries. Next we consider the governance mechanisms analyzed in the literature and discuss whose interests are pursued in practice. Finally we consider nonprofits and mutuals. Much of the information that is used comes from Charkham (1994), Prowse (1995), and from the 1996 report of a study group at the Institute of Fiscal and Monetary Policy of the Japanese Ministry of Finance.

### 2.1. Legal Definitions of the Corporation

The precise legal details of the corporation differ somewhat across countries. Company law of the United States is similar to company law of the

25

United Kingdom because they share a common origin. The managers in both countries have a fiduciary duty to the shareholders. In other words, they have a strong legal requirement to act in the interests of shareholders. A classic illustration of this is provided by a case involving Ford Motor Company early in its history. Henry Ford announced a special dividend but said that it would be discontinued in the future in order to allow funds to be diverted for the benefit of employees. One of the major shareholders sued on the grounds that the corporation exists for the benefit of shareholders and the management did not have the right to pursue the interests of workers. Ford Motor Company lost the case. (Subsequently it appeared that Henry Ford's announcement was designed to manipulate the stock price so that he could purchase blocks at a lower level than would otherwise be necessary!)

The channel through which shareholders exercise control of company affairs is the board of directors. The board is elected by the shareholders, typically on a one share–one vote basis. Sometimes multiple classes of shares exist, the main difference between classes being the number of votes each share has attached to it. The board of directors consists of a mix of outside directors and inside directors, the latter being the top executives of the firm. It is rare that the chief executive officer is not on the board. In both the United States and United Kingdom the CEO often acts as chairman as well. Once elected, the board of directors specifies the business policies to be pursued by the firm. The role of management is to implement the policies determined by the board. Shareholders have very little say in the affairs of the company beyond electing directors. For example, it is the directors who decide on their own compensation, without any input from shareholders. A committee of outside directors determines senior management's compensation. Except in unusual circumstances, such as a proxy fight, outside directors are nominated by the incumbent management and thus typically owe their allegiance to the CEO. Table 2.1 shows the total number of directors and (in parentheses) the number of outside directors for a typical sample of large firms in each of the countries. The size of boards is roughly the same in the United States and the United Kingdom, usually around 10–15 people. In the United States a majority are typically from outside the firm, while in the United Kingdom a minority are from outside.

The U.S. Occupation Forces had a heavy influence on the development of the Japanese legal system and the structure of its institutions after the Second World War. As a result, Japan resembles the United States in terms of the legal form of corporations. Some important differences do exist, however. Historically, nonfinancial corporations faced elaborate restrictions that prevented them from establishing holding companies.

26

Table 2.1. *Number of Members on Boards of Directors*

| United States[a] | | United Kingdom[a] | | Japan[a] | | France[a] | | Germany[b] | |
|---|---|---|---|---|---|---|---|---|---|
| Ford | 15 (10) | Glaxo | 16 (7) | Toyota | 60 (1) | Saint Gobain | 16 | Hoechst | 21 (11) |
| IBM | 14 (11) | Hanson | 19 (8) | Hitachi | 36 (3) | AGF | 19 (5) | BASF | 28 (10) |
| Exxon | 12 (9) | Guinness | 10 (6) | Matsushita | 37 (6) | Usinor Sacilor | 21 (5) | Robert Bosch | 20 (11) |
| Mobil | 16 (10) | British Airways | 10 (6) | Nissan | 49 (5) | Alcatel Alsthom | 15 | Krupp | 22 (7) |
| Philip Morris | 16 (4) | Allied Domecq | 12 (4) | Toshiba | 40 (3) | Elf Aquitaine | 11 | Bayer | 22 (11) |
| RJR Nabisco | 9 (6) | Grand Metropolitan | 14 (1) | Honda | 37 (3) | Renault | 18 | Daimler Benz | 20 (8) |
| Texaco | 13 (11) | BTR | 10 (4) | Sony | 41 (6) | Thomson | 8 | Volkswagen | 20 (7) |
| Johnson & Johnson | 14 (12) | Associated British Foods | 7 (1) | NEC | 42 (5) | | | Tyssen | 23 (27) |
| GAP | 11 (8) | British Steel | 8 (0) | Fujitsu | 36 (7) | | | Siemens | 20 (15) |
| | | | | Mitsubishi Electric | 37 (3) | | | | |
| | | | | Mitsubishi Motors | 43 (4) | | | | |
| | | | | Mitsubishi Heavy Industries | 43 (3) | | | | |
| | | | | Nippon Steel | 53 (1) | | | | |
| | | | | Mazda | 45 (8) | | | | |
| | | | | Nippon Oil | 22 (0) | | | | |

[a] Figures in parentheses: United States: Outside directors. United Kingdom: Nonexecutive (outside) directors. Japan: Outside directors (including cross-directorships). France: Directors from the government.

[b] For Germany the first column represents the members of the Supervisory Board and the second is the members of the Management Board.

*Source:* Institute of Fiscal and Monetary Policy (1996), Chart III-3-3, p. 69.

One of the changes in the reform of the Japanese financial system, the so-called Big Bang, is to allow nonfinancial corporations to form holding companies. The rights of Japanese shareholders are in theory greater than those of shareholders in the United States and United Kingdom. For example, in Japan it is easier for shareholders to nominate directors directly and to elect them. Also, management remuneration must be decided at general meetings of shareholders. These differences in rights and the role of the shareholders' meeting has led to a unique feature of Japanese corporate life, namely, the *sokaiya*. The *sokaiya* are racketeers who demand payments in exchange for not disrupting shareholders' meetings.

Despite these differences in shareholders' rights, the structure of Japanese boards of directors is such that shareholders do not in fact have much influence. It can be seen from Table 2.1 that the size of Japanese boards is much larger than in other countries. There are a handful of outside directors, but they have very little influence. The overwhelming majority of directors are from inside the company. Their number is such that they include many people in addition to the most senior members of management. Nominations of individuals for board directorships are essentially controlled by the company's CEO. This together with the unwieldy size of the board and its composition means CEOs hold tremendous power. Provided the financial position of a Japanese corporation is sound, it is essentially the CEO and those closest to him who control the company's affairs.

Germany has a very different type of governance structure than the United States, United Kingdom, or Japan. This is the system of *codetermination*, which has a long history. Pistor (1996) argues it arose in the late nineteenth century from an attempt to overcome the contradiction between the reality of industrialization and liberal ideas about the self-determination and the rights of individuals. Its legal origins date from 1891 when an amendment to the law on entrepreneurial activities (*Gewerbeordnung*) provided that workers' councils could be established on a voluntary basis. The Weimar Constitution formally recognized code-termination, but the principle was suppressed by the Nazis. It steadily reemerged after the Second World War and currently the most important legislation governing it is the Codetermination Act (*Mitbestimmungsgesetz*) of 1976. This generally applies to companies with more than 2,000 employees.

Firms to which the Act applies have two boards, the supervisory board and the management board. The supervisory board is the controlling body. As outlined in Schneider-Lenné (1992) and Prowse (1995), half of its representatives are elected by shareholders and half by the employees. The shareholders' general meeting elects the shareholder representatives. Two-thirds of the employee representatives work for the company, while the other third are trade union representatives. The supervisory board elects a chairman and deputy chairman from its members. A majority of two-thirds of the votes is required for a candidate to be elected. If this is not attained in two polls, the shareholders elect the chairman from among themselves and the employee representatives similarly elect the deputy. As a result, the chairman is usually from the shareholder side, while the deputy chairman is from the employee side. In the event of a tie in the voting of the supervisory board the chairman has a casting vote. It is in this sense that shareholders have ultimate control. However, members of the supervisory board legally must represent the interests of the company as a whole and not just the groups they represent. It can be seen from Table 2.1 that supervisory boards typically number just over 20 persons in size and so are slightly bigger than boards in the United States and United Kingdom but smaller than in Japan.

The management board is appointed by the supervisory board. Nobody can be a member of both boards, and cross-company board memberships are restricted. The management board is responsible for the operation of the company, while the supervisory board supervises its activities. The management board provides information to the supervisory board. This can obviously lead to abuse, because the management has an incentive to distort the information it provides to make the firm appear more successful than it actually is. This problem is often mitigated by the fact that the chairman of the supervisory board is a retired former CEO of the company, with wide experience of its operations and many informal contacts. Table 2.1 shows that the management board is usually fairly small, smaller than the supervisory board and the boards in other countries.

The German system provides an interesting contrast to the Anglo-American and Japanese systems. It is often argued that the dual board system better represents outside shareholders and ensures that management must take account of their views. In addition, employees' views are also represented, their bias presumably being to ensure the long-run viability of the firm.

The French system contains elements similar to those of both the Anglo-American and the German systems. Firms can choose from two types of boards of directors. The first type, which is more common, is single-tiered as in the Anglo-American system. The board elects the *président directeur-général* (PDG), who is like a CEO but is more powerful. He or she has the sole right to "represent" the company and is the only person who can delegate this power. Single-tiered boards mostly consist of outside directors who are shareholders and representatives from financial institutions with which the firm has transactional relationships. As in the Anglo-American model, the board determines business policies, which are then carried out by the PDG and management.

The second type of board has two tiers, as in Germany. *The conseil de surveillance* is like the German supervisory board except that employees do not have the right to representation. However, one feature of the French system that makes it more akin to the German system is that, whichever type of board the firm has, the workers' representatives have the right to attend board meetings as observers in all companies with at least 50 employees. The *conseil de surveillance* appoints the *directoire*, who have responsibility for the management of the company. One of the members of the *directoire* is designated *président de directoire* by the others.

It can be seen from Table 2.1 that the size of French boards is roughly similar to the United States. Complete or partial government ownership of corporations is more common than in other countries and, as Table 2.1 indicates, in some cases this leads to government representation on boards.

## 2.2. Regulatory Restrictions and the Pattern of Share Ownership

In addition to having different legal structures for the firm, different countries also place different restrictions on the holding of shares by financial institutions and nonfinancial corporations. Table 2.2 summarizes these restrictions. These restrictions have had important implications for the countries' patterns of share ownership, which are shown in Table 2.3.

Restrictions on institutional holdings of shares are one area where the United States differs significantly from the United Kingdom. In the United States, the Glass-Steagall Act (repealed in November 1999) has prevented banks from holding equity stakes in companies except in unusual circumstances, such as when a firm has gone bankrupt. Insurance companies are regulated by state laws. New York State regulations affect a large proportion of companies, not only because many companies are headquartered there, but also because other states tend to follow New York's lead. Historically, New York regulations prevented insurers from holding any equity. However, in more recent times, life insurance companies have been able to hold a limited amount. To ensure diversification, mutual and pension funds are also restricted in the amount of

*Table 2.2. Regulations on Shareholding of Financial Institutions and Nonfinancial Corporations*

| | United States | United Kingdom |
|---|---|---|
| Banks | Banks: Cannot hold shares of other corporations (Glass-Steagall Act). Bank holding companies: Holdings are limited to a maximum of 5% of the shares of nonfinancial corporations Trusts: Holdings are limited to a maximum of 10% of the fund's assets in any one company's shares. | No special regulations on holdings. However, in the case of large-volume acquisitions of shares, advance permission of the Bank of England is required. A report to the Bank of England is required when exposure (all claims including shares invested) exceeds 10% of a bank's total capital.[a] |
| Life insurance companies | Varies by state. For instance, under New York State Law (which applies to 60% of all insurance companies), investments must be less than 20% of assets or a maximum of 50% of surpluses. Holdings of the shares of any single company are limited to 2% of total assets. | Voluntary self-limitation of holding of stock in any single company (normally 2.5% of assets), for the purpose of portfolio diversification. A maximum (normally 5% of assets) is imposed on the amount of stock in any single company which a pension fund or insurance company can hold on its own. |
| Other insurance companies | Prohibition on holding a noninsurance company in its entirety. | Same as above. |
| Mutual funds | Tax penalty imposed on holdings in excess of 10% of the stock of any single company. | Under laws regulating financial services holding of stock for the purpose of controlling a company is prohibited. |
| Pension funds | Under the Employee Retirement Income Securities Act, investment diversification is required. Holdings in excess of 10% of the pension fund's own stock are prohibited. | Same as for insurance companies. |

*Table 2.2. (cont.)*

| | Japan | France | Germany |
|---|---|---|---|
| Other | Holding of stock which results in restricting competition is prohibited. | | Under "The City Code on Takeovers and Mergers," the mutual holding of shares the purpose of which is to prevent the transfer of control of stock is prohibited. |
| Banks | Under Article 11 of the Anti-Monopoly Law holdings are limited to 5% of the total number of issued shares of a domestic company. | The holding of shares of any single nonfinancial corporation is limited to a maximum of 15% of the bank's capital. Total holdings of all shares cannot exceed 60% of all the bank's capital. | Holdings greater than 10% are permitted, but only up to the value of the bank's capital.[a] |
| Life insurance companies | Under the Anti-Monopoly Law, holdings are limited to a maximum of 10% of the total number of issued shares of any single company. | | Holding of shares up to 20% of total assets is permitted. |
| Other insurance companies | Same as above. | | No regulations. |
| Mutual funds | No regulations. | | No regulations. |
| Pension funds | | | No regulations. |
| Other | Establishment of holding companies is prohibited (Article 9 of the Anti-Monopoly Law). A subsidiary whose parent company | A company can hold a maximum of 10% of the total number of issued shares of another company. Subsidiaries can also hold up to | A subsidiary whose parent company owns more than half of its stock cannot hold stock in its parent company. |

owns more than half of its stock cannot hold stock in its parent company (Commercial Code Article 211 [2]).

When one company controls another through shareholdings the controlled company has no voting rights with respect to the controlling company's stock (Commercial Code, Article 241 [3]).

A corporation which engages in nonfinancial business and has capital assets worth at least 10 billion yen, or net assets worth at least 30 billion yen, is prohibited from holding shares in domestic companies exceeding the value of its capital or net assets, whichever is greater (Anti-Monopoly Law, Article 9 [2]).[b]

10% of the stock of parent companies but cannot vote.

Mutual holding of shares is possible, but voting rights are limited to 25% of all voting rights, even when a company owns more than 25% of the stock of another company. Establishment of holding companies is permitted (in the case of pure holding companies and management holding companies).

[a] The United Kingdom and Germany are scheduled to make modifications to their regulations as EU integration progresses.
[b] Japan is scheduled to make changes to its laws on holding companies as part of the "Big Bang" reform of its financial system.
Source: Institute of Fiscal and Monetary Policy (1996), Chart III-2-3, p. 60.

Table 2.3. *Comparison of Shareholders by Sector (% of Total)*[a]

| | Individuals | Pension Funds, etc. | Financial Institutions | Nonfinancial Corporations | Public Sector | Foreign Individuals and Institutions | Other |
|---|---|---|---|---|---|---|---|
| United States | 50 | 20 | 5 | 14 | 0 | 5 | 6 |
| United Kingdom | 20 | 31 | 30 | 3 | 4 | 12 | |
| Japan | 23 | | 41 | 25 | 1 | 4 | 6 |
| France | 34 | | 23 | 21 | 2 | 20 | |
| Germany | 17 | | 22 | 42 | 5 | 14 | |

[a]Data is for 1990 except for France, which is for 1992.

*Source*: Prowse (1995), Table 2, p. 13 for United States and Institute of Fiscal and Monetary Policy (1996), Chart III-2-1, p. 59 for the other countries.

34

any single stock they can own. It can be seen from Table 2.3 that these regulations have meant that the pattern of share ownership in the United States is significantly different from the pattern in other countries. Only a small amount of equity, 5 percent, is held by financial institutions, whereas in the other countries the average holding is 29 percent. Instead, the proportion owned by individuals is much higher than elsewhere and the proportion owned by mutual and pension funds is higher than in Japan, Germany, and France. The main restriction on the holding of shares by nonfinancial corporations is the requirement that this not restrict competition in any way. This has been interpreted fairly strictly. In a famous case, the Supreme Court forced DuPont to sell its 25 percent holding in General Motors and cut all other ties. The United States's 14 percent ownership of shares by nonfinancial corporations is much lower than for Japan, Germany and France, but it is comparable to the United Kingdom.

It can be seen from Table 2.2 that the United Kingdom has far fewer formal regulations than the United States does. Banks can hold equity if they wish and need only obtain permission from the Bank of England if they are purchasing large blocks. Insurance companies are limited only by the need to diversify, which is a self-imposed limitation. With regard to holdings of nonfinancial corporations, the only limitation is that firms must not hold each other's shares to prevent a transfer of control. This lack of regulation in the United Kingdom creates a pattern of ownership in which financial institutions hold more and individuals less relative to the United States. Compared to Japan, Germany, and France, the holding of shares by nonfinancial corporations is much less and the holdings of pension funds much greater in the United Kingdom.

As Tables 2.2 and 2.3 indicate, Japan, Germany, and France are all somewhat similar in terms of the regulatory restrictions on shareholdings and the patterns of ownership. In all three countries, banks can hold the equity of companies. There are regulations on the proportions of the equity of firms that banks can hold in Japan. In Germany and France, there are restrictions on holdings of equity relative to bank capital. As mentioned above, holding companies were traditionally not permitted in Japan. In Germany and France, there are limitations on the percentages of firms that can be owned.

Complex interactions of holding companies occur in both Germany and France. Van Hulle (1996) contains an account of European holding groups. In Japan, the interactions in terms of crossholdings are relatively simple. Figure 2.1, from Prowse (1995), shows the ownership tree of Daimler-Benz AG. Here the nature of the interactions between firms is

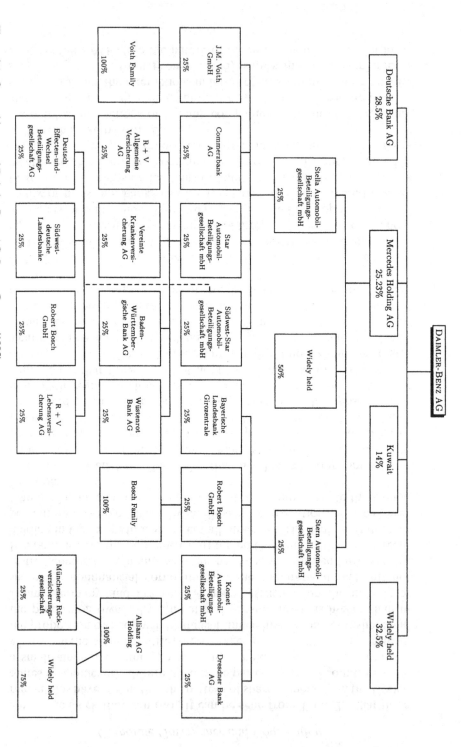

Figure 2.1. Ownership tree of Daimler-Benz AG. *Source:* Prowse (1995).

necessarily somewhat more subtle than in Japan because of their complexity, but they have similar effects.

## 2.3. *Governance Mechanisms*

There are a number of ways in which the main issue of how shareholders can ensure managers act in their interests has been answered in the literature. The most important of these are the following:

   i   The board of directors
   ii  Executive compensation
  iii  The market for corporate control
  iv  Concentrated holdings and monitoring by financial institutions
   v  Debt

We consider each of these in turn.

### *Board of Directors*

The board of directors is, in theory at least, the first method shareholders have to control managers and ensure the company is run in their interest. As discussed in Subsection 2.1 above, the way that boards are chosen and structured differs in significant ways across countries. In the United States and United Kingdom shareholders elect directors and have to rely on them to set business policies and supervise management. A balance of inside and outside directors on the board is supposed to ensure the board is at the same time knowledgeable about the company and independent from management. The extent to which this theory works in practice is widely debated. Since management, and in particular the CEO, effectively determines who is nominated for the board, it is not entirely clear that the board is as independent as it might be. Mace (1971), Weisbach (1988), and Jensen (1989) document the weakness of U.S. boards in disciplining managers. Bhagat and Black (forthcoming) survey the literature on the relationship between board composition and firm performance. The evidence indicates that firms with a majority of independent directors on their board do not perform better than firms without such boards. However, it does seem that having a moderate number of inside directors is associated with greater profitability.

In Japan the independence of the board of directors is mitigated by the large size of boards, the very limited number of outside directors, and the extreme power of the CEO to determine nominations for directors. Even though shareholders in theory have more power to control the board of directors than in other countries, this does not mean much in practice.

The two-tiered nature of German boards represents an attempt to formalize the different roles of outside and inside directors, since the supervisory board consists of people outside the current management while the management board consists of serving managers. Informational problems are minimized by including former managers on the supervisory board, though this dilutes the independence of the supervisory board. If the supervisory board contains former managers, how independent from current management can it be? Typically, the current management will have been chosen by the former management and many of the policies they will be implementing will have originated with the previous regime. There is also the complication that the supervisory board has employee representatives. It is interesting to note that in France, where both single-tiered and two-tiered boards are allowed, single-tiered boards tend to predominate.

Although the structure of boards is so different across countries, the limited empirical evidence available suggests that they are equally effective or ineffective at disciplining management. Kaplan (1994a,b) has conducted studies of the relationship between management turnover and various performance measures in Japan, Germany, and the United States. His findings indicate a similar relationship in each of the countries. Kang and Shivdasani (1995) confirm these results for Japan and also provide evidence on the effectiveness of different types of governance mechanisms. Among other things, they find that the presence of outside directors on the board has no effect on the sensitivity of top executive turnover to either earnings or stock-price performance. In contrast, concentrated equity ownership and ties to a main bank do have a positive effect. For Germany, Franks and Mayer (1997) find a strong relationship between poorly performing companies and turnover on management boards but not with turnover on supervisory boards.

*Executive Compensation*
An additional method of ensuring that managers pursue the interests of shareholders is to structure compensation appropriately. Diamond and Verrecchia (1982) and Holmstrom and Tirole (1993) have developed models where the interaction of capital markets and contingent compensation achieve this. Provided investors have an incentive to gather information and stock market prices partially reflect this, incentives can be provided by making managers' compensation depend on the company's share price. Examples of the form this dependence can take are direct ownership of shares, stock options, and bonuses dependent on share price. Provided share prices contain enough information about the anticipated future profitability of the firm, effective automatic incentive

systems can, in theory, be designed to ensure that managers maximize shareholder wealth.

Share prices are not the only contingency that can be used to motivate managers. Accounting-based performance measures are also frequently used. The advantage of the share price is that it is not as easily manipulable by management as accounting data. In addition to making compensation directly contingent on the share price, there is the possibility of dismissal for bad performance. If other firms perceive that the performance was due to incompetence, the manager may find it difficult to find another job. On the other hand, managers who perform extremely well may be bid away at higher compensation levels to other companies. The managerial labor market thus also plays an important part in providing incentives to managers.

In addition to providing incentives for increased effort, contingent compensation may have another, less desirable, effect. If executive compensation is sensitive to the share price and executives have limited liability, they will have an incentive to take excessive risks. They benefit greatly from good performance, but the penalty they bear for poor performance is limited.

There has been some debate about the optimal sensitivity of executive compensation to the share price in practice. Jensen and Murphy (1990) confirm previous findings of a positive relationship between executive pay and performance in the United States and estimate that CEO compensation varies by about $3 for every $1,000 change in a firm's value. They suggest that this figure is much too small. Haubrich (1994) has calibrated an appropriately designed principal–agent model that takes into account risk aversion and argues that a small sensitivity is optimal for reasonable parameter values. For other countries, the number of empirical studies is small. Kaplan (1994a,b) considers the sensitivity of pay and dismissal to performance in Germany and Japan. He finds that Germany and Japan are similar to the United States in this respect.

The dramatic increase in executive compensation in the United States in recent years, partly in response to arguments such as those of Jensen and Murphy, has led to the opposite concern of whether boards of directors have been captured and are paying themselves exorbitant amounts. It is interesting to note that there is a considerable difference in levels of compensation across countries. In the United States, executive compensation is very high. At the other extreme, Japan executives appear to make a small fraction of what their counterparts in the United States do. The European countries lie in between these two extremes.

## The Market for Corporate Control

Manne (1965) argues that an active market for corporate control is essential for the efficient operation of capitalist economies. It allows able management teams to gain control of large amounts of resources in a small amount of time. Inefficient managers are removed and replaced with people who are better able to do the job. The existence of a market for corporate control also provides one means of disciplining managers. If a firm is pursuing policies that do not maximize shareholders' wealth, it can be taken over and the managers replaced.

There are three ways in which the market for corporate control can operate: through proxy contests, friendly mergers, and hostile takeovers. Proxy contests involve a group of shareholders trying to persuade the remaining shareholders to act in concert with them and unseat the existing board of directors. For example, if someone wishes to change a firm's policies, he can have himself and others with similar views voted onto the board of directors at a shareholders' meeting. In order to do this, he solicits proxies from other shareholders, which allows him to vote their shares. Proxy fights are usually difficult to win, because holdings are often spread among many people. As a result, they do not occur very frequently in any of the countries under consideration. Recent theoretical analyses of proxy fights, which throw some light on the problems involved with shareholder voting, are Bhattacharya (1997), Yilmaz (1997), and Maug (1998).

Friendly mergers occur when both firms agree that combining them would create value. In this case there are a number of ways that the transaction can occur. There may be an exchange of stock or one firm may make a tender offer for the other's stock. Friendly mergers and takeovers occur in all the countries under consideration and account for most of the transaction volume that occurs. Prowse (1995) reports that in the United States friendly transactions constituted 82.2 percent of transactions, in the United Kingdom 62.9 percent and in the rest of Europe 90.4 percent.

The third way in which the market for corporate control can operate is through hostile takeovers. These occur when there is conflict between the acquirers and acquirees over the price that should be paid, the effectiveness of the policies that will be implemented, and so forth. Hostile tender offers allow the acquirers to go over the heads of the target management and appeal directly to their shareholders. This mechanism is potentially very important in ensuring an efficient allocation of resources in the way Manne (1965) suggests. However, as Hansmann (1996) points out, hostile tender offers first appeared in 1956 and were not widely used until the 1960s, so they are a relatively recent innovation. Corporations with widely held shares were a commonplace for many decades before that. It is not clear that hostile tender offers have induced a significant change in the efficiency with which corporations are managed.

Grossman and Hart (1980) have pointed to a problem with the operation of the takeover mechanism of corporate governance that may help to explain why takeovers are not more effective in disciplining management. Existing shareholders will have a strong incentive to free ride on raiders who plan to increase the value of the firm. If, on the one hand, the price offered by the raider is below the price that the new policies will justify and the shareholder believes that the offer will succeed, then it is better for him to hold the shares than to tender them; but then every shareholder should hold onto the shares and the offer cannot succeed. On the other hand, if the shareholders believe that the offer will not succeed, they should tender their shares; but then the offer will succeed and, again, these beliefs are inconsistent with equilibrium. The only equilibrium is one in which the raider's offer price is equal to the price the new policies will justify. The problem is that in this equilibrium the raider's profit is zero before allowing for any costs incurred in undertaking the bid. If these costs are included, the profit will be negative and there will be no incentive to undertake any takeovers.

A number of solutions to the free-rider problem have been suggested. Grossman and Hart's (1980) solution is that corporate charters should be structured so that raiders can dilute minority shareholders' interests after the takeover occurs. This means the raider can offer a price below the post-takeover value of the firm to him and the bid will still succeed. Existing shareholders know that if they retain their shares, the raider will dilute their interest. Shleifer and Vishny (1986) pointed out that if the raider can acquire a block of stock before attempting a takeover at the low pretakeover price, there will be a profit on this block even if all the remaining shares are purchased at the full price justified by the raider's plans. Burkart (1995) shows that it is privately optimal for a large shareholder to overbid and this results in an inefficient equilibrium.

In addition to the Grossman and Hart free-rider problem, there are a number of other problems with the operation of the market for corporate control. A second problem arises because of competition among bidders. Suppose there are substantial (sunk) costs of identifying a takeover target initially. Once the takeover bid is announced, other raiders will realize it is an attractive target and will bid. This competition will eliminate any profits by ensuring the target will sell at its full value. This means the initial bidder will realize a loss if the initial costs of identifying the target are taken into account. Unlike the free-rider problem, allowing ex post dilution will not have the desired effect of providing an incentive for takeovers. Competing raiders will take into account the benefits of dilution and include them in their bids. In contrast, owning a block of stock purchased at the pretakeover price will allow a raider to make a profit.

A third problem in the operation of the market for corporate control is the possibility of management entrenchment. Managers may be incompetent and want to prevent a takeover to preserve their jobs. There are a number of ways they can achieve this. First, they have a significant informational advantage over outsiders. For example, they may plausibly claim the raider is not offering enough and the firm would be better to continue under current policies or wait for another bidder. Second, there are a number of antitakeover tactics they can use. Examples in the U.S. are poison pills, staggered election of directors, and dual-class recapitalizations. "Poison pills" involve issuing rights to shareholders to buy stock in the company at a significantly reduced price in the event of a takeover. Staggered election of directors ensures that only a fraction of directors, often one-third, can be replaced in any year. So, even if a raider acquires all the votes, it will still take some time to acquire control of the board. Dual-class recapitalizations involve issuing a second class of share with superior voting rights and requiring they be exchanged for regular shares before being sold. This ensures that votes become concentrated in managers' hands.

Despite all these problems, hostile takeovers do occur fairly frequently in the United States and United Kingdom. Prowse (1995) points out that in the United States almost 10 percent of companies in the Fortune 500 in 1980 have since been acquired in a transaction that was hostile or started off as hostile. For the United Kingdom, Franks and Mayer (1992) report that there were 35 successful hostile bids made over two years in the mid-1980s. This is much higher than in Germany, France, or Japan. In Germany, Franks and Mayer (1993) report that there have only been three hostile takeovers between 1945 and 1994 and document them. Franks and Mayer (1997) document a substantial market in share stakes, but their analysis suggests such sales do not perform a disciplinary function. In Japan, Kester (1991) argues that there were no hostile takeovers among large firms in the 1945–94 period. In France, hostile takeovers are also rare.

Why are there such differences in the number of hostile takeovers between the United States and United Kingdom, on the one hand, and France, Germany, and Japan, on the other? A common belief is that it is because of regulatory restrictions. In fact, there are few explicit restrictions on takeover attempts in Germany, France, or Japan. In some ways, the regulations are more conducive to takeovers than in the United States and United Kingdom. For example, in Germany the threshold at which a large equity stake must be disclosed is 25 percent compared to 5 percent in the United States and United Kingdom. This means that the barriers caused by Grossman and Hart's free-rider problem and competition among bidders should be less significant in Germany than in the United States and United Kingdom.

A more plausible explanation for the difference in the occurrence of takeovers across countries is the prevalence of cross shareholdings in Japan and the structure of holding companies and cross shareholdings in Germany and France. The structure of ownership in these countries makes it difficult to acquire the number of shares necessary for a takeover.

Another important question is the extent to which the market for corporate control leads to an improvement in efficiency in the way Manne's (1965) argument suggests it should. There have been numerous empirical studies of takeovers in an attempt to understand whether they create value. Jensen (1993) estimates the total increase in the stock market value of target firms in the United States from 1976 to 1990 to be $750 billion. It seems that the increase in value for bidding firms was zero and possibly even negative. Overall, the stock market data suggests that total value (i.e., the sum of the target and bidding firms' values) did increase significantly. There is an issue of whether this was caused by the mergers and takeovers or was simply a reflection of a previous undervaluation in the stock market. Another possibility, suggested by Shleifer and Summers (1988), is that gains from takeovers may be the result of violating implicit contracts with workers and other suppliers.

A number of studies have attempted to use accounting data to identify the reason why the value of the targets increased. For example, Ravenscraft and Scherer (1987) and Herman and Lowenstein (1988) have found little evidence that operating performance improves after takeovers. Franks and Mayer (1996) analyzed a sample of U.K. firms and found that hostile takeover targets did not underperform before acquisition, but were subject to the redeployment of assets afterwards. There are some studies, such as Kaplan (1989), Bhagat, Shleifer, and Vishny (1990), Kaplan and Weisbach (1991), and Healy, Palepu, and Ruback (1992, 1997), that do find changes and improvements in operations that can at least partially explain takeover premia. So, the evidence is mixed.

*Concentrated Holdings and Monitoring by Financial Institutions*
Stiglitz (1985) has argued that concentrated ownership of the firm's shares is one of the most important ways through which value maxi-

mization by firms can be ensured. At one extreme, a single person or family owns the firm and there are significant incentives to maximize its value. At the other extreme, shares are held by a large number of people, no one of whom holds a large stake. In this case, nobody has an incentive to monitor the management and ensure they are running the firm in the shareholders' interests. In the intermediate case, where one or more shareholders owns a large stake and many small shareholders hold a few shares, the large shareholders may have an incentive to monitor the firm's management and ensure it maximizes share value.

A number of recent theoretical analyses have considered important aspects of concentrated ownership. Burkart, Gromb, and Panunzi (1997) consider the costs and benefits of monitoring by large shareholders. They show that such monitoring may restrict the misuse of resources ex post but may also blunt ex ante managerial initiative. There is a trade-off between control and initiative. Bolton and von Thadden (1998a,b) develop a framework to analyze the trade-off between liquidity and control. Ownership of a large block provides incentives to monitor but also leads to a lack of liquidity. Pagano and Röell (1998) consider the trade-off between public and private ownership and monitoring. With private ownership, there is monitoring because of shareholder concentration, but no liquidity. Public ownership results in the costs of going public and less monitoring, but greater liquidity.

The differences in concentration of share ownership in the different countries are illustrated in Table 2.4. This shows the percentage of outstanding shares owned by the largest five shareholders in the United States, United Kingdom, Japan, and Germany for a sample of large nonfinancial companies. The United States and United Kingdom have relatively low concentration, while Japan and particularly Germany have a high concentration. Table 2.5 shows the frequency of majority ownership and identity of the majority shareholder. In the United Kingdom in particular, and the United States to some extent, majority ownership is mainly due to family and individual holdings of large blocks. Often the founding family retains a significant amount of the shares after the firm has gone public. In Japan, majority ownership is less frequent. The difference there between the concentration indicated by the largest five shareholders and majority ownership is probably due to the fact that holdings by banks and insurance companies of the shares in any one firm are restricted to 5 percent and 10 percent, respectively. In Germany, majority ownership, like the holdings of the largest five shareholders, is particularly high.

The importance of equity ownership by financial institutions in Japan and Germany and the lack of an effective market for corporate control

*Table 2.4. Summary Statistics of Ownership Concentration of Large Non-financial Corporations. Percentage of Outstanding Shares Owned by the Largest Five Shareholders*

|  | United States | United Kingdom | Japan | Germany |
|---|---|---|---|---|
| Mean | 25.4 | 20.9 | 33.1 | 41.5 |
| Median | 20.9 | 15.1 | 29.7 | 37.0 |
| Standard deviation | 16.0 | 16.0 | 13.8 | 14.5 |
| Minimum | 1.3 | 5.0 | 10.9 | 15.0 |
| Maximum | 87.1 | 87.7 | 85.0 | 89.6 |
| Mean firm size (millions of US$, 1980)[a] | 3,505 | 1,031 | 1,835 | 3,483 |
| Mean firm size (millions of US$, 1980)[b] | 1,287 | N.A. | 811 | 1,497 |

[a] Measured by total assets.
[b] Measured by market value of equity.
[c] Samples: United States: 457 nonfinancial corporations in 1980.
        United Kingdom: 85 manufacturing corporations in 1970.
        Japan: 143 mining and manufacturing corporations in 1984.
        Germany: 41 nonfinancial corporations in 1990.
*Source*: Prowse (1995), Table 9, p. 25.

*Table 2.5. Frequency of Majority Ownership and the Identity of the Majority Shareholder (%)*

|  | United States | United Kingdom | Japan | Germany |
|---|---|---|---|---|
| Frequency of majority ownership[a] | 10.8 | 9.8 | 8.4 | 25.1 |
| Identity of majority owner:[b] |  |  |  |  |
|     Individual | 5.1 | 6.7 | 2.1 | 6.4 |
|     Financial Institution |  | 0 | 3.6 | 3.7 |
|     Nonfinancial firm | 5.7 | 1.8 | 2.7 | 8.7 |
|     Other[c] |  | 1.3 | N.A. | 6.4 |

[a] Number of majority-owned firms as a percentage of total number of firms in the sample. For the United States, number of majority-owned firms identified from the total of all listed companies.
[b] Number of firms majority-owned by a certain shareholder class as a percentage of all firms in the sample.
[c] Includes foreign and government majority-owned companies. For Japan, foreign-owned companies are subsumed in the other categories.
*Source*: Prowse (1995), Table 10, p. 29.

has led to the suggestion that the agency problem in these countries is solved by financial institutions acting as the outside monitor for large corporations.

In Japan, this system of monitoring is known as the *main bank system*. According to Teranishi (1994) and Hoshi, Kashyap, and Loveman (1994) this system grew out of the close relationships between banks and firms that were fostered by the way credit was allocated during the war. The main characteristics of this system are the long-term relationship between a bank and its client firm, the holding of both debt and equity by the bank, and the active intervention of the bank should its client become financially distressed. It has been widely argued that this main bank relationship ensures the bank acts as delegated monitor and helps to overcome the agency problem between managers and shareholders. Hoshi, Kashyap, and Scharfstein (1990a,b, 1993) provide evidence that the main bank system helps firms by easing liquidity constraints and reduces agency costs. They also document that firms reduced their bank ties in the 1980s as access to the bond market became easier. In contrast, Hayashi (1997) finds no evidence that main bank ties ease liquidity constraints. He suggests Hoshi, Kashyap, and Scharfstein's results are probably due to the poor quality of their capital stock estimate. Kang and Shivdasani (1997) find that companies restructure to a greater extent in response to adverse circumstances the greater the ownership of the main bank. Aoki and Patrick (1994) contains a number of studies suggesting that until recently the effectiveness of the main bank system has been high. A dissenting view is contained in a paper by Ramseyer (1994), who suggests that the traditional emphasis in the literature on the importance of this system in achieving effective corporate governance is too strong. He argues that if the system really worked in the way described, explicit contracts should be used much more than they are in practice. Over all, the main bank system appears important in times of financial distress and less important when a firm is doing well.

In Germany, the data on concentration of ownership probably understate the significance of the banks' effective position. The reason is that many bank customers keep their shares "on deposit" at banks and allow banks to exercise proxies on their behalf. As a result, banks control a higher proportion of voting equity and have more representation on boards of large industrial enterprises than their direct holdings suggest. A 1978 Monopoly Commission study found that, of the top 100 corporations, banks controlled the votes of nearly 40 percent of the equity and were represented on two-thirds of the boards. German banks thus tend to have very close ties with industry and form long-run relationships with firms. This is known as the *hausbank* system. A number of studies have provided evidence on the effectiveness of the outside monitoring of German banks. Elston (1993) finds firms with strong ties to a bank are not as tightly liquidity-constrained as firms with weaker ties. Cable (1985) and Gorton and Schmid (1996) find evidence that firms with a higher proportion of equity controlled by banks do better. This evidence is consistent with the hypothesis that bank involvement helps firms.

A number of issues arise in evaluating the effectiveness of banks as outside monitors in Japan and Germany. The first is that banks are themselves subject to the same agency problems as firms. Charkham (1994, p. 36) points out that, in effect, the big three banks essentially control themselves: "At general meetings in recent years, Deutsche Bank held voting rights for 47.2 percent of its shares, Dresdner for 59.25 percent and Commerzbank for 30.29 percent." In addition, other large shareholders are often widely held themselves. Schreyögg and Steinman (1981) compare a sample of 300 large German firms according to whether there is concentration in terms of direct ownership or ultimate ownership taking into account the holding company structure. They find that in terms of ultimate ownership there is significantly less concentration. The problem is illustrated by Figure 2.1. Although it would appear at first sight that Daimler-Benz has concentrated ownership, the block shareholders are themselves held by groups of small shareholders.

Diamond (1984) has referred to this as the problem of "Who monitors the monitor?" In his model he suggests intermediaries can overcome this problem by having a diversified portfolio and promising a fixed return to depositors. If the intermediary does not monitor, then it will be unable to pay the promised return to depositors. Prowse (1995) suggests that there are a number of problems with the application of Diamond's argument to Japanese and German banks. First, the effect of deposit insurance is not considered. Second, in addition to debt, banks in these countries also have equity holdings that have significant nondiversifiable risk associated with them. This means a bank can claim bad outcomes are due to this risk rather than to a lack of monitoring.

Edwards and Fischer (1994) have argued that in Germany the corporate governance role of banks has been overemphasized in the literature. They provide a variety of evidence that banks do not have the degree of influence as lenders, shareholders, or voters of proxies that is usually supposed. For example, they find that the number of votes controlled in a company is only weakly related to the number of representatives the bank has on the supervisory board.

Wenger and Kaserer (1998) point to Metallgesellschaft and Daimler-

Benz as extreme examples of the failure of the German corporate governance system. Metallgesellschaft had losses of over $ 1 billion when it wound up a large position in oil futures. This position had been undertaken as part of a plan to sell home heating oil in the United States at a fixed price. It appears that the supervisory board, despite being chaired by a representative of Deutsche Bank, did not fully understand the strategy until they were forced to by the sequence of events that unfolded. In the late 1980s and early 1990s, Daimler-Benz adopted a strategy of becoming a conglomerate, despite the fact that U.S. auto companies had already been unsuccessful with this strategy. Even though Daimler-Benz's supervisory board was chaired by Deutsche Bank's CEO, there was no attempt to prevent what turned out to be a significant waste of resources.

Hellwig (1991) has also stressed the importance of moral hazard on the part of the monitoring bank, and Hellwig (Chapter 3) discusses the possibility of collusion between the monitoring bank and the firms being monitored.

La Porta, López-de-Silanes, and Shleifer (1998) consider the incidence of widely held corporations in 27 wealthy economies, including those that are the focus of this essay. They find that, with the exception of countries such as the United States and United Kingdom, where minority investors are well protected, corporations are not widely held but instead are controlled by families or the State. Another exception is Germany, where banks play a significant role in the governance of some large corporations through their ownership of shares. La Porta, López-de-Silanes, Shleifer, and Vishny (1998) suggest a possible reason for the common occurrence of large blocks of stock, which is different from the standard monitoring explanation. They find a negative correlation between the extent of minority shareholder protection and concentrated equity ownership. The implication is that, when legal protection is poor, the best protection against abuse of minority shareholders is to hold large blocks of stock.

*Debt*
An important strand of the corporate governance literature has focused on the role of debt as a means of disciplining managers. Grossman and Hart (1982) were the first to argue that managers could commit themselves to working hard by using debt rather than equity. Similarly, Jensen's (1986) free cash flow theory suggested that debt could be used to prevent managers from squandering resources. In the late 1980s and early 1990s it was widely argued that leveraged buyouts (LBOs), in which managers or other groups purchased firms using a large proportion of

debt financing, were an efficient response to agency problems. However, debt can have undesirable as well as desirable effects on managers' behavior. Jensen and Meckling (1976) pointed out that managers have an incentive to take risks and may even accept projects that destroy value, if significant amounts of debt are used. Myers (1977) pointed to the debt overhang problem, where firms may forgo good projects if they have significant debt outstanding. The reason is that for a firm facing financial distress a large part of the returns to a good project go to bond-holders.

One of the concerns of the literature on debt has been how lenders can ensure that borrowers actually make repayments on the debt they issue. One of the standard answers has been reputation. For example, Eaton and Gersovitz (1981), Allen (1983), and Diamond (1989) provide models of debt where reputation plays an important role in ensuring repayment. Bulow and Rogoff (1989) point out that reputation alone often will not work.

Hart and Moore (1989) and Hart (1995) have stressed the importance of the right to liquidate in the event of default as a method of ensuring repayment. The threat of liquidation ensures that some funds can always be extracted except in the final period. Their theory and its extensions provides a plausible theory of entrepreneurial firms but is not directly applicable to corporations, because outside equity cannot be used. Fluck (1998) has shown how this framework can be extended to allow for infinitely lived, outside equity by incorporating a right for equity holders to dismiss management.

Perhaps the most important weakness of the argument that debt is important for ensuring effective governance in corporations is the fact that retained earnings are the most important source of finance for corporations (see, e.g., Mayer 1988). Typically, large corporations do not have a problem meeting their debt payments.

*Analysis*

Why are there such marked differences in corporate governance in different countries? Prowse (1990, 1995) has stressed that governance develops subject to legal and regulatory constraints. Roe (1994) has argued that in understanding the different structure of corporate governance across countries it is important to consider political factors in the development of the legal system and its regulation. In particular, he argues that the United States chose to have a financial system where the power of financial institutions such as banks and insurance companies was very limited. As a result, they could not play a significant role in corporate governance. In Germany and Japan a different political climate allowed financial institutions to become involved in corporate governance.

Political factors are important without a doubt but there is a question of the extent of their importance. The United Kingdom presents an interesting contrast to the United States. It has a similar separation of ownership and control in corporations but very different financial institutions. In particular, the banking system is concentrated and, although the Bank of England has wide powers of intervention, there are few if any explicit restrictions on the activities that banks may undertake, as Table 2.2 indicates. Nevertheless banks have chosen not to become involved in corporate governance. Insurance companies have also not been barred from playing an important governance role but have not done so. If banks and insurance companies in the United Kingdom chose not to become involved in corporate governance, then the same might be true in the United States if the banks and insurance companies there had had the ability to become involved. This comparison is difficult to reconcile with the idea that it is politics and legal and regulatory constraints that are the only determinants of differences in corporate governance across countries.

## 2.4. Whose Company Is It in Practice?

How important are these differences in governance mechanisms? To what extent are managers in different countries constrained by governance mechanisms to act in shareholders' interests? One view is that governance mechanisms do not constrain firms very much, at least in some countries. For example, in Japan managers do not appear to view themselves as working for the shareholders. This is illustrated by the mission statement of Asahi Breweries contained in Table 2.6. The statement is revealing in that shareholders' interests are only mentioned in the final section and seem fairly unimportant: "We at Asahi . . . desire to fulfill our responsibilities to the stockholders and the local communities in which we operate."

The view that Japanese corporations have relatively little responsibility toward their shareholders is confirmed in surveys of managers. Figure 2.2 shows the choices of senior managers at a sample of major corporations in the five countries between the following two alternatives:

a   A company exists for the interest of all stakeholders (black bar).
b   Shareholders' interest should be given the first priority (gray bar).

In Japan the overwhelming response by 97.1% of those asked was that all stakeholders were important. Only 2.9% thought shareholders' inter-

## Table 2.6. *Corporate Philosophy of Asahi Breweries, Ltd.*

We at Asahi Breweries, Ltd., through our business activities including alcoholic and non-alcoholic beverages, food, and pharmaceuticals, wish to contribute to the health and well-being of people the world over. By thus contributing to society as a whole, the company seeks to attain the trust and confidence of the consumer and develop still further.

*1. Consumer Orientation*
   Identifying the best interests of consumers, we endeavor to meet their demands by creating products suited for contemporary tastes and lifestyles.

*2. Quality First*
   Open to consumer opinion of our products, we consistently enhance quality level and extend technological capabilities in order to market the finest products in the industry.

*3. Respect for Human Values*
   Our Company firmly believes that human beings are the core of the business, and follows the principle of human values through developing human resources and implementing fair personnel management. Each employee is encouraged to fully utilize his or her own potential, and work to realize an open, positive thinking corporate culture.

*4. True Partnership between Labor and Management*
   Our Company aims to strengthen harmonious relations between labor and management based on mutual understanding and trust. Both parties work hand in hand for corporate development as well as the welfare of all employees.

*5. Cooperation with Business Associates*
   We seek to build strong relations with all our business associates and affiliates in a spirit of co-existence and co-prosperity based in mutual trust. At the same time, we are determined to accept and fulfill our responsibilities as the core of the Asahi group of companies.

*6. Social Responsibilities*
   We at Asahi, through securing and expanding the base of our operations, desire to fulfill our responsibilities to stockholders and the local communities in which we operate. Also in carrying out business activities, we sincerely observe the moral principles of management based on social standards.

*Source*: Asahi Breweries, Ltd. Case, 1989, Harvard Business School, 9-389-114.

ests should be put first. At the other end of the spectrum managers in the United States and United Kingdom by majorities of 75.6% and 70.5%, respectively, stated that shareholders were the most important stakeholders. Germany and France are more like Japan in that 82.7% and 78%, respectively, viewed the firm as being for all stakeholders.

The same survey also asked the managers what their priorities were with regard to dividends and employee layoffs. The specific alternatives they were asked to choose between were:

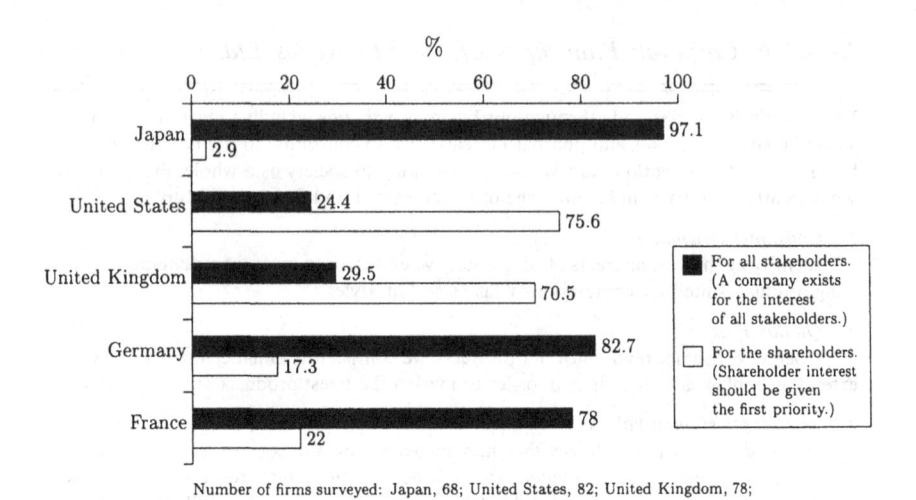

Number of firms surveyed: Japan, 68; United States, 82; United Kingdom, 78; Germany, 110; France, 50.

Figure 2.2. Whose company is it? *Source*: Yashimori (1995).

a Executives should maintain dividend payments, even if they must lay off a number of employees (black bar).
b Executives should maintain stable employment, even if they must reduce dividends (gray bar).

Figure 2.3 shows the results. As before, there is a sharp difference between Japan and the United States and United Kingdom, with Germany and France closer to Japan but not quite as extreme.

The evidence on managers' views of the role of the firm is upheld by the way that wages are structured in the different countries. In the United States and United Kingdom, wages are based on the nature of the job done. Employees' personal circumstances generally have no effect on their compensation. In Japan and Germany, it is common for people to be granted family allowances and special allowances for small children. In France, vacation allowances are common. These differences underline the fact that in the United States and United Kingdom the firm is designed to create wealth for shareholders, whereas in Japan and to some extent Germany and France, it is a group of people working together (see p. 57 of the report of the study group of the Institute of Fiscal and Monetary Policy of the Japanese Ministry of Finance).

These differences in the role of the firm, together with the limited evidence on the effectiveness of internal and external governance mecha-

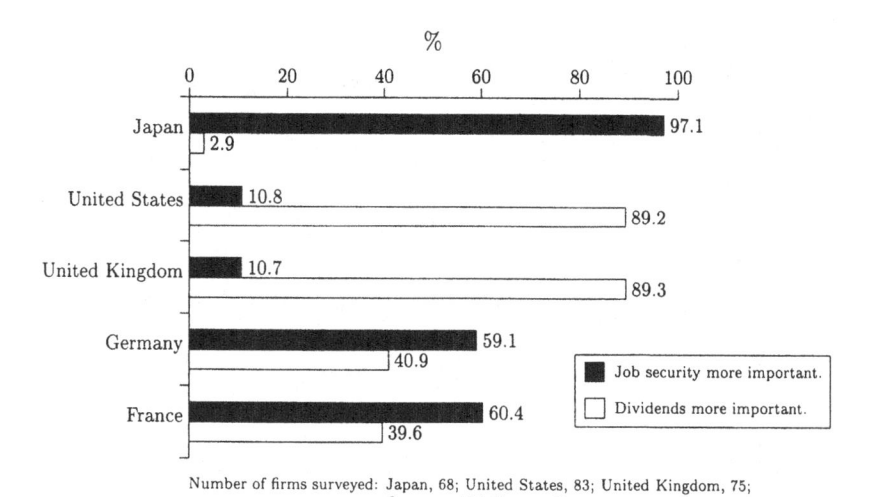

Number of firms surveyed: Japan, 68; United States, 83; United Kingdom, 75; Germany, 105; France, 68.

Figure 2.3. Job security or dividends. *Source*: Yashimori (1995).

nisms, raise the question of whether the traditional agency view of the firm is the correct way to think about companies. Before turning to this issue, we next consider the operation of nonprofit organizations, where, even in the United States and United Kingdom, the specific goal of the organization is different from pursuing profit.

### 2.5. Nonprofits and Mutuals

Traditional neoclassical theory recognizes two types of organization. These are the profit-maximizing firm and the government. In reality the range of organizational forms encountered in most countries is significantly greater. Some of these, such as workers' cooperatives, represent a very small portion of economic activity. However, others are significant. Nonprofit firms are important in many countries. In the United States nonprofits are important in health care, education, social services, and cultural activities. In these industries nonprofits compete directly with for-profit organizations. Table 2.7 shows the main sectors where taxable and tax-exempt organizations coexist and the relative shares of each (see also James and Rose-Ackerman 1986 and Hansmann 1996). It can be seen that in the sectors shown, both forms of organization coexist and compete successfully.

The industries where nonprofits compete with for-profits have

Table 2.7. Service Industries Where Taxable and Nontaxable Firms Co-exist: U.S. Totals 1992[a]

| SIC Code | Kind of business or operation | Taxable Firms[b] | | Tax-exempt Firms[c] | | Tax-exempt Firms' Share of Total | |
|---|---|---|---|---|---|---|---|
| | | Establishments (number) | Receipts[d] ($1,000) | Establishments (number) | Revenue[e] ($1,000) | Establishments (%) | Revenue (%) |
| **Health Services:** | | | | | | | |
| 8011 | General medical clinics | 4,736 | 12,590,420 | 3,187 | 16,548,253 | 40 | 57 |
| 8021 | Dental clinics | 604 | 351,169 | 115 | 73,640 | 16 | 17 |
| 805 | Nursing and personal care facilities | 14,954 | 33,989,607 | 5,925 | 15,220,487 | 28 | 31 |
| 8062 | General medical and surgical hospitals | 704 | 24,162,290 | 4,920 | 254,391,214 | 87 | 91 |
| 8063,9 | Specialty hospitals | 699 | 6,920,685 | 797 | 25,344,022 | 53 | 79 |
| 808 | Home health care services | 8,045 | 10,413,844 | 2,215 | 5,713,903 | 22 | 35 |
| 809 | Misc. health and allied services, n.e.c. | 11,457 | 9,604,620 | 6,492 | 7,122,298 | 36 | 43 |
| **Educational Services:** | | | | | | | |
| 823 | Libraries | 232 | 30,141 | 1,572 | 527,347 | 87 | 95 |
| 824 | Vocational schools | 4,615 | 3,892,230 | 1,052 | 548,601 | 19 | 12 |
| 829 | Schools and educational services, n.e.c. | 9,888 | 3,320,018 | 3,659 | 1,897,224 | 27 | 36 |
| **Social Services:** | | | | | | | |
| 83 | Total | 59,123 | 13,349,165 | 81,726 | 53,671,936 | 58 | 80 |
| 835 | Child day care services | 35,327 | 5,269,980 | 15,970 | 3,691,637 | 31 | 41 |
| 832,3,6,9 | Other social services | 23,796 | 8,079,185 | 65,756 | 49,980,299 | 73 | 86 |
| **R&D, Management and Related Services:** | | | | | | | |
| 8731 | Commercial physical & biological research | 3,826 | 11,788,343 | 344 | 4,978,474 | 8 | 30 |
| 8732 | Commercial economical, sociological and educational research | 5,165 | 6,138,318 | 536 | 352,374 | 9 | 5 |
| 8734 | Testing laboratories | 4,540 | 4,763,614 | 164 | 371,169 | 3 | 7 |

| | | | | | | |
|---|---|---|---|---|---|---|
| 8741 | Management services | 19,733 | 21,728,354 | 453 | 598,290 | 2 | 3 |
| 8742 | Management consulting services | 33,762 | 22,628,984 | 342 | 326,373 | 1 | 1 |
| 8743 | Public relations services | 5,103 | 2,890,250 | 205 | 63,935 | 4 | 2 |
| 8748 | Business consulting services, n.e.c. | 12,628 | 4,573,223 | 694 | 1,258,292 | 5 | 22 |
| Amusement, Recreation and Related Services: | | | | | | | |
| 7922 | Theatrical producers and misc. services | 4,255 | 4,433,701 | 1,669 | 1,296,809 | 28 | 23 |
| 7929 | Bands, orchestras, actors and other entertainers and entertainment groups | 5,831 | 4,191,788 | 1,420 | 1,522,885 | 20 | 27 |
| 7991 | Gymnasiums and athletic clubs | 1,697 | 880,109 | 183 | 145,255 | 10 | 14 |
| 7997 | Membership sports and recreation clubs | 7,275 | 5,018,717 | 7,452 | 5,609,613 | 51 | 53 |
| 841 | Museums and art galleries | 356 | 134,612 | 2,749 | 2,602,725 | 89 | 95 |
| 842 | Arboreta & botanical or zoological gardens | 119 | 57,085 | 329 | 595,818 | 73 | 91 |
| 7032 | Sporting and recreational camps | 1,840 | 603,079 | 1,205 | 373,727 | 40 | 38 |

*Source*: "The 1992 Census of Service Industries"; U.S. Department of Commerce, Bureau of the Census.

[a] For detailed definition of terms, refer to the table source.

[b] The two classifications are based on the federal income tax filing requirement for the establishment or organization. Establishments which indicated that all or part of their income was exempt from federal income tax under provisions of Section 501 of the IRS code were classified as tax-exempt; establishments indicating no such exemption were classified as taxable. All government-operated hospitals were classified as tax-exempt.

[c] The basic dollar volume measure for taxable service establishments includes receipts from customers or clients for services rendered, from the use of facilities, and from merchandise sold during 1992, except for health practitioners and legal, architectural, engineering and surveying services, which reported on a cash basis. Receipts are net after deductions for refunds and allowance for merchandise returned by customers. They do not include taxes collected from customers and remitted directly to a local, state, or federal tax agency, nor do they include income from contributions, gifts, grants, dividends, interest, and investments; or sale or rental of real estate.

[d] Basic dollar volume measure for tax-exempt firms. Includes revenue from customers or clients for services rendered and merchandise sold during 1992. Also included are income from interest, dividends, gifts, grants, rents, royalties, etc. Receipts from taxable business activities of firms exempt from federal income tax (unrelated business income) are also included in revenue. Revenue does not include taxes collected and directly paid, sale of real estate, investments, or other assets.

[e] n.e.c.: Not elsewhere classified.

particularly interesting implications for corporate governance. As seen above, standard views of corporate governance based on the agency theory of the firm suggest that governance mechanisms involving monitoring by outsiders are crucial in ensuring that organizations are run efficiently. However, in the sectors in Table 2.7, nonprofits compete quite successfully with for-profits. The formal governance mechanisms in these nonprofits appear very weak. There is no market for corporate control. There are typically self-perpetuating boards of trustees and directors who usually receive little if any compensation for their oversight facilities. However, these firms are able to compete successfully with for-profit entities, which are subject to the full rigors of the market for corporate control and other disciplining devices.

The financial sector provides a particularly interesting example of the coexistence of different organizational forms. Hansmann (1996) points out that, in the nineteenth century in the United States, mutual savings banks were a very successful form of organization. The term "mutual" in their title is misleading, since in fact they are legally nonprofits. The depositors do not have the right to vote on the affairs of the bank and they are governed by self-perpetuating boards. Of course mutual organizations where the depositors formally control the organization are also important in the financial sector. Mutual savings and loans have this structure. In the insurance industry, mutual organizations are also important. Nonprofits and mutuals have played a significant role in the financial sector not only in the United States but also in most other countries.

## III. The Role of Competition

It has been argued (see, e.g., Alchian 1950 and Stigler 1958) that competition in product markets is a very powerful force for ensuring good corporate governance. If the managers of a firm waste or consume large amounts of resources, the firm will be unable to compete and will go bankrupt. There seems little doubt that competition, particularly international competition, is a powerful force in disciplining management.

### 3.1. Managerial Slack

One idea studied in the corporate governance literature is that competition between different organizational *forms* may be helpful in limiting efficiency losses. If a family-owned business has the sole objective of maximizing share value, it may force all the corporations in that industry to do the same thing. An early attempt to model product-market competition as a mechanism to discipline managers is found in Hart (1983).

On the supply side, Hart assumes that there is a large number of small firms. A fraction $v$ are traditional profit maximizers; these are called *entrepreneurial* firms. The remaining fraction $1 - v$ are operated by managers who maximize their own interests; these are called *managerial* firms. The firms have identical cost functions $C(w, q, L)$, where $w$ is the input price, $q$ is the output level, and $L$ is the level of managerial effort. Managerial effort and input prices are assumed to be substitutes, in the sense that greater effort compensates for higher input costs:

$$C(w, q, L) = \hat{C}(\Phi(w, L), q).$$

The cost index $\Phi(w, L)$ is increasing in the input price $w$ and decreasing in managerial effort $L$. Ex ante, the input prices are independently and identically distributed across firms. Ex post, there is no aggregate uncertainty: the cross-sectional distribution of input prices is nonstochastic and proportional to the ex ante probability distribution.

The manager takes output and input prices as given and decides how much output to produce and how much managerial effort to exert in order to maximize his own preferences. An incentive problem arises because the manager can observe his input price $w$ and his effort $L$, but the shareholders cannot. Thus, a manager who faces a low input price may choose to shirk: instead of achieving high profits for the shareholders he exerts a low level of effort and claims that profits are low because the input price is high.

The manager's preferences are assumed to be additively separable in income and effort: the von Neumann–Morgenstern utility function is $H(U(I) - V(L))$, where $I$ is the manager's income and $L$ is his effort. The manager is infinitely risk averse: his utility-of-income function is very flat above $\bar{I}$ and very steep below $\bar{I}$. The manager's reservation utility is $\bar{U}$. In order to be acceptable to the manager, a managerial contract must guarantee the manager an income that is at least $\bar{I}$ and never call on the manager to make an effort greater than $\bar{L}$, where

$$U(\bar{I}) - V(\bar{L}) = H^{-1}(\bar{U}).$$

These restrictive assumptions are chosen to make the problem analytically tractable, but it turns out that they are crucial for the substantive results as well, as we shall see below.

Since the manager must be paid a fixed income and exert a fixed amount of effort to achieve his reservation utility, this is the only outcome that is consistent with efficiency. If the shareholders could observe the manager's effort $L$, they could achieve the first best by offering the manager a contract that pays him $\bar{I}$ as long as he exerts an effort $L = \bar{L}$. Since they cannot do this, they must settle for the second best. It is assumed that the shareholders know the distribution function $F(w)$ and the equilibrium product price $p$ and can observe the firm's ex post profit level. Let $\pi(p, \Phi)$ denote the maximum profits when the product price is $p$ and the cost index is $\Phi$. If the manager follows the first best rule of setting $L = \overline{L}$, the profits vary between a low of $\pi(p, \Phi(w_{max}, \overline{L}))$ and a high of $\pi(p, \Phi(w_{min}, \overline{L}))$. The manager must receive a salary of $\overline{I}$ (otherwise he gets less than his reservation utility $\overline{U}$) and there is no point giving him more (since his utility function is flat above $\overline{I}$). Thus, the best that the owners can do is to offer him a salary of $\overline{I}$ as long as profits are equal to $\pi(p, \Phi w_{max}, \overline{L}))$ or greater. The managers will accept this contract, which requires them to work flat out (i.e., choose $L = \overline{L}$) when $w = w_{max}$; but for any lower price $w < w_{max}$ they can slack by taking less effort. Precisely, for any $w < w_{max}$ the manager chooses $L(w)$ so that

$$\pi\left(p, \Phi(w, L(w))\right) = \pi\left(p, \Phi(w_{max}, \overline{L})\right).$$

Under this contract, the equilibrium level of aggregate output will be strictly lower and the output price will be strictly higher than in the first best.

This analysis assumes that the input prices for different firms are independent, so the law of large numbers implies that there is no aggregate uncertainty. Suppose, instead, that the input prices are perfectly correlated across firms. Then the equilibrium product price is stochastic and positively correlated with input prices. It is assumed that the shareholders cannot observe the equilibrium price or the profits of other firms in the industry. As before, it is optimal for the shareholders to pick some input price $\hat{w}$ and insist that the manager work flat out at that price. For any other price $w \neq \hat{w}$, the manager will continue to produce the same profits but will engage in some slack.

The amount of managerial slack in an individual firm is measured by the proportional increase in input prices that could be absorbed without any change in profits if slack could be eliminated. The average amount of slack is denoted by $X^{ind}$ in the market with independent input prices and $X^{corr}$ in the market with perfectly correlated input prices. Given an equilibrium of the kind described above and some additional assumptions, it can be shown that $X^{corr} \leq X^{ind}$. In the independent case, the product price is constant across states of nature, because the cross-sectional distribution of input prices is nonstochastic. When an individual manager faces an input price $w < w_{max}$, he can reduce his effort because he only needs to produce profits greater than or equal to $\pi(p, \Phi(w_{max}, \overline{L}))$, the amount that he would produce by working flat out when the input price is $w_{max}$. However, when input prices are perfectly correlated, there is a second effect to consider. Suppose that $\hat{p}$ is the product price in the state with the input price $\hat{w}$. In a state of nature where $w <$ $\hat{w}$, the output price $p$ will be lower than $\hat{p}$. This is because all the entrepreneurial firms also face a lower input price $w < \hat{w}$ and are producing more output, thus pushing down the output price. The manager has to exert more effort to compensate for the fall in the output price, and this effect offsets his ability to slack as a result of the fall in input price.

It can be shown that $X^{ind}$ is the same as the amount of slack that would be realized in a monopolistic firm whose owners were faced by the same incentive problem in controlling the manager. In this sense, competition does not have an effect on managerial slack in the independent case. However, it can be shown that an increase in the fraction of entrepreneurial firms $v$ does reduce $X^{corr}$. The more entrepreneurial firms there are in the market, the stronger the incentive effect of competition on managers will be.

We remarked above that the simplifying assumptions about the managers' risk aversion turn out to be crucial for the substantive conclusions of Hart's analysis. Scharfstein (1988) shows that the result that increased competition reduces managerial slack can be reversed when the manager's marginal utility of income is strictly positive. Perhaps this should not be too surprising. Consider a different model, say a Cournot oligopoly model in which managerial effort is unobserved and the manager receives a fixed share of profits. Greater competition (in the form of a larger number of firms in the market) will reduce profits and hence the managers' incentive to work. There is a trade-off, of course, between the interest of the shareholders in greater profits and the interest of consumers in getting more output at a lower price, so this is not to say that greater competition is a bad thing. Still, it suggests that the effects of competition will generally be ambiguous.

The role of the market in Hart (1983) and Scharfstein (1988) is to provide information. If the owners could observe the profits of the entrepreneurial firms, they could use that information as a benchmark to condition the rewards to the managers. This is the approach taken by Holmstrom (1982) and Nalebuff and Stiglitz (1983), for example. In Hart's model this information is unavailable, so an indirect channel must be used. Competition translates a fall in input prices into a fall in output prices, which in turn are translated into lower profits unless the managers work harder to keep profits up.

In a recent study, Schmidt (1997) addresses a related question in a model without hidden information. Schmidt (1997) observes that increased competition may threaten the survival of a firm by forcing it into bankruptcy and asks what effect this will have on managerial slack. Schmidt's model assumes that the manager is risk neutral and wealth constrained and that he suffers a penalty (lost rents, forgone opportunities) when the firm goes bankrupt. The manager is required to engage in efforts that reduce future production costs. Costs are assumed to take on two values, high or low, and greater effort reduces the probability of high costs. The actual costs are observed after the manager has made the effort, and at that point the owner decides whether to liquidate the firm or not. Greater competition lowers the price that the firm receives for its output and, other things being equal, increases the risk that the owner will find it optimal to liquidate the firm.

Schmidt discovers that greater competition has two effects on the manager's optimal effort. The first is the threat-of-liquidation effect that we expect to find: the manager has a directly increased incentive to work harder to avoid liquidation. There is also an indirect effect, since the cost to the owner of providing incentives to take high effort is reduced. So the threat-of-liquidation effect unambiguously raises managerial effort.

The second effect is ambiguous and results from the fact that increased competition reduces profits and may reduce the benefits of a cost reduction. As a result, the owner may be disinclined to pay the manager the high rents necessary to achieve a cost reduction. If the value of a cost reduction is decreasing in the degree of competition, the net effect of increased competition may be to lower managerial effort.

The second effect occurs only if the manager is paid more than his reservation level. Schmidt (1997) cites a study by Aghion, Dewatripont, and Rey (1995) that treats a special case of his model. In their model, the manager is always paid his reservation level and so the effect of increased competition is unambiguous.

These studies describe a mechanism by which competition in the product market helps discipline managers, but they are restrictive in several respects:

- First, they all take the agency approach, in which the main obstacle to achieving efficiency is the principal–agent relationship between the manager and the shareholders. As we have indicated, some organizations appear to function successfully even in the absence of external governance mechanisms.
- Second, the focus of the models on cost minimization seems to be too narrow. While cost minimization may be a useful proxy for other important managerial activities, it is not clear that this model captures all the important features of managerial behavior.
- Third, casual empiricism suggests that "effort" is something that managers supply quite readily. The failure of management to maximize the shareholders' interests may come from sources other

than lack of effort. With an alternative source of management failure, such as differences in inherent ability (adverse selection), risk shifting, or private benefits, the effects of competition may be different.

- Fourthly, the entrepreneurial firms that force the managers to provide greater effort are a deus ex machina in these models. What happens in industries where *all* the firms are managerial? Perhaps competition among managerial firms will only ensure that corporate governance is equally inefficient across firms. For example, if all the firms in a market are corporations that face an agency problem, they will all be able to survive if the inefficiencies associated with corporate governance problems affect all firms equally. Competition between them may not lead to full efficiency (Jensen and Meckling 1976).

- Fifthly, the arguments of Hart and his followers assume that markets are perfectly competitive. As we have seen, things could be quite different in markets that are imperfectly competitive. Many markets in which Fortune 500 companies operate are oligopolistic. These companies compete on the product market, but it is not clear what effect imperfect competition has on managerial slack. Possibly collusion among a small number of firms will take the form of high levels of managerial slack rather than high monopoly profits.

Nonetheless, the idea that competition enhances the performance of managerial firms may have a broader application than these models suggest. We next review the empirical evidence on the effect of competition on performance. Although limited in quantity, this suggests that competition is important. We then go on to develop an alternative to the principal–agent approach.

## 3.2. The Effectiveness of Competition as a Control Mechanism

The empirical evidence on the role of competition in ensuring corporate performance is sparse. Nickell (1996) suggests that the most persuasive evidence consists of broad-brush observations. The first of these is the low level of productivity in Eastern Europe compared to Western Europe after competition was suppressed in the East under communist regimes. The second is the importance of domestic competition in ensuring that firms are internationally competitive, demonstrated by Porter (1990). The third is that deregulation is generally followed by productivity gains. Graham, Kaplan, and Sibley (1983) document this for the case of the U.S. airline industry.

A number of studies have provided detailed evidence of the effect of competition on performance. One question is the effect of competition on innovation. Geroski (1990) and Blundell, Griffith, and Van Reenen (1995) find that the more concentrated an industry and the higher are other measures of monopoly power, the lower is the rate of innovation. Another is the relationship between competition and technical efficiency. Caves and Barton (1990), Green and Mayes (1991), and Caves (1992) find that above a certain level of market concentration technical efficiency is reduced. Caves (1980) points to the evidence in the management literature that competition leads to more efficient decision-making structures in firms. Finally, Nickell (1996) and Nickell, Nicolitsas, and Dryden (1997) find evidence that the higher is the level of competition, the higher is the level of growth in productivity. Moreover, the latter paper documents that competition is a substitute for other corporate governance mechanisms.

## IV. An Evolutionary Approach

The neoclassical theory of the firm regards the firm as a collection of inputs and outputs. The role of the manager is simply to make the choice that maximizes profits. Coase (1937) introduced the notion of transaction costs to explain the existence and the size of the firm. Jensen and Meckling (1976) introduced the agency-cost approach. Williamson (1985) explained the nature of the firm in terms of strategic problems and, subsequently, Grossman and Hart (1986) developed the theory of the firm in terms of the control of assets. All of the recent approaches stress a struggle for control between insiders and outsiders who have conflicting interests. Jensen (1986) and Hart and Moore (1989) stress the struggle between managers and shareholders or external claimants for the control of earnings. Our perspective on the firm is rather different. It seems to us that the agency approach, broadly defined, is somewhat exaggerated and hard to reconcile with the successful performance (by some standards) of actual firms. This alternative perspective can be summarized in the following points:

- In the United States, at least, the upper level of management is remarkable for the amount of effort it makes. While there may be some conflict of interest between shareholders and managers, it appears to be the case that managers do regard the success of the firm, as measured by earnings or growth, as part of their own objective function. Managers, in other words, work hard and appear to be quite "entrepreneurial."

- A manager, at the top level, is not merely an employee who exerts effort on behalf of an absentee employer, the shareholders. The top managers in a company act like entrepreneurs. They choose the direction of the firm and assign crucial tasks to their subordinates. They identify new opportunities and coordinate the managerial team as it seeks to exploit these opportunities. In this sense, the manager in our view is very similar to Frank Knight's entrepreneur (Knight 1964).
- Shareholders may not know better than the manager what needs to be done. A manager is not merely a stand-in for the shareholder, making decisions that the shareholder could make for him or herself. The manager has entrepreneurial skills that the shareholder in all probability lacks. The major concern for the shareholder is likely to be not whether the manager is working hard enough (his colleagues will see to that), or whether the manager is following instructions, but whether the manager has "the right stuff," the entrepreneurial skills and talents to achieve success for the firm.

To the extent that shareholders have a view about the suitability of the management of a company, they can express it through the stock market, buying shares in companies whose management is "undervalued" and selling shares in companies whose management is "overvalued." This vote of confidence may be the only way of expressing their information about the quality and performance of the management, given the absence of effective mechanisms for replacing or disciplining management. However, even this view may overstate the role of shareholders in choosing management. There may be important cases where the shareholders' information about the competence or skill of management is very limited because of lack of experience. This will be particularly true of start-up companies with a new and relatively inexperienced management. It may also be true of an established company with an experienced management when the company is undertaking an expansion into a new area, for example, developing a highly innovative product or diversifying into an unrelated market. In these cases, it may not be possible for shareholders to say with any degree of confidence which managements will succeed and which will fail.

This view does not require us to assume that shareholders are stupid or that managers have superior information about their own competence. It may be that no one knows what is the optimal strategy for the firm. More precisely, there may be a lack of common knowledge about the optimal strategy so that, while each potential manager thinks his strategy would be the best, equally well-informed shareholders and potential managers may disagree. In this case, the issue is not how to give the shareholders control but how to decide who ought to be given control. As we have argued in Allen and Gale (1999), one of the functions of a stock market is to match managers and shareholders with similar views of the world, in cases where there is diversity of opinion; that is, individuals agree to disagree. Placing a company in the hands of a manager and giving him freedom to manage may be the only way to determine whether a particular strategy or style of management is going to be successful. In other words, trial and error is the only way to identify the best management. Managers may be no better able to distinguish skill levels than shareholders; alternatively, the managers may all think they are brilliant, which is not much more helpful. This is different from the adverse selection problem that arises when managers know their skill levels but shareholders do not. In a world with diversity of opinion, clever incentive schemes and selection processes tend not to be very effective.

There are costs as well as benefits of control. Burkart, Gromb, and Panunzi (1997) argue that too much monitoring (without commitment to reward the manager) will rob the manager of the incentives to exert effort on behalf of the shareholders. Allen and Gale (forthcoming) argue that superior information about the running of the firm may make it optimal to give the manager "almost complete" discretion about the running of the firm, even if the manager has private benefits that cause his interests and preferences to diverge systematically from those of the shareholders. Here we focus on the question of which manager is best suited to run the firm. A manager is regarded as a highly motivated automaton, who will run the firm in the way that he is "programmed" to run it. He probably feels that this is the best way to run the firm, but that is irrelevant. From the point of view of shareholders and other stakeholders, the relevant question is how things will turn out under this or that choice of manager.

In a dynamic market, one with constantly changing products, processes, and prices, it may not be possible to say with precision at any point in time which management is best suited to succeed in the future. From this point of view, the absence of effective discipline through takeovers may not be a drawback. The theory of the takeover as a means of disciplining management rests on the assumption that there exists a raider who knows how to run the firm more efficiently. There may well be lots of people who think that they can run the firm more efficiently, but they are not necessarily right in believing that. More precisely, it may not be common knowledge that a given raider will do better. If the raider is investing his own money, there is no reason why he should not try to take over the firm and run it as he sees fit. But if he is investing someone else's money, it is not clear why his (uninformed) backers should believe that he will do a better job. In fact, an unnoticed obstacle to the takeover as a management discipline device may be the difficulty of putting together a coalition of investors who can agree on a better strategy with some confidence.

It is precisely in this case, where the information of outsiders is limited, that competition in the product market is most important. In the absence of well-informed shareholders and effective means of controlling management decisions, competition among companies has two functions; it disciplines managements and at the same time reveals which managements are the strongest. The company with the strongest management will develop the best products, produce the highest earnings and growth and drive companies with weaker management out of business or, at least, leave them with a much smaller share of the market.

In the absence of good information about the preferred management strategy, the second-best optimum may be to let various managements compete and see which one succeeds. This suggests an evolutionary perspective in which competition does not merely lead to static value maximization asymptotically as time goes to infinity, but actually leads to incentive-efficient selection of managements in the short run.

Evolutionary arguments have been used in the past to suggest that competition among firms will select a population of firms that maximize profits (or value), even if none of them consciously make the attempt to do this (Friedman 1953; Machlup 1967). Some recent models have confirmed this hypothesis under particular assumptions (Luo 1995). Others (Radner 1995) have found, not surprisingly, that firms that maximize other objectives, such as probability of survival, may last longer on average and gradually come to dominate the population. The analysis of Radner (1995) considers the survival of a firm that accumulates capital until its net worth is zero (the bankruptcy point). Firms are subject to exogenous "productivity" shocks, but there is no direct competition among firms. There does not seem to be any general theoretical justification for the Friedman–Machlup hypothesis, but it may be that within particular, empirically relevant, environments it can be shown to hold.

Our view differs from the traditional application of evolutionary ideas in several respects:

- We have in mind a particular kind of competition, where firms compete for control of a market or compete to develop a new or better product before its rivals. In a dynamic market, this kind of competition may have a winner-take-all characteristic, where one product or management style or form of organization may drive out others.
- Fixed costs are important in most modern industries, and this also reinforces the winner-take-all characteristic of competition. Fixed costs also make growth important. When firms are growing this helps to ensure that shareholders receive a return since assets are being acquired.

The form of competition is important. As we noted earlier, competition does not merely take the relatively innocuous form of reducing prices and profits. A firm can lose its entire market to a stronger competitor. In fact, this kind of competition may be seen as an alternative to the takeover. Instead of having a raider take control of the assets of a company with a weak management, replace the management, and change the target firm's strategy, a competing firm takes control of the market of a company with a weak management and dispenses with the whole firm.

It may be argued that this form of discipline is inefficient to the extent that it wastes the assets (physical and human capital) of the now defunct firm. But this argument is not necessarily correct. If the defunct firm has assets that are specific to a product or technology that failed, the assets would have to be abandoned in a takeover as well. If the assets are non-specific, they can be used by the firm that takes over the market too. So taking over the firm's market need not be any less effective than taking over the firm itself.

Finally, we need to mention the internal finance problem. The absence of effective external controls on managers and the reliance of the typical firm on internally generated funds (retained earnings) for investment purposes, means that the managerial firm is largely autonomous. This is even more true in countries like Japan and Germany than it is in the United States and the United Kingdom. There may be some reason to expect companies that have been very successful in the past to have an entrepreneurial team of managers and to be successful in the future. Therefore, a firm that has generated large amounts of cash may be very good at identifying and exploiting opportunities for investment. To the extent that there is a good match between the earnings generated in the past and the profitability of investment in the firm, this system of financing investment internally through retained earnings may be fairly efficient.

In a dynamic market, however, where the environment is constantly changing, the possibility of a serious mismatch between the allocation of funds and the allocation of investment opportunities cannot be ignored. There will be start-up companies with little cash and great opportunities for growth and mature companies with a lot of cash and limited opportunities for growth. The crucial question is whether this mismatch can be identified or, more precisely, whether it is common knowledge, and hence whether anything can be done about it. For the same reasons that we earlier questioned the efficiency of the takeover mechanism, even if it were effective in changing managements, we here question the possibility of improving on internal finance. In both cases, an improvement assumes that outsiders (shareholders, raiders) have better information about the right choice than management and can agree on what should be done. If this assumption is not satisfied, internal finance may be the best that can be done subject to the diversity of opinion that characterizes the stock market.

## V. Competition for Markets: A Parable

In his seminal contribution on the role of takeovers in corporate governance, Manne (1965) conceived of firms as being run by management teams of different qualities. The takeover was conceived of as a mechanism for displacing underperforming management teams. A firm that was being run by a good team could take over a firm that was being run by a bad team, get rid of the bad team, and improve the firm's performance. We also think the quality of the management team is crucial to the success of the firm, but competition in the product market plays the role of takeovers: the firm with the stronger management team captures the product market from the firm with the weaker management team. A simple formal example will clarify these ideas and provide a test of theoretical coherence.

Firms are set up by teams of managers. There is an exogenously specified set of teams $i = 1, \ldots, n$ and each team sets up a single firm. The aim of the firm or team is to develop a product that will be produced and sold in the future. The value of the product depends on the amount of capital invested and on the quality of the management team.

There are two dates, $t = 0, 1$. At date 0, the management of firm $i$ chooses an amount of capital $k_i \geq 0$ to invest in the development of a product. Investment in the firm is provided by a large number of risk-neutral outside investors, who play no active role in the management of the firm. The opportunity cost of capital is denoted by $R$: for every unit of capital invested at date 0 the investors give up a safe return of $R$ units at date 1.

At date 0 there is uncertainty about the quality of the management team and the decisions they make. However, there is no *asymmetry* of information: managers and investors have the same information about the quality of the management team and, hence, about the future payoffs of the firm. This uncertainty is resolved at date 1 when the quality of the management teams and their products is revealed. Uncertainty about the quality of the teams is represented by the state of nature $w$, which is unknown at date 0 and becomes common knowledge at date 1.

The value of the product developed by team $i$ is given by $V_i(k_i, w)$. Because there is symmetric information about the quality of the team, insiders and outsiders know the function $V_i(\cdot)$ and the investment $k_i$ and have the same probability distribution $F(\cdot)$ over the states of nature $w$. We assume that $V(0, w) = 0$ for all $w$ so capital is essential to the development of a useful product. In general, the more capital that is provided, the greater is the probability that the value of the product is high. We assume that once the new product is developed it can be produced at constant marginal cost and, without essential loss of generality, we set the marginal cost equal to zero.

Managers are assumed to be risk neutral and maximize the expected terminal value of the investors' net wealth. Note that there is no moral hazard problem. The managers work as hard as they can to maximize the expected returns of the investors. They also commit to pay all the profits to the investors.

At date 1 there is assumed to be a continuum of identical consumers whose measure is normalized to one. Each consumer wants to consume at most one unit of a new product.

## 5.1. Equilibrium

At date 0 the firms jointly choose their investment strategies $k = (k_1, \ldots, k_n)$. At the beginning of date 1, the state of nature $w$ is realized and the firms observe the quality of the product they have developed

$$V(k, w) = (V_1(k_1, w), \cdots, V_n(k_n, w)).$$

Then the firms engage in Bertrand competition. Since the qualities are continuously distributed (for $k_i > 0$) the probability of ties can be ignored. Then Bertrand competition will lead to an outcome in which the best product captures the entire market and the price charged for this product is equal to the difference between the value of the first and second-best products. The price for every other product is zero. At this price, consumers are indifferent between the first- and second-best products, but they will demand only the first-best product in equilibrium (if a positive fraction of consumers were expected to choose the second-best product, the firm with the first-best product would have chosen a slightly lower price to capture the entire market). Formally, for any firm $i$ let

$$V_{-i}(k_{-i}, w) = (V_1(k_1, w), \cdots, V_{i-1}(k_{i-1}, w), V_{i+1}(k_{i+1}, w), \cdots, V_n(k_n, w))$$

denote the vector of the qualities of goods $j \neq i$; let

$$k_{-i} = (k_1, \cdots, k_{i-1}, k_{i+1}, \cdots, k_n)$$

denote the allocation of investment in goods $j \neq i$; and let

$$V_{-i}^*(k_{-i}, w) = \max_{j \neq i}\{V_j(k_j, w)\}$$

denote the highest value in the vector $V_{-i}(k_{-i}, w)$. Then, in the second-period equilibrium, the price charged for the $i$th product is denoted by $p_i(k, w)$ and satisfies

$$p_i(k, w) = \max\{V_i(k, w) - V_{-i}^*(k_{-i}, w), 0\}, \forall i.$$

Since the demand is equal to one for the best product and zero for the rest, the revenue of firm $i$ is also equal to $p_i(k, w)$.

At the first date, we look for a Nash equilibrium in the investment levels. The $i$th team chooses $k_i$ to maximize $E[p_i(k_i, k_{-i}, w)] - Rk_i$, taking as given the investment levels of the other management teams, $k_{-i}$. So a Nash equilibrium is a vector $k^*$ such that

$$k_i^* \in \arg \max_{k_i \geq 0}\{E[p_i(k_i, k_{-i}^*, w)] - Rk_i\},$$

for each $i$.

## 5.2. Optimum

Since the cost of production at date 1 is zero, the surplus generated by consuming the $i$th product is $V_i(k_i, w)$. Surplus is maximized by having all consumers consume the best product, so the total surplus at date 1 is

$$V^*(k, w) \equiv \max_{i=1, \cdots n}\{V_i(k_i, w)\}.$$

Assuming that the consumers are also risk neutral and that lump-sum transfers are possible, the first-best efficient allocation is found by maximizing net surplus, that is, by solving the planner's problem:

$$\max_{k \geq 0} V^*(k) - R \sum_{i=1}^{n} k_i,$$

where $V^*(k) \equiv E[V^*(k, w)]$ is the expected value of $V^*(k, w)$.

Define $V_{-i}^*(k_{-i}) \equiv E[V_{-i}^*(k_{-i}, w)]$. Then the objective function $V^*(k)$ can be written equivalently as

$$V^*(k) = E\left[\max\left\{V_i(k_i, w) - V_{-i}^*(k_{-i}, w), 0\right\} + V_{-i}^*(k_{-i}, w)\right]$$

$$= E\left[\max\left\{V_i(k_i, w) - V_{-i}^*(k_{-i}, w), 0\right\}\right] + V_{-i}^*(k_{-i})$$

and the planner's problem can be rewritten equivalently as

$$\max_{k \geq 0} E\left[\max\left\{V_i(k_i, w) - V_{-i}^*(k_{-i}, w), 0\right\}\right] + V_{-i}^*(k_{-i}) - R \sum_{i=1}^{n} k_i,$$

Suppose that $k^*$ is a solution to the planner's problem above. A necessary condition is that $k_i^*$ maximizes

$$E\left[\max\left\{V_i(k_i, w) - V_{-i}^*\left(k_{-i}^*, w\right), 0\right\}\right] - Rk_i$$

$$= E\left[p_i\left(k_i, k_{-i}^*, w\right)\right] - Rk_i.$$

But this means that $k_i^*$ satisfies the equilibrium condition for the firm's choice of $k_i$. Hence, we have the following result.

*Proposition 1. If $k^*$ is a solution to the planner's problem, then $k^*$ is a Nash equilibrium of the firm's investment "game."*

The proposition tells us that an optimum can be decentralized as a market equilibrium through the uncoordinated investment decisions of the firms. The converse may not be true, however. A market equilibrium, in which each firm maximizes expected present value, need not be an optimum. Here is a trivial example to illustrate this. For ease of exposition it is kept very simple. With a few changes, it could be made to satisfy the assumptions of the model.

Suppose there are two firms $i = 1, 2$ and that for each firm a fixed cost $F > 0$ is required to produce a good of value $\overline{V}$ (there is no uncertainty). Innovation is efficient because $\overline{V} > RF$, but there is no point in having both firms innovate. There are two asymmetric Nash equilibria in which precisely one of the firms innovates (and earns the monopoly profits $\overline{V} - RF$) and the other remains passive. Both of these equilibria are efficient. There is also a symmetric, mixed-strategy equilibrium, in which both firms innovate with probability $0 < \lambda < 1$. If a firm innovates it must pay the fixed cost $F$ at date 0; but it only earns positive revenue at the second date if the other firm fails to innovate, which happens with probability $(1 - \lambda)$. If both firms innovate, they engage in Bertrand competition at the second date and both earn zero revenue. Thus, the expected profits from innovating are $(1 - \lambda)\overline{V} - RF$ and this is equal to the profit from not innovating if and only if

$$(1-\lambda)\overline{V} - RF = 0$$

$$\Rightarrow (1-\lambda) = \frac{RF}{\overline{V}} \in (0,1).$$

The Nash equilibrium defined by this equation is inefficient because there is a positive probability $\lambda^2$ that both firms innovate and a positive probability $(1 - \lambda)^2$ that neither firm innovates.

Without symmetry, we can have inefficient pure strategy equilibria. For example, suppose that there are two firms $i = 1, 2$ and that firm 1 is more efficient than firm 2: each can produce a product of value $\overline{V}$, but the cost is higher for firm 2; that is, $F_1 < F_2$. Suppose that $RF_2 < \overline{V}$ so that both firms can produce positive surplus. Then there are two pure strategy equilibria, an efficient one in which firm 1 develops the new product and firm 2 does not, and an inefficient equilibrium in which firm 2 develops the product and firm 1 does not.

## 5.3. Learning and Evolution

The simple model underlying Proposition 1 captures the idea that in a winner-takes-all environment, equilibrium can be efficient. With Bertrand pricing and inelastic demand, the market is a kind of *Vickrey mechanism* that awards the winner with revenue exactly equal to his marginal contribution to the surplus in the economy. Although the framework is special, it is worth noting that Proposition 1 does not require any special assumptions on the development technology $V_i(\cdot)$ or on the distribution of the state of nature $w$. Nonetheless, the static version of the model ignores many of the interesting questions of corporate governance, which require a multiperiod framework for their analysis.

Suppose there is a finite sequence of dates $t = 0, 1, \ldots, T$ and that firms can invest at date $t < T$ to develop new products at date $t + 1$. As before, there are $n$ firms $i = 1, \ldots, n$ and the investment of firm $i$ at date $t$ is denoted by $k_{it}$. The state of nature $w = (w_0, w_1, \ldots, w_{T-1})$ is composed of $T$ components, where $w_t$ represents the uncertainty in the development process at date $t$. The management teams have symmetric beliefs about the distribution of $w_t$ at date 0 and that they all receive the same information at date $t > 0$. The value of the good developed at date $t$ is denoted by $V_i(k_{it}, w_t)$. Note that the value of the product depends only on the component $v$ and not on the full vector $w$ as before. The function $V_i(\cdot)$ does not depend explicitly on $t$, but there is no loss of generality in this since we have not specified the distribution of $w_t$.

Once the new goods are available at dates $t$, the firms compete in Bertrand fashion for the unit demand from consumers. There is no discounting over time, so the firms seek to maximize the sum of their expected net profits over the $T$ dates.

Each period is thought of as a development cycle in which a new generation of goods appears. There is no competition between the goods developed at date $t$ and date $t + 1$. Thus, at each date $t$ the firms are playing the same game; only the distribution of $w_t$ has changed. At each date equilibrium is defined in the same way as in the previous section.

The distribution of $w_t$ changes over time for two reasons. First, there may be exogenous changes over time (technological progress). Second, the observation of the quality of the products developed by the firms at date $t$ reveals something about the state $w_t$ and this will change the conditional distribution of $w_{t+1}$ to the extent that $w_t$ and $w_{t+1}$ are correlated. For example, suppose that $w_t = (w_{1t}, \ldots, w_{nt})$, where $w_{it}$ is a noisy signal of the quality of firm $i$'s management team and let

$$\log w_{it} = t \log A + \log \theta_i + \log \varepsilon_{it}$$

where $t \log A$ is a deterministic trend term representing technological progress ($A \geq 1$), $\log \theta_i \sim N(\mu_i, \sigma_i^2)$ is the true quality of the management team, uncertain but constant over time, and $\log \varepsilon_{it} \sim N(0, \sigma_\varepsilon^2)$ is a noise term.

In what follows, assume that the technology is given by

$$V_i(k_{it}, w_t) = v_i(k_i)w_{it}.$$

Then observing the value of $V_i(k_{it}, w_t)$ is equivalent to observing $w_{it}$, a noisy signal of $\theta_i$, and all the management teams will update their beliefs symmetrically. The investment decision at date $t$ is conditioned on all the information that has become available over time. If firm $i$ has developed products with low values, the probability distribution of $\theta_i$ will be shifted to the left; if it has developed high-value products, the probability distribution of $\theta_i$ will be shifted to the right. Other things being equal, the optimal and equilibrium investment in firm $i$ will increase or decrease as the public estimate of the quality of that firm's management improves or worsens. In this sense, the industry evolves: better managements get higher investment and worse managements get lower investment over time. Some firms may have to shut down altogether.

As long as $k_{it} > 0$ for all dates $t < T$, the information revealed at each date is independent of the value of $k_{it}$. Positive investment is optimal, for example, if

$$v_i'(k_{it}) \to \infty \quad \text{as} \quad k_{it} \to 0, \forall i,$$

because the distributions of $w_{it}$ are unbounded. Consequently, the surplus maximization problem at each date is independent of the others and solving the static problem at each date yields an optimum over the $T +$ 1 period horizon. Conversely, if $k^* = (k_0^*, \ldots, k_{T-1}^*) >> 0$ is an optimum then it must be an equilibrium, by the argument used to prove Proposition 1, since each firm maximizes long-run profits if and only if it maximizes profits at each date. Hence, we have the following result.

*Proposition 2. Suppose that $k^*$ is a solution to the planner's problem of maximizing surplus over a $T + 1$ period horizon and suppose that $k_{it}^* > 0$ for every i and $t < T$. Then $k^*$ is a subgame perfect equilibrium of the firm's investment "game."*

As we stressed at the outset, our focus is on selection rather than moral hazard. To make this clear, we have adopted the extreme assumptions that every management team works "flat out" and seeks to maximize the interests of their shareholders by maximizing net present value. Furthermore, managers and investors have symmetric information about the quality of management teams and the value of the strategies they follow. The crucial problem is to identify the best managements and this can only be done by experience, by observing the outcome of their managerial strategies.

So far, we have not mentioned the thorny problem of internal finance in this context. It has been implicitly assumed that management does whatever it can to maximize the expected wealth of the outside investors, including reallocating the profits from the first round of profit development in the firms that are expected to be the most profitable in the second round. So if firm $i$ develops the best product at date $t$ and earns large profits but does not have good prospects at date $t + 1$, those profits will be turned over to some other firm $j$ to invest in its own development projects. There are conditions in which 100 percent internal financing is optimal. For example, if the highest quality management team earns the highest profits at date $t + 1$ because it developed the best product at date $t$, then it may be optimal for this firm to reinvest its profits in product development at date $t + 1$. These are extreme conditions, however, and in general things will be much more complicated. The firm that has the largest pot of cash at date $t + 1$ may not have the best ideas for developing a new product. How can we get this firm to give up its cash to allow another entrepreneur the chance to develop a better product? How do we get Bill Gates to invest his money in Sun Microsystems to develop Java? There may be a role for antitrust policy to break up monopolies at some point.

Inefficient internal finance appears to be a problem in diversified firms. Lamont (1997) found that investment by oil companies in nonoil divisions was reduced when oil prices fell sharply in 1986. His evidence was consistent with diversified companies overinvesting and subsidizing underperforming segments of the firm. Shin and Stulz (1998) consider a wide range of firms operating in multiple businesses. They also find evidence of cross subsidization and argue this is inefficient because it is unrelated to the investment opportunities of the divisions as measured by Tobin's Q. Berger and Ofek (1995) find that diversified firms sell at a discount and identify the extent of the discount with the extent to which divisions invest in low-Q industries. Finally, Scharfstein (1998) provides evidence of "socialism" in capital allocation in conglomerates. Divisions in high-Q manufacturing industries tend to invest less than stand-alone peers while in low-Q manufacturing industries the reverse is true. All this suggests that internal capital markets may allocate resources worse than external markets.

This problem is more complicated if we recognize that there may be *diversity of opinion* about what is the best product or the best strategy for developing a better product (see Allen and Gale 1999). In the presence of diversity of opinion, the efficient allocation depends on the beliefs of the individuals involved. Because of the divergence of their beliefs, it is harder to make everyone better off, there are more efficient allocations, and this increases the possibility that the market equilibrium is efficient. These are issues that cannot be pursued here, but it indicates the difficulty of passing judgment on efficiency of the allocation of resources we observe in a world of autonomous management teams.

## 5.4. Competition within the Product Cycle

The assumption that a single period corresponds to a complete product cycle is crucial. If the products developed in one period compete with the products developed in the next period, things become much more complicated. The fact that a good product has been developed at date $t$ makes it harder to develop a profitable new product at date $t + 1$. The bar has been raised and any new product must exceed the value of the existing product to capture the market. It may well happen that the product developed at the first date $t$ is so good that it is not worthwhile for any firm to invest in developing a product at date $t$. In this framework there many not exist any subgame perfect equilibrium that is efficient. A three-period example will make this point.

There are two identical firms $i = 1,2$. There is no uncertainty: $w_0 = 0$ and $w_1 = 1$. At date 0 the development technology is

$$V_i(k_i, w_0) = \begin{cases} 5 & k_i \geq 9 \\ 0 & k_i < 9 \end{cases}$$

and at date 1 it is

$$V_i(k_i, w_1) = \begin{cases} 5 & k_i \geq 2 \\ 0 & k_i < 2 \end{cases}$$

The only function of the states here is to shift the technology, making it more efficient at date 1 than at date 0. The opportunity cost of investment is $R = 1$. Since the technology is deterministic, there is no advantage to having both firms invest at a single date. The question is whether to invest 9 at date 0 or 2 at date 1. The former yields a surplus of $2 \times 5 - 9 = 1$ and the latter a surplus of $5 - 2 = 3$, so the efficient decision is to develop the product at date 1. However, there is no subgame perfect equilibrium that achieves this. Suppose that firm $i$ invests $k_i = 2$ at date 1 in equilibrium and that no firm invests at date 0. Then firm $j \neq i$ earns zero profits and can do better by investing $k_j = 9$ at date 1. To see this, note that once firm $j$ has developed the product, firm $i$'s best response at date 1 is to invest $k_i = 0$, because if firm $i$ also develops the product they will both earn no revenue at date 2 as a result of Bertrand competition, and that means that firm $i$'s profit is $0 - 2 = -2$. By preempting firm $i$, firm $j$ captures all the surplus and earns a profit of $2 \times 5 - 9 = 1$, which is greater than 0.

This preemption motive does not occur in the two-period version of the model, because firms choose their investments at the same time. The three-period example above is special, but the fact that development activity in the current period affects future investment in development is a robust feature of models with more than two periods when successive generations of products compete directly.

An interesting question is whether there are particular classes of games in which an analogue of Proposition 1 holds. One example will make this possibility clear. Suppose we have a structure like a patent race in which the firms compete to produce a product of fixed value $\bar{V}$. At each period, either one of the firms has produced this product and the game stops, or the product is not yet developed and the game continues.

Then conditional on the game continuing, there is no competing product in existence and the structure of the game does not change over time, except that the time horizon gets shorter and the potential surplus shrinks proportionately.

Given that product-market competition is one of the more plausible governance mechanisms, it is surprising how little formal analysis has been done in this area. Much work remains to be done on this topic.

## VI. Concluding Remarks

Since Berle and Means (1932) pointed to the separation of ownership and control in the modern corporation, the literature on corporate governance has concentrated on the agency problem between shareholders and managers. It has been widely agreed that the board of directors is an ineffective way of overcoming this problem. The focus instead has been on external governance mechanisms. As we have seen, the theoretical and empirical evidence suggests they do not work very well.

In the United States and United Kingdom the main external mechanism for corporate control is the market. The three ways in which this operates are through proxy contests, friendly mergers, and hostile takeovers. Like boards of directors, proxy contests are also widely agreed to be ineffective as a means of disciplining managers. Friendly mergers allow efficiency gains to be made but do not solve the agency problem. This leaves hostile takeovers as the main way in which managers can be disciplined. However, as Hansmann (1996) points out these are a relatively recent invention and were not widely used until the 1960s. The efficiency of firms did not apparently change very much at this juncture. There are also theoretical problems with the operation of the takeover mechanism such as the Grossman and Hart (1980) free-rider problem which were detailed above. Finally, the empirical evidence is mixed. There are increases in stock market values as a result of mergers and takeovers, but it is not clear why these increases occur. The evidence from studies of accounting data suggest changes in operating efficiency are hard to find. Alternative explanations are that the increase in stock values is due to a recognition by the market of previous undervaluation or a transfer from other stakeholders as suggested by Shleifer and Summers (1988).

In Japan and Germany, the absence of a market for corporate control has led to an alternative theory of how the agency problem is overcome. In Japan it has been suggested that the main bank system performs this role. The idea is that a firm's major bank, which is typically also a holder of a block of equity, can exercise considerable influence. In Germany, the *hausbank* system operates in a similar way. The main difference is that, in addition to loans and the direct ownership of equity, German banks are also able to vote the proxies of customers' shares. How effective are these mechanisms in ensuring that managers pursue shareholders' interests? At a theoretical level there is an issue of why the banks should undertake the role of pursuing maximization of shareholder value. As with the corporations themselves, they are public companies and there seems no reason why they do not also suffer from an agency problem. An illustration is the fact that the managers of the big three German universal banks have proxies for such a large proportion of their own bank's shares that they have effective voting control. At an empirical level the evidence for the effectiveness of this type of system is that, when a firm does have financial problems, its main bank or hausbank does intervene and the firm is able to do better than firms in a similar situation that do not have a link to a bank. Otherwise, there is little evidence of involvement.

Another focus of the literature on corporate governance has been on the use of debt finance as a mechanism for overcoming the agency problem. Grossman and Hart (1982), Jensen (1986), and others argue that by forcing the firm to pay out large amounts of their earnings as interest on debt managers are committing to work hard and avoid squandering shareholders' money. Again this argument is not entirely persuasive. Empirically, the problem is that the most common form of finance is retained earnings. Debt is relatively little used. Most corporations have very little difficulty meeting their interest payments.

In the countries considered, there are many types of private organization other than for-profit corporations. These include nonprofit firms. The governance mechanisms for these organizations provide additional insights. There is no market for corporate control and no external monitoring by financial institutions. The only apparent external oversight is through boards of trustees and directors. Despite this lack of a solution to the agency problem, these organizations are able to compete with for-profit corporations and in some sectors such as higher education are dominant.

To summarize, the standard corporate governance mechanisms that are the focus of much of the literature do not appear to work very effectively. However, despite this lack of outside discipline and monitoring, most firms seem to operate fairly efficiently. In all the countries considered there are many firms that compete effectively in international markets and their shareholders have historically received high rates of return. Many nonprofits also compete effectively with for-profit organizations.

How can firms operate efficiently and generate returns for shareholders when standard corporate governance mechanisms are ineffective? We have argued that a broader perspective than the standard agency view of governance is necessary. What is crucial is dynamic competition in product markets. In order for firms to survive in competitive markets in constantly changing environments, they must have entrepreneurial management teams that do more than cost minimize. They must make good decisions about the future direction the firm should move in. Managers are more than just stand-ins for shareholders; they must take the initiative. In such circumstances there is likely to be considerable diversity of opinion and the standard agency framework is not valid. Monitoring by potential raiders and managers is not relevant. The best that may be achievable is to allow management teams to compete and see which are successful and survive. Rather than having a raider take over an ineffective firm and change its policies, what happens is that the best firms take over the market. This broader view can explain why firms with such different explicit internal and external governance mechanisms are able to operate reasonably efficiently and provide a return to shareholders.

## References

Aghion, Philippe, Matthias Dewatripont, and Patrick Rey. (1995). "Competition, Financial Discipline, and Growth." Working Paper, Université Bruxelles Libre.

Alchian, Armen. (1950). "Uncertainty, Evolution, and Economic Theory." *Journal of Political Economy* 58: 211–21.

Allen, Franklin. (1983). "Credit Rationing and Payment Incentives." *Review of Economic Studies* 50: 639–46.

Allen, Franklin, and Douglas Gale. (1999). "Diversity of Opinion and Financing of New Technologies." *Journal of Financial Intermediation* 8: 68–89.

(Forthcoming). *Comparing Financial Systems*. Cambridge, Mass.: MIT Press.

Aoki, Masahiko, and Hugh Patrick. (1994). *The Japanese Main Bank System: Its Relevance for Developing and Transforming Economies*. New York: Oxford University Press.

Berger, Philip, and Eli Ofek. (1995). "Diversification's Effect on Firm Value." *Journal of Financial Economics* 37: 39–65.

Berle, Adolf, and Gardiner Means. (1932). *The Modern Corporation and Private Property*. New York, Chicago: Commerce Clearing House, Inc.

Bhagat, Sanjai, and Bernard Black. (Forthcoming). "The Uncertain Relationship between Board Composition and Firm Performance." In Klaus Hopt, Mark Roe, and Eddy Wymeersch (Eds.), *Corporate Governance: The State of the Art and Emerging Research*. New York: Oxford University Press.

Bhagat, Sanjai, Andrei Shleifer, and Robert Vishny. (1990). "Hostile Takeovers in the 1980's: The Return to Corporate Specialization." *Brookings Papers on Economic Activity*, pp. 1–72.

Bhattacharya, Utpal. (1997). "Communication Costs, Information Acquisition, and Voting Decisions in Proxy Contests." *Review of Financial Studies* 10: 1065–97.

Blundell, Richard, Rachel Griffith, and John Van Reenen. (1995). "Dynamic Count Data Models of Technological Innovation." *Economic Journal* 105: 333–44.

Bolton, Patrick, and Ernst-Ludwig von Thadden. (1998a). "Blocks, Liquidity, and Corporate Control." *Journal of Finance* 53: 1–25.

(1998b). "Liquidity and Control: A Dynamic Theory of Corporate Ownership Structure." *Journal of Institutional and Theoretical Economics* 154: 177–223.

Bulow, Jeremy, and Kenneth Rogoff. (1989). "A Constant Recontracting Model of Sovereign Debt." *Journal of Political Economy* 97: 155–78.

Burkart, Mike. (1995). "Initial Shareholdings and Overbidding in Takeover Contests." *Journal of Finance* 50: 1491–515.

Burkart, Mike, Denis Gromb, and Fausto Panunzi. (1997). "Large Shareholders, Monitoring, and the Value of the Firm." *Quarterly Journal of Economics* 112: 693–728.

Cable, J. R. (1985). "Capital Market Information and Industrial Performance." *Economic Journal* 95: 118–32.

Caves, Richard. (1980). "Industrial Organization, Corporate Strategy and Structure." *Journal of Economic Literature* 18: 64–92.

(1992). *Industrial Efficiency in Six Nations*. Cambridge, Mass.: MIT Press.

Caves, Richard, and David Barton. (1990). *Efficiency in US Manufacturing Industries*. Cambridge, Mass.: MIT Press.

Charkham, Jonathan. (1994). *Keeping Good Company: A Study of Corporate Governance in Five Countries*. Oxford: Clarendon Press.

Coase, Ronald. (1937). "The Nature of the Firm." *Economica* 4: 386–405.

Diamond, Douglas. (1984). "Financial Intermediation and Delegated Monitoring." *Review of Economic Studies* 51: 393–414.

(1989). "Reputation Acquisition in Debt Markets." *Journal of Political Economy* 97: 828–62.

Diamond, Douglas, and Ro Verrecchia. (1982). "Optimal Managerial Contracts and Equilibrium Security Prices." *Journal of Finance* 37: 275–87.

Eaton, Jonathan, and Mark Gersovitz. (1981). "Debt with Potential Repudiation: Theoretical and Empirical Analysis." *Review of Economic Studies* 48: 289–309.

Edwards, Jeremy, and Klaus Fischer. (1994). *Banks, Finance and Investment in Germany*. Cambridge: Cambridge University Press.

Elston, J. A. (1993). Firm Ownership Structure and Investment: Theory and Evidence from German Panel Data. Unpublished manuscript.

Fama, Eugene, and Michael Jensen. (1983a). "Separation of Ownership and Control." *Journal of Law and Economics* 26: 301–25.

(1983b). "Agency Problems and Residuals Claims." *Journal of Law and Economics* 26: 327–49.

Fluck, Zsuzsanna. (1998). "Optimal Financial Contracting: Debt versus Equity." *Review of Financial Studies* 11: 383–418.

Franks, Julian, and Colin Mayer. (1992). "Corporate Control: A Synthesis of the International Evidence." IFA Working Paper No. 165–92, London Business School, London.

(1993). "German Capital Markets, Corporate Control and the Obstacles to Hostile Takeovers: Lessons from Three Case Studies." Working Paper, London Business School, London.

(1996). "Hostile Takeovers and the Correction of Managerial Failure." *Journal of Financial Economics* 40: 163–81.

(1997). "Ownership, Control and the Performance of German Corporations." Working Paper, London Business School.

Friedman, Milton. (1953). *Essays in Positive Economics*. Chicago: University of Chicago Press.

Geroski, Paul. (1990). "Innovation, Technological Opportunity, and Market Structure." *Oxford Economic Papers* 42: 586–602.

Gorton, Gary, and Frank A. Schmid. (1996). "Universal Banking and the Performance of German Firms." National Bureau of Economic Research, Working Paper 5,453, Cambridge, Mass.

Graham, David, Daniel Kaplan, and David Sibley. (1983). "Efficiency and Competition in the Airline Industry." *Bell Journal of Economics* 14: 118–38.

Green, Alison, and David Mayes. (1991). "Technical Inefficiency in Manufacturing Industries." *Economic Journal* 101: 523–38.

Grossman, Sanford, and Oliver Hart. (1980). "Takeover Bids, the Free-Rider Problem, and the Theory of the Corporation." *Bell Journal of Economics* 11: 42–64.

(1982). "Corporate Financial Structure and Managerial Incentives." In J. McCall (Ed.), *The Economics of Information and Uncertainty*. Chicago: University of Chicago Press.

(1986). "The Costs and Benefits of Ownership: A Theory of Vertical and Lateral Integration." *Journal of Political Economy* 94: 691–719.

Hansmann, Henry. (1996). *The Ownership of Enterprise*. Cambridge, Mass.: Harvard University Press.

Hart, Oliver. (1983). "The Market Mechanism as an Incentive Scheme." *Bell Journal of Economics* 14: 366–82.

(1995). *Firms, Contracts and Financial Structure*. Oxford: Clarendon Press.

Hart, Oliver, and John Moore. (1989). "Default and Renegotiation: A Dynamic Model of Debt." Working Paper, Harvard University.

Haubrich, Joseph. (1994). "Risk Aversion, Performance Pay, and the Principal-Agent Problem." *Journal of Political Economy* 102: 258–76.

Hayashi, Fumio. (1997). "The Main Bank System and Corporate Investment: An Empirical Reassessment." NBER Working Paper 6172, Cambridge, Mass.

Healy, Paul, Krishna Palepu, and Richard Ruback. (1992). "Does Corporate

Performance Improve after Mergers?" *Journal of Financial Economics* 31: 135–75.

(1997). "Which Takeovers Are Profitable? Strategic or Financial?" *Sloan Management Review* (Summer): 45–57.

Hellwig, Martin. (1991). "Banking, Financial Intermediation, and Corporate Finance." In Alberto Giovannini and Colin Mayer (Eds.), *European Financial Intermediation*. Cambridge: Cambridge University Press, pp. 35–63.

Herman, Edward, and Louis Lowenstein. (1988). "The Efficiency Effects of Hostile Takeovers." In John Coffee, Jr., Louis Lowenstein, and Susan Rose-Ackerman (Eds.), *Knights, Raiders, and Targets: the Impact of the Hostile Takeover*. New York: Oxford University Press.

Holmstrom, Bengt. (1982). "Moral Hazard in Teams." *Bell Journal of Economics* 13: 324–40.

Holmstrom, Bengt, and Jean Tirole. (1993). "Market Liquidity and Performance Monitoring." *Journal of Political Economy* 101: 678–709.

Hoshi, Takeo, Anil Kashyap, and Gary Loveman. (1994). "Financial System Reform in Poland: Lessons from Japan's Main Bank System." In Aoki and Patrick.

Hoshi, Takeo, Anil Kashyap, and David Scharfstein. (1990a). "Bank Monitoring and Investment: Evidence from the Changing Structure of Japanese Corporate Banking Relationships." In R. Glenn Hubbard (Ed.), *Asymmetric Information, Corporate Finance and Investment*. Chicago: Chicago University Press.

(1990b). "The Role of Banks in Reducing the Costs of Financial Distress in Japan." *Journal of Financial Economics* 27: 67–8.

(1993). "The Choice between Public and Private Debt: An Analysis of Post-Deregulation Corporate Finance in Japan." National Bureau of Economic Research Working Paper 4,421, Cambridge, Mass.

Institute of Fiscal and Monetary Policy. (1996). *Socio-Economic Systems of Japan, the United States, the United Kingdom, Germany and France*. Ministry of Finance, Japan.

James, Estelle, and Susan Rose-Ackerman. (1986). *The Nonprofit Enterprise in Market Economics*. New York: Harwood Academic Publishers.

Jensen, Michael. (1986). "Agency Costs of Free Cash Flow, Corporate Finance, and Takeovers." *American Economic Review* 76: 323–9.

(1989). "The Eclipse of the Public Corporation." *Harvard Business Review* 67: 60–70.

(1993). "The Modern Industrial Revolution, Exit, and the Failure of Internal Control Systems." *Journal of Finance* 48: 831–80.

Jensen, Michael, and William Meckling. (1976). "Theory of the Firm: Managerial Behavior, Agency Costs and Ownership Structure." *Journal of Financial Economics* 3: 305–60.

Jensen, Michael, and Kevin Murphy. (1990). "Performance Pay and Top-Management Incentives." *Journal of Political Economy* 98: 225–64.

Kang, Jun-Koo, and Anil Shivdasani. (1995). "Firm Performance, Corporate Governance, and Top Executive Turnover in Japan." *Journal of Financial Economics* 38: 29–58.

———. (1997). "Corporate Restructuring during Performance Declines in Japan." *Journal of Financial Economics* 46: 29–65.

Kaplan, Steven. (1989). "The Effects of Management Buyouts on Operating Performance and Value." *Journal of Financial Economics* 24: 581–618.

———. (1994a). "Top Executives, Turnover, and Firm Performance in Germany." *Journal of Law, Economics, and Organization* 10: 142–59.

———. (1994b). "Top Executive Rewards and Firm Performance: A Comparison of Japan and the United States." *Journal of Political Economy* 102: 510–46.

Kaplan, Stevren, and Michael Weisbach. (1991). "The Success of Acquisitions: Evidence from Divestitures." *Journal of Finance* 47: 107–38.

Kester, Carl. (1991). *Japanese Takeovers: The Global Contest for Corporate Control.* Boston: Harvard Business School Press.

Knight, Frank. (1964). *Risk, Uncertainty and Profit.* New York: A. M. Kelley.

Lamont, Owen. (1997). "Cash Flow and Investment: Evidence from Internal Capital Markets." *Journal of Finance* 52: 83–109.

La Porta, Rafael, Florencio López-de-Silanes, and Andrei Shleifer. (1998). "Corporate Ownership Around the World." Working Paper, Harvard University.

La Porta, Rafael, Florencio López-de-Silanes, Andrei Shleifer, and Robert Vishny. (Forthcoming). "Law and Finance." *Journal of Political Economy.*

Luo, Guo Ying. (1995). "Evolution and Market Competition." *Journal of Economic Theory* 67: 223–50.

Mace, M. L. (1971). *Directors, Myth and Reality.* Boston: Harvard Business School Press.

Machlup, Fritz. (1967). "Theories of the Firm: Marginalist, Behavioral, Managerial." *American Economic Review* 57: 1–33.

Manne, Henry. (1965). "Mergers and the Market for Corporate Control." *Journal of Political Economy* 73: 110–20.

Maug, Ernst. (1998). "How Effective Is Shareholder Voting? Information Aggregation and Conflict Resolution in Corporate Voting Contests." Working Paper, Duke University.

Mayer, Colin. (1988). "New Issues in Corporate Finance." *European Economic Review* 32: 1167–88.

Myers, Stewart. (1977). "Determinants of Corporate Borrowing." *Journal of Financial Economics* 5: 147–75.

Nalebuff, Barry, and Joseph Stiglitz. (1983). "Information, Competition, and Markets." *American Economic Review* 73: 278–83.

Nickell, Stephen. (1996). "Competition and Corporate Performance." *Journal of Political Economy* 104: 724–46.

Nickell, Stephen, Daphne Nicolitsas, and Neil Dryden. (1997). "What Makes Firms Perform Well?" *European Economic Review* 41: 783–96.

Pagano, Marco, and Ailsa Röell. (1998). "The Choice of Stock Ownership Structure: Agency Costs, Monitoring and the Decision to Go Public." *Quarterly Journal of Economics* 113: 187–225.

Pistor, Katherina. (1996). "Co-determination in Germany: A Socio-Political Model with Governance Externalities." In *Conference on Employees and Corporate Governance*, Columbia Law School, November 22.

Porter, Michael. (1990). *The Competitive Advantage of Nations*. London: Macmillan.

Prowse, Stephen. (1990). "Institutional Investment Patterns and Corporate Financial Behavior in the United States and Japan." *Journal of Financial Economics* 27: 43–66.

——— (1995). "Corporate Governance in an International Perspective: A Survey of Corporate Control Mechanisms among Large Firms in the U.S., U.K., Japan and Germany." *Financial Markets, Institutions and Instruments* 4: 1–63.

Radner, Roy. (1995). *Economic Survival* (1995 Nancy L. Schwartz Memorial Lecture), Evanston, IL: Kellogg School of Management, Northwestern University.

Ramseyer, J. Mark. (1994). "Explicit Reasons for Implicit Contracts: The Legal Logic to the Japanese Main Bank System." In Aoki and Patrick.

Ravenscraft, David, and Frederic Scherer. (1987). *Mergers, Selloffs and Economic Efficiency*. Washington, D.C.: Brookings Institution.

Roe, Mark. (1994). *Strong Managers, Weak Owners: The Political Roots of Corporate Finance*. Princeton, N. J.: Princeton University Press.

Scharfstein, David. (1988). "Product Market Competition and Managerial Slack." *RAND Journal of Economics* 19: 147–55.

——— (1998). "The Dark Side of Internal Capital Markets II: Evidence from Diversified Conglomerates." NBER Working Paper 6352.

Schmidt, Klaus. (1997). "Managerial Incentives and Product Market Competition." *Review of Economic Studies* 64: 191–214.

Schneider-Lenné, Ellen. (1992). "Corporate Control in Germany." *Oxford Review of Economic Policy* 8: 11–23.

Schreyögg, G., and H. Steinmann. (1981). "Zur Trennung von Eigentum und Verfügungsgewalt – Eine Empirische Analyse der Beteiligungsverhältnisse in Deutschen Grossunternehman." *Zeitschrift für Betriebswirtschaft*, 51: 533–56.

Shin, Hyun-Han, and René Stulz. (1998). "Are Internal Capital Markets Efficient?" *Quarterly Journal of Economics* 113: 531–52.

Shleifer, Andrei, and Lawrence Summers. (1988). "Breach of Trust in Hostile Takeovers." In A. Auerbach (Ed.), *Corporate Takeovers: Causes and Consequences*. Chicago: University of Chicago Press, 33–56.

Shleifer, Andrei, and Robert Vishny. (1986). "Large Shareholders and Corporate Control." *Journal of Political Economy* 94: 461–88.

——— (1997). "A Survey of Corporate Governance." *Journal of Finance* 52: 737–83.

Stigler, George. (1958). "The Economies of Scale." *Journal of Law and Economics* 1: 54–71.

Stiglitz, Joseph. (1985). "Credit Markets and the Control of Capital." *Journal of Money, Credit and Banking* 17: 133–52.

Teranishi, Juro. (1994). "Loan Syndication in War-Time Japan and the Origins of the Main Bank System." In Aoki and Patrick.

Van Hulle, Cynthia. (1996). "On the Nature of European Holding Groups." Working Paper 9609, Department of Applied Economics, Katholieke Universiteit, Leuven.

Weisbach, Michael. (1988). "Outside Directors and CEO Turnover." *Journal of Financial Economics* 20: 431–60.

Wenger, Ekkehard, and Christoph Kaserer. (1998). "The German System of Corporate Governance: A Model Which Should Not be Imitated." In S. Black and M. Moersch (Eds.), *Competition and Convergence in Financial Markets: The German and Anglo-American Models*. Amsterdam: North-Holland Elsevier Science, pp. 41–78.

Williamson, Oliver E. (1985). *The Economic Institutions of Capitalism: Firms, Markets, Relational Contracting*. New York: Collier Macmillan.

Yilmaz, Bilge. (1997). "Strategic Voting and Proxy Contests." Working Paper, University of Pennsylvania.

# Discussion

## Comments on Allen and Gale, "Corporate Governance and Competition"[1]

### A. Atilano Jorge Padilla

Corporate governance is currently a hot topic in Europe, where corporate governance reform appears to be in the agenda of several countries. Roughly speaking, the European reform agenda takes the U.S. model of corporate governance as a standard for comparison. This agenda is centered on two issues: (a) implementing an effective market for corporate control, and (b) strengthening internal control in corporations, that is, designing optimally the companies' boardrooms. For instance, in Spain a code of conduct for boards of directors, known as Informe Olivencia, was drafted early this year. Immediately afterwards, the Comisión Nacional del Mercado de Valores (CNMV), the stock exchange watchdog in Spain, recommended to all companies listed in the Spanish stock exchange the adoption of this code. It also made mandatory for listed companies to report publicly at the end of each fiscal year whether or not they had adopted and implemented the code. In so doing, the CNMV aims to ensure that the boards of directors of listed companies in Spain under-

---

[1] I wish to thank the valuable comments and assistance of María Gutiérrez, who has helped me to understand the subtleties of corporate governance.

take what the CNMV understands as their three main responsibilities: (a) defining the firm's long-term strategy, (b) monitoring and disciplining management, and (c) building a bridge between managers and shareholders. Similar changes have taken place in many other European countries: in some countries corporate laws have been broadly rewritten, and in many others the requirements for participation on stock exchanges are under review (see Berglöf 1997). Indeed, the Informe Olivencia is to a large extent an intellectual heir of the reports produced by the Cadbury and Greenbury Committees in the United Kingdom.

In recent years, economists have studied the properties of alternative corporate governance mechanisms from a theoretical and empirical viewpoint. Since the seminal work by Berle and Means (1932), the literature has focused on the so-called agency problem: the conflict of interest between the suppliers of funds to the firm and the firm's managers. This approach assumes that managers try to exert control over the use of the funds supplied by outside investors in order to accomplish their personal aims, which may be in conflict with the outside investors' basic interest in obtaining an adequate return on their supplied funds. The agency approach to corporate governance thus focuses on how the conflicting interests of managers and outside investors, mainly shareholders, can be aligned.

The contribution of the paper by Allen and Gale to this literature is both illuminating and controversial. Their message can be briefly summarized in the following three points:

1. *The agency approach to corporate governance is somewhat inadequate.* This claim is based on the following reasons. First, this approach takes an excessively narrow focus. It ignores that in many instances managers are not only responsible to outside investors. Other stakeholders, such as employees, may be legally entitled to exert control on the firm's policy. Second, the separation of ownership and control is a much less frequent phenomenon than a reading of the academic literature suggests. Indeed, La Porta, López-de-Silanes, and Shleifer (1998) find that "except in economies with very good shareholder protection, relatively few ... firms are widely held. ... Rather, these firms are typically controlled by families or the State. ... The results suggest that the central agency problem in large corporations around the world is that of restriction of minority shareholders by controlling shareholders, rather than that of restricting empire building by professional managers unaccountable to shareholders." Third, managers, in particular top managers, are rather entrepreneurial. For Allen and Gale, shareholders may not be as much concerned with the manager's incentives to exert effort as with his entre-

preneurial abilities. Fourth, shareholders may not have better knowledge than the manager does about the optimal course of action for the firm. Hence, interference by shareholders may end up reducing shareholders' value, in contradiction with one of the main tenets of the agency approach.

2. *The existing mechanisms for corporate governance, whether based on external market discipline or internal monitoring, are not particularly effective.* Allen and Gale conclude from the available evidence that the internal and external governance mechanisms in place do not seem to work very well. In spite of wide differences between the corporate governance systems in various countries, there do not seem to be comparable cross-country differences in the way firms operate or in their profitability. Furthermore, nonprofit firms are quite successful, even outperforming for-profit firms, notwithstanding the absence of external or internal discipline on their managers. On the one hand, there is no market for the corporate control of nonprofits. On the other, their boards of trustees are everlasting and hardly motivated to monitor management.

3. *Competition in product and input markets is the main factor in ensuring efficient resource allocation.* The reason is that firms run by opportunistic, or plainly incompetent, managers will not be able to survive in a competitive environment. In the absence of good information about the optimal management strategy, where standard governance mechanisms are ineffective almost by definition, a Darwinian process of competition may serve to select best management teams. It is important to notice that their argument in defense of competition differs from previous theories of how competition may lead to static value maximization, which were based on the agency approach.

In what follows, I will reflect on these three points.

*1.* I am quite sympathetic with the authors' assertion that too much emphasis has been placed on moral hazard problems in corporate finance. This is particularly true for the plethora of theoretical models on executive compensation and capital structure that assume that managers are intrinsically lazy and thus should be motivated to exert effort. In this respect, I agree with Allen and Gale that top managers tend to work very hard. I would dare to say that they might even work too hard from a social welfare standpoint. But there are other moral hazard problems apart from the undersupply of effort. Perhaps the most important for our purposes are the well-known "asset substitution problem" and the "managerial conservatism problem." Depending on the informational setting

86

and also on the way managerial compensation is structured, a manager may choose investment projects that involve too much or too little risk from the shareholders' viewpoint. There seems to be evidence of both types of behavior.

I also think that excessive weight has been awarded to theories of asymmetric information, where managers know their own idiosyncratic talents and abilities and shareholders cannot distinguish among different managerial types. In my view, managers, like most other entrepreneurs, tend to think too highly of themselves and act according to their misperceived abilities and fortunes. These misperceptions are well documented in the psychological literature: overconfidence seems to be a common characteristic of the healthy mind and entrepreneurs are reported to be among the most optimistic individuals. Overconfidence may induce managers to: (a) work too hard; (b) undertake excessively bold investment projects; (c) severely misallocate internal resources, saving an excessively large proportion of their wealth or posting too much collateral in risky endeavors; and (d) distort competition in product and input markets.[2] In sum, overconfidence produces many evils. It may also be beneficial in early moments of market development, when hard work is needed, as well as during recessions, when bold behavior may be needed to solve coordination problems.[3]

The negative effects of overconfidence may be successfully addressed through the prevailing mechanisms for internal control. The board of directors may put some discipline on overconfident managers. The role of the board is not to detect and punish opportunistic behavior from the manager, but to ensure that his investment decisions are not corrupted by his misperceptions. To obtain the board's approval, the manager must clearly state the premises under which his or her profitability estimates are calculated. This may allow the board to challenge the manager's optimistic expectations. One may argue that there is no reason to believe that directors are less overconfident than managers. This is a fair point. Yet, boards are composed of several members whose views are likely to be heterogeneous, in particular if independent directors are part of the board. The aggregation of the conflicting opinions of the various directors may wash away a number of misperceptions and substitute a costly process of learning through trial and error. Further research is needed on this point, however.

---

[2] See the papers by Gromb, Manove, and Padilla (1998), Kyle and Wang (1997), Heaton (1998), Manove (1998), and Manove and Padilla (1998).
[3] See Bernardo and Welch (1997), and Gromb, Manove, and Padilla (1998).

2. Allen and Gale make a convincing case regarding the lack of empirical evidence supporting the effectiveness of internal and external governance mechanisms. I am not sure, though, whether their overview of the evidence leads us to conclude that not much can be expected from existing corporate governance mechanisms or, instead, points the need for further empirical research in this area. In this respect, I tend to share the opinion of Röell (1997) that there are still too few studies on the relationship between corporate governance and economic performance. Focusing on the role of directors, most studies have analyzed the relationship between board composition and managerial turnover in financially distressed firms. But board composition measures (such as the proportion of independent directors within the board) are only part of the story; it seems necessary to control for other determinants of boards' behavior, such as the liability protection awarded to directors.

3. Competition plays, no doubt, a fundamental role in shaping markets. However, I am not all that sure that competition is the one and only medicine we need here. Maybe this is because of my skepticism about "promised paradises." I do believe that there are some legitimate objective concerns that can be raised against the authors' suggestion that we may well rely on competition as a perfect substitute for the existing corporate governance institutions. First, as the authors recognize, the transition period may be long and also socially and economically costly. Many firms will underperform or even disappear due to inadequate management during the convergence process.

Most important, convergence is not warranted. For instance, I have already argued that overconfident entrepreneurs make all sorts of allocation errors. Yet, in a world where both overconfident and realist entrepreneurs coexist, there is no guarantee that the market will force optimists out of business. Manove (1998) has shown that, under minor conditions, there is a long-term steady state in which the overconfident control all business. The reason is that optimists save more and thus invest more, so that their companies grow faster and eat up their rivals who are run by realists. Convergence may also fail if there is no heterogeneity in the first place and the initial conditions are unsatisfactory, for example because all companies are run by dilettantes, who are happy with their quiet lives.

In sum, I share the point of view of Roe that "governance can be seen as competition's assistant; good governance speeds along competitive adaptation; bad governance slows it down" (Roe 1994, p. 233).

I would like to conclude by judging the essay by Allen and Gale from a more general, and perhaps also more abstract viewpoint. In this essay, a corporate governance system appears to be defined as the set of institutions that guide the firm's policies and strategies to maximize shareholders' value. According to this definition, the main function of a corporate governance system is to improve ex ante efficiency by providing adequate incentives for value-enhancing investments. This is a popular definition, which is consistent with the traditional view of the firm as a "nexus of contracts."

This view of corporate governance has been persuasively challenged by Zingales (1998) as too narrow. Zingales, for whom corporate governance is only meaningful in the presence of contractual incompleteness, defines a corporate governance system as the complex set of constraints that shape the ex post bargaining over the quasirents generated by a firm. Consequently, for him, a corporate governance system has not only efficiency effects, but also determines the distribution of rents within the firm. Furthermore, under this new definition, ex ante efficiency is no longer the only efficiency objective of a corporate governance system. Corporate governance must also aim to minimize inefficiency in ex post bargaining. These two objectives are perfectly compatible in a world of incomplete contracts, but this is precisely the world in which Zingales locates the habitat for corporate governance.

Competition may be an appropriate substitute for corporate governance under the first definition, but both institutions can only be regarded as complements if, instead, we accept as valid the incomplete contracting approach outlined by Zingales. I am afraid that there are still many questions to ask, many theories to develop and much evidence to collect and analyze . . .

### References

Berglöf, E. (1997). "Reforming Corporate Governance: Redirecting the European Agenda." *Economic Policy,* 24: 93–117.

Berle, A., and G. Means. (1932). *The Modern Corporation and Private Property.* New York, Chicago: Commerce Clearing House, Inc.

Bernardo, A., and I. Welch. (1997). "On the Evolution of Overconfidence and Entrepreneurs." UCLA Working Paper.

De Meza, D., and C. Southey. (1996). "The Borrower's Curse: Optimism, Finance and Entrepreneurship." *Economic Journal,* 106: 375–86.

Gromb, D., M. Manove, and A. J. Padilla. (1998). "Entrepreneurial Optimism." MIT Sloan School of Management, manuscript.

Heaton, J. (1998). "Managerial Optimism and Corporate Finance." The University of Chicago Graduate School of Business, manuscript.

Kyle, A. S., and F. A. Wang. (1997). "Speculation Duopoly with Agreement to Disagree: Can Overconfidence Survive the Market Test?" *Journal of Finance,* 52: 2073–90.

La Porta, R., F. López-de-Silanes, and A. Shleifer. (1998). "Corporate Ownership around the World." Harvard University, manuscript.

Manove, M. (1998). "Entrepreneurs, Optimism and the Competitive Edge." Boston University, manuscript.

Manove, M., and A. J. Padilla. (1998). "Banking (Conservatively) with Optimists." CEPR. Discussion Paper 1918.

Roe, M. (1994). *Strong Managers, Weak Owners: The Political Roots of Corporate Finance.* Princeton, N.J.: Princeton University Press.

Röell, A. A. (1997). "Comments to 'Reforming corporate governance: redirecting the European agenda' by E. Berglöf." *Economic Policy,* 24: 119–20.

Zingales, L. (1998). "Corporate Governance." In Peter Newman (Ed.), *New Palgrave Dictionary of Economics and the Law.* London: Macmillan Reference Ltd.

## Comment on Allen and Gale, "Corporate Governance and Competition"

### B. Monika Schnitzer

This is a very illuminating, but also a disturbing essay. It is illuminating because it provides a comprehensive and very knowledgeable overview of how different corporate governance mechanisms work in theory and how effective they are in practice. It is disturbing because it concludes that the standard corporate governance mechanisms, on which we spend so much time in the classroom and in our research, do not appear to work very effectively. If nevertheless most firms operate rather efficiently, so the authors argue, it is because dynamic competition in product markets forces them to do so.

In this comment I want to focus on three questions. The first is about the empirical evidence for Allen and Gale's proposition that competition rather than governance systems discipline managers. What evidence do we have that competition indeed has a positive impact on the performance of firms? It seems that such evidence is not too difficult to find. The authors refer to a few broad-brush examples reported by Nickell (1996) like the effects of deregulation that is accompanied by an increase in competition and which is typically followed by significant productivity gains. Similarly, World Bank studies confirm that an increase in competition due to trade liberalization in developing countries has a positive impact on productivity growth in these countries.

The authors also refer to a number of econometric studies that focus on this issue. A much studied question is the relationship between market structure and R&D intensity. One of the problems here is that industries differ not only with respect to market structure but also with respect to R&D opportunities. Geroski (1990) uses panel data and controls for technological opportunities by using fixed industry effects. He finds that concentration tends to reduce the rate of innovation, confirming the positive role of competition. Nickell (1996) analyzes the relationship between the number of competitors and total factor productivity with data of U.K. firms. His results suggest that competition has a positive impact on total factor productivity growth.

The examples listed here are certainly not rare exceptions and I think I can safely proceed with my comment on the presumption that there exists evidence confirming Allen and Gale's proposition. But even if this so, my second question asks about the mechanisms by which competition improves the performance of firms. What theoretical arguments can be given for competition to have a disciplinary effect on managers? In their paper, Allen and Gale refer to a number of theoretical models, in particular by Hart (1983), Scharfstein (1988), and Schmidt (1997). One prominent argument in the theoretical literature that is mentioned only briefly in their essay is the possibility of relative performance evaluation. The argument formalized by Holmstrom (1982) and Nalebuff and Stiglitz (1998) goes as follows. If the shocks affecting each firm's costs are correlated, then more information becomes available as the number of competitors increases. This information can be used to mitigate moral hazard problems. But in order to exploit this information the manager's wage has to be made contingent on the profits not only of his own firm but also on the profits of competing firms.

Appealing as this argument is theoretically, it seems to have not much empirical relevance. For quite some time, the prevailing view was that CEO compensation responds very little to increases in its own firm's value, let alone other firms' value (Jensen and Murphy 1990). Baker, Jensen, and Murphy (1998) discuss possible explanations for this observation. However, some new evidence suggests a stronger relationship between firm performance and CEO compensation (Hall and Liebman 1998). Still, the evidence on relative performance evaluation (RPE) in practice is much weaker. Gibbons and Murphy (1992) and Hall and Liebman (1998) find some evidence that CEO salary and bonus changes are negatively related to market returns. However, Hall and Liebman point out that changes in direct pay that include such a RPE component are tiny as compared to changes in the value of stock and stock option holdings that do not include such a RPE component. In fact, there is even

91

evidence that executive compensation responds positively to both own and rival performance (Aggarwal and Samwick 1999). Aggarwal and Samwick argue that strategic interaction among firms can explain the lack of relative performance-based compensation, because of the need to soften product market competition. They find that the positive sensitivity of compensation to rival firm performance is increasing in the degree of competition in the industry.

Of course, even if such a RPE component is not reflected in managerial compensation schemes, it is possible that managerial turnover follows such a relative performance scheme. It would be worthwhile to check the empirical evidence on the hiring and firing decisions and whether it is related to the relative performance of a firm.

Let me come to my third question. Even if we may not understand completely how competition disciplines managers, can we feel confident that all nonperforming managers are exposed to competitive pressure? To put it more bluntly, how can we be sure that enough firms have access to the financial resources needed to enter the market and drive out nonperforming firms? Allen and Gale may be right in arguing that governance systems are of little relevance as long as there is enough competition. However, having enough competition may in turn depend on effective governance systems that provide the necessary outside finance for market entry. If external control on managers is as little effective as Allen and Gale put it, one should be skeptical that new entrants can acquire enough funds to compete successfully and drive out nonperforming firms.

How do firms finance themselves given the ineffective external control? The typical picture is that firms rely on retained earnings to finance their investments. Do firms with internal funds use them efficiently? Insofar as high past earnings reflect high managerial skills, internal financing need not be bad, Allen and Gale argue. They are optimistic that inside financing is efficient if there is a good match between past earnings and the profitability of investment in the firm. But even if this is not the case, so the argument goes, internal finance may be best as long as outsiders have no better information where to invest.

The empirical evidence on internal capital markets draws a less optimistic picture. Let me cite again just two recent empirical studies. Shin and Stulz (1996) investigate the divisional investment policies of diversified firms. They fail to find support that diversified firms allocate more funds to divisions in industries with better investment opportunities. Similarly, Scharfstein (1998) examines capital allocation in diversified conglomerates. He reports that conglomerate divisions in industries with high Tobin's Q invest less than their stand-alone peers and vice versa. In contrast, Billett and Mauer (1998) find that the value-enhancing impact of profitable cross subsidies in diversified firms is significantly larger than the value-destroying impact of unprofitable cross subsidies.

My overall impression is that the empirical evidence confirms Allen and Gale's positive view that competition has a positive impact on managerial performance. What we still need to understand better are the mechanisms by which this is achieved. Relative performance evaluation, for example, though convincing on theoretical grounds, is empirically not relevant. If nevertheless I am less optimistic about the role of competition than Allen and Gale are, it is because I do not see what guarantees that competition is in fact working when needed. This would require that new market entrants have access to external funds. However, for this, effective governance mechanisms may be required after all.

### References

Aggarwal, Rajesh K., and Andrew A. Samwick. (1999). "Executive Compensation, Strategic Competition, and Relative Performance Evaluation: Theory and Evidence." *Journal of Finance*, 54: 1999–2043.

Baker, George P., Michael C. Jensen, and Kevin J. Murphy. (1998). "Compensation and Incentives: Practice versus Theory." *Journal of Finance*, 43: 593–616.

Billet, Matthew T., and David C. Mauer. (1998). "Cross Subsidies, External Financing Constraints, and the Contribution of the Internal Capital Market to Firm Value." Mimeo, University of Iowa.

Geroski, Paul A. (1990). "Innovation, Technological Opportunity, and Market Structure." *Oxford Economic Papers*, 42: 586–602.

Gibbons, Robert, and Kevin J. Murphy. (1992). "Optimal Incentive Contracts in the Presence of Career Concerns: Theory and Evidence." *Journal of Political Economy*, 100: 468–505.

Hall, Brian J., and Jeffrey B. Liebman. (1998). "Are CEOs Really Paid Like Bureaucrats?" *Quarterly Journal of Economics*, 113: 653–91.

Hart, Oliver. (1983). "The Market Mechanism as an Incentive Scheme." *Bell Journal of Economics*, 366–82.

Holmstrom, Bengt. (1982). "Moral Hazard in Teams." *Bell Journal of Economics*, 13: 324–40.

Jensen, Michael C., and Kevin J. Murphy. (1990). "Performance Pay and Top-Management Incentives." *Journal of Political Economy*, 98: 225–64.

Nalebuff, Barry J., and Joseph E. Stiglitz. (1983). "Information, Competition and Markets." *American Economic Review, Papers and Proceedings*, 73: 278–83.

Nickell, Stephen J. (1996). "Competition and Corporate Performance." *Journal of Political Economics*, 104: 724–46.

Scharfstein, David S. (1988). "Product Market Competition and Managerial Slack." *RAND Journal of Economics*, 19: 147–55.

—— (1998). "The Dark Side of Internal Capital Markets II: Evidence from Diversified Conglomerates." NBER Working Paper 6352.

Schmidt, Klaus M. (1997). "Managerial Incentives and Product Market Competition." *Review of Economic Studies*, 64: 191–213.

Shin, Hyun-Han, and René M. Stulz. (1996). "An Analysis of Divisional Investment Policies." NBER Working Paper 5639.

CHAPTER 3

# On the Economics and Politics of Corporate Finance and Corporate Control

MARTIN HELLWIG

## I. Introduction

The purpose of this essay is to call for a reassessment of the significance of corporate finance for corporate control and for a reorientation of the theory of corporate governance. The long-running repertory play "Banks versus Markets" should be taken off the playbill for a while, to be replaced perhaps by a new offering "Career Patterns, Intrigues, and Resource Allocation in Insider Systems with Mutual Interdependence."

According to the recent authoritative survey by Shleifer and Vishny (1997), "corporate governance deals with the ways in which suppliers of finance to corporations assure themselves of getting a return on their investment." Through suitable governance mechanisms, "advanced countries . . . have assured the flow of enormous amounts of capital to firms, and actual repatriation of profits to the providers of finance." This view rests on the notions that (i) the corporate sector needs external funds for investment, (ii) the financial system channels such funds to the corporate sector from the household sector, and (iii) in this system the interests of external providers of funds are safeguarded through control rights giving them scope for interfering with management misbehavior.

With this view of corporate governance, the literature has studied the incentive implications of different governance mechanisms for company management and financiers. Attention has focused in particular on the free-rider problem that arises if a company has many outside financiers and the resources that any one of them devotes to monitoring and controlling the company's management provides benefits to all of them jointly. This free-rider problem is seen as being reduced if finance as well as control are somewhat concentrated – as in the case of a company having a large shareholder (Shleifer and Vishny 1986; Admati Pfleiderer, and Zechner 1994) or a company having an exclusionary "main bank"

Paper presented at the Conference on Corporate Governance, Sitges, October 23–4, 1998. I am grateful for comments received from the conference participants, in particular, the discussants, Andrei Shleifer and Andreu Mas-Colell. Research support from the Schweizerischer Nationalfonds through the University of Basle and from the Deutsche Forschungsgemeinschaft is gratefully acknowledged.

relation (Diamond 1984; Mayer 1988; Hellwig 1991). A similar albeit temporary concentration of finance and control is seen at work in disciplinary hostile takeovers (Manne 1965; Grossman and Hart 1980; Jensen and Ruback 1983).[1] The different mechanisms have different allocative implications, so a large research program proposes to develop comparative welfare assessments of the different mechanisms by working out the details of their allocative implications; for an example see the recent comparison by Bolton and von Thadden (1998) of outside finance with a large shareholder and dispersed outside finance through an organized market with a takeover mechanism.

Methodologically this theory of corporate governance can be seen as a branch of applied contract theory. A typical study proceeds by describing a set of interrelated incentive problems, then considering the allocative implications of different contractual arrangements, and finally suggesting that prior negotiations will induce the different parties to choose an arrangement that is incentive-efficient, i.e., Pareto-efficient under the various relevant incentive compatibility constraints. This line of analysis is common to both, the "complete-contracts" approach of the early literature (e.g., Jensen and Meckling 1976; Grossman and Hart 1980; Diamond 1984) and the "incomplete-contracts" approach of the more recent literature (e.g., Aghion and Bolton 1992; Dewatripont and Tirole 1994; Hart 1995; see also the systematic treatment in Tirole 1998). Analyses using an incomplete-contracts approach typically allow for endogenous role assignments or the possibility of subsequent renegotiation of contracts, but otherwise they resemble the complete-contracts approach in starting from given game forms and assuming that contracts inducing incentive-efficient outcomes in these game forms provide the clue to understanding institutional arrangements in the real world. In both approaches, initial contracts, in combination with the participants' expectations about their implications for subsequent events, play the role of a constitution that governs all that happens in the course of the relationship that is analyzed.

I do not want to question the importance of the insights that this literature has yielded. I would, however, like to suggest that there are some important phenomena that it fails to capture. As an example, consider the evolution of shareholders and shareholder rights at Union Bank of Switzerland (UBS) since the seventies. In 1975, UBS introduced the

---

[1] The observation that the three types of governance structure, those involving large shareholders, those involving banks, *and* those involving the threat of takeovers, *all* involve a certain amount of concentration in the provision of finance and the exertion of control is brought out very clearly by Shleifer and Vishny (1997).

instrument of name shares with a right for management to disapprove any transfer of title in these shares without giving reasons. Ostensibly this was done to demonstrate to the authorities the "Swiss" character of the bank, but in fact the right to refuse somebody as a new name shareholder applied to anybody, regardless of nationality. Bearer shares were maintained as a means of retaining shareholders from abroad, but relative to its nominal value and its dividend rights a bearer share had only one-fifth of the voting power of a name share; moreover aggregate voting rights of bearer shares were kept below 50 percent, safeguarding a majority for name share holders. A decade and a half later corporate managers in Switzerland found that management discretion over the registration of name shareholders created adverse political reactions in Switzerland and abroad; so, after Nestlé had taken the lead, in 1990 UBS abolished this regulation, but at the same time it instituted a 5 percent rule: No one shareholder and no group of shareholders acting in concert may vote more than 5 percent of the votes of outstanding shares at a shareholders' meeting. In the context of a subsequent shareholders' meeting the President of the Administration Council actually suggested that commonness of opposition to management proposals was evidence of concerted voting and hence reason to invoke the 5 percent limit. In the meantime, in the early nineties another bank trying to play the role of the large shareholder of our governance theories had assembled a significant block of name shares, estimated at some 18 percent of overall votes. When this bank claimed a say on UBS policies, in 1994 UBS management discovered that the preferential voting rights of name shares were fundamentally unfair to the holders of bearer shares and got a shareholders' meeting to abolish this "discrimination."[2]

Each change of rules anew was approved by the requisite two-thirds majority of shareholders represented. However, significant portions of votes were not cast by shareholders in person, but by banks representing them. These proxy votes were subject to a legal stipulation that the banks casting them *had to* vote for the proposals of management unless the shareholders in question had given explicit instructions to the contrary. The 1994 vote on the abolition of voting-rights privileges for name shares also involved a large block of name shares from UBS's own portfolio being voted by a private individual to whom UBS had "sold" this

---

[2] This 1994 vote at UBS was contested in court on the grounds that as the matter concerned a redistribution of rights between classes of shareholders, there should have been separate votes of the different classes. The matter was still pending when the SBC/UBS merger was announced. Following this merger, the lawsuit was withdrawn for being moot.

block, while using a simultaneous forward "repurchase" to insulate this person from whatever losses the elimination of voting-rights premia from name share prices might entail.

Generalizing from the example, I draw three main conclusions:

- The "charter" of an institution with a certain length of life should be interpreted as the result of the institution's history rather than prior contracting. As such it will be shaped by interim strategic considerations rather than an ex-ante concern for incentive efficiency.
- Whatever control rights assignments the charter may stipulate, management must be expected to actively try to immunize itself against control from outsiders. To the extent that it succeeds, this serves to neutralize governance mechanisms based on active outsider involvement.
- The notion of a given game form representing a given set of interrelated incentive problems does not capture the essence of the strategic situation. Management's ability to invent new moves *and* new rules may be an essential element of the overall relation between a company and its outside shareholders.

An analogy from incomplete-contracts theory may be helpful. Grossman and Hart (1986) introduced the notion of incomplete contracting in order to understand the significance of "ownership." In their interpretation, ownership represents a "residual control right," that is, the right to dispose of the object in question in all those circumstances for which no other control rights assignment has been specified. In the actual modeling, the word "residual" loses some of its meaning because in fact the contract that is described specifies control rights assignments for *all* circumstances that can arise within the model. Even so, the notion of residualness is regarded as an important theoretical innovation in their work.

The preceding account of governance at UBS over the past 25 years suggests that perhaps one should apply the notion of residualness to management's power to disenfranchise outside shareholders, that is, assume, without bothering to specify any particular game form, that in all circumstances not otherwise provided for, management has the effective power to set the rules of decision making so as to immunize itself against unwanted interference from outsiders. Proceeding further from the example, in this essay I shall argue that such a residual power of management to disenfranchise outsiders is to be found in many systems; significant elements of it are to be found even in the United States, according to La Porta et al. (1998) the country with the strongest "antidirector rights" of shareholders.

Given this observation, the essay will explore the functioning of a system in which the residual power of corporate management to immunize itself against interference from outsiders is virtually unchecked. I shall argue that, contrary to what the initial quotation from Shleifer and Vishny (1997) might lead one to expect, such a system is not necessarily hampered by a scarcity of funds in the corporate sector. It may, however, be affected by a *misallocation of funds* in that some firms may have inefficiently low investments while others may be wasting "free cash flow." In such an economy the task of the financial system may not be the traditional one of channeling funds from households to firms, but rather channeling funds from firms with excessive cash flow to firms with insufficient cash flow.

Politics is an important part of the system. In the UBS example a major role was played by the law requiring banks to cast their clients' proxy votes on the side of management unless the clients give orders to the contrary. By such a law, the political establishment aligns itself with incumbent management; such an alignment is to be found in many countries. It is therefore important to understand why this takes place, what are its implications for the functioning of the political system, and what are its implications for the allocation of resources; presumably the support of incumbent corporate management by the political system is not altogether gratuitous.

In the remainder of the essay, I shall first discuss in detail why I consider traditional notions of control of firms by the financial system to be exaggerated. I shall then discuss the allocative implications of the analysis. Finally, I shall consider the political economy of corporate finance and corporate control.

As may be apparent from the UBS example, much of the argument is developed from the perspective of continental Europe. One may therefore wonder to what extent it can be applied to, for example, the United States. Shouldn't one be looking at differences between continental Europe and the United States so as to get some understanding of the relative performance of different systems? This has been the standard research strategy of comparative institutional analysis in finance, from the discussions of the "main bank relation" by Gerschenkron (1962) or Mayer (1988, 1990) to the more recent systematic accounts by La Porta et al. (1997, 1998, 1999a,b) of "law and finance" in different countries.

To some extent I shall pursue the opposite strategy, dwelling on similarities rather than differences, or, more precisely, similarities behind apparent differences. I shall argue that seemingly different institutional arrangements in different countries may serve similar functions, catering to similar interests. For instance, a poison pill provision in the charter of a U.S. company incorporated in the State of Delaware serves the same purpose as the provision in charters of Swiss companies that give management the right to refuse the registration of a new holder of a name share. A comparative institutional analysis that takes observed differences at face value may miss these functional similarities and overlook the universality of, for example, a phenomenon like management working to emancipate itself from the control of its financiers. Institutions and regulations may be different in different countries with political and legal environments, but some of the differences may be apparent rather than real in the sense that a given purpose of a given interest group may be achieved by different means in different environments.

I do not actually want to suggest that governance systems in different countries are all the same. However, it is sometimes quite difficult to pinpoint precisely what the differences are and why they are there. Underlying this difficulty is an identification problem. Whereas the traditional comparative approach takes institutions and regulations as given and studies their impact on behavior and performance, institutions and regulations are not in fact exogenous. At least in part they reflect the pressures of organized interests, including the interests of corporate management and the financial sector, on political and judicial decision making. To the extent that they do, a comparative approach that considers only the one-way causality of the effects of institutions and regulations on corporate control and corporate finance is subject to simultaneity bias. To understand the differences in corporate governance across countries, one has to look at differences in regulations and in the reality of governance *jointly* as the result of more fundamental differences in social, political, and legal traditions. For this purpose it is important to take account of the political economy of corporate governance and to appreciate the mechanisms affecting the evolution of institutions and regulations as well as the mechanisms linking regulations to finance and governance.

## II. Corporate Finance and Corporate Control

### 2.1. Do Firms Trade Control for Finance?

The notion that outside financiers exert control over firms rest on the hypothesis that firms are systematically willing to trade power of control for finance. This notion is problematic. It overlooks the fact that (i) even in advanced economies a significant portion of investment is financed from retained earnings, (ii) investment and financing strategies are frequently chosen with a view to preserving the independence of incumbent control, and (iii) even in cases where previous contracts have provided control rights to outside financiers, subsequent developments may provide management with an opportunity to void these contracts.

The importance of retained earnings corresponds to the "pecking order" discussed by Myers and Majluf (1984): New investments are financed first by retained earnings, then by loans, and only in the last instance by new share issues. Some firms will restrict their investments to what they can finance by retained earnings; others will restrict them to what they can finance by retained earnings and loans. Few firms look at the stock market as a regular source of new funds.[3] Indeed for publicly listed firms in the United States, Rajan and Zingales (1998) show that the stock market plays a role for external finance at and shortly after the initial public offering, but not thereafter; for mature firms the financing contribution of the stock market is negative as shares are repurchased, for example, in the context of leveraged buyouts. Interestingly, for mature firms, the financing contribution of loan finance is also negative as loan renewals fall short of loan repayments.

Myers and Majluf relate the "pecking order" of finance to differential costs of adverse selection in a model in which management has private information about investment prospects. A simpler explanation may be based on differential implications of the different sources of finance for control: Reinvestments of retained earnings are effectively decided upon by management acting autonomously. Even if the approval of a shareholders' meeting is needed, this is taken for granted in a world in which shareholders find it difficult and expensive to organize an opposition against management. In contrast, investments financed by loans require the approval of the lender who has to put up the money; moreover they entail a risk that if things turn out badly one may become dependent upon the lender's goodwill to continue the enterprise. Finally, new share finance requires the surrender of further voting rights to outsiders, which may enhance the risk of a loss of control by incumbent management or incumbent block shareholders.

In a recent survey of small and medium size privately held German companies, Harhoff (1998) asked – inter alia, see also Harhoff and

---

[3] The reader who is used to teaching MBA students about the social usefulness of the New York Stock Exchange as a source of investment finance may want to puzzle about the following statement from an official of a major Swiss corporation: "We don't regard shares as a source of funds. We have issued shares because we want the public to have a stake in our company. In a direct democracy, with popular votes on substantive questions, this is important."

Körting (1998) – whether respondents would have profitable investment projects to pursue if they had a profit windfall amounting to about 10 percent of the preceding year's sales. Out of 1,509 respondents, 819 answered affirmatively. A follow-up question asked whether they would also pursue these investment projects if at current market rates they were offered additional loans of comparable size. More than one-half of those who had answered yes to the first question now answered no! Only 334 respondents answered yes. The same pair of questions referring to innovation projects yielded 564 affirmative responses if funds were available from windfall profits and 220 if funds were available from additional loans. These response patterns correspond to the findings of earlier surveys by Fischer (1990), Edwards and Fischer (1994), and Gerke et al. (1995), in which respondents consistently expressed an aversion to external finance based on a fear of losing control of their companies.

At the level of share finance, the fear of losing control is a major reason for the fragmentation of share classes that has been prevalent in continental Europe until very recently. Nonvoting shares, bearer shares with reduced voting rights, name shares with restricted transferability – all these are tools by which incumbent entrepreneurs/managers try to retain control over the majority at the shareholders' meeting. Retentions of large blocks serve the same purpose; they too enable incumbent insiders to retain control. This device is most effective when combined with a hierarchical company structure: Even a large industrial compound can be controlled with a relatively small investment if the insider has a controlling stake, say 50 percent, in one company, which in turn has a 50 percent share in another company, etc.; the significance of such arrangements is discussed by Barca (1995) for the case of Italy, by Franks and Mayer (1995, 1998) as well as Becht and Böhmer (1997) for the case of Germany.[4]

The importance of concentrated shareholdings that La Porta et al. (1998, 1999a) observe in many countries may reflect such holdings by insiders rather than the kind of solution to the free-rider problem that is studied in the literature on large shareholders as monitors and

---

[4] These considerations raise serious identification problems for empirical research. Apart from the obvious difficulty of distinguishing between large shareholders who are associates of management and large shareholders who are controllers of management, there is the deeper difficulty of distinguishing between investor-driven and management-driven correlations in financial data. If La Porta et al. (1997) observe that, e.g., countries with violations of the rule of one-share–one-vote also have relatively low stock market capitalizations of equity held by outsiders, does this reflect the market's view that outside equity holders with reduced voting power will be badly treated or does it reflect the neuroses of a management that uses both retentions of large blocks and shares with reduced (or no) voting rights to make sure that it cannot lose control?

controllers of corporate management (see, e.g., Shleifer and Vishny 1986; Admati et al. 1994; Bolton and von Thadden 1998). Even where we do observe a separation of concentrated shareholdings and management, this may be the result of generation change and inheritance arrangements rather than any exchange of control for finance. In the second or third generation, the heirs of the founder may not want to or may not be able to run the company on a day-to-day basis. At the same time they may not want to sell it, for example, because the market for companies is impaired by lemons considerations and they expect to get significantly less than the company's value. Then they need to hire a manager to run the company. The ultimate control right, namely the right to fire the manager, does not actually change hands in this transaction.

Relations between the controlling family and the manager in this setting will have some of the features of an agency relation, but this does not imply that the block holders who monitor and control the manager will do so on behalf of all shareholders. To the extent that there are conflicts of interest between them and the outside shareholders, they will want the manager to act as *their* agent and to defend their position against the outsiders. In particular, they will want him to maintain the value of their controlling position, avoiding any possibility of dilution of their power by the outsiders. Depending on how effective they are at controlling him, the manager may follow suit, or he may try to become more independent by playing the different classes of shareholders off against each other, transforming the blockholders themselves into "outsiders" (along with the other outsiders). In the final analysis, such power struggles may have more to do with dynastic infighting in a feudal system than with the notion of a systematic exchange of control for finance and the exertion of control by outside financiers.

## 2.2. Do Firms Surrender Control to Banks to Get Loans?

Entrepreneurs' fears of losing control concern loan finance as well as share finance. For the case of Germany in the 1980s, this is amply laid out in Fischer (1990) or Edwards and Fischer (1994). According to their findings, based on interviews with a small sample of firms and banks, firms – almost regardless of size – tried very consciously to avoid borrowing strategies that would put the banks into the driver's seat. Moreover they went out of their way to cultivate multiple banking relations in order to avoid dependence on any one bank. While one of the banks might be designated "the main bank" (Hausbank), according to Edwards and Fischer, this designation would not provide the bank with significant power. For instance, loan rates were by and large the same for main banks and other banks, reflecting the firms playing the different banks off against each other in loan negotiations. Deviations from this pattern tended to involve firms in difficulties that managed to exploit the fact that "their banks" were committed to them, having been unable to withdraw in time. In these instances, the very prominence of the main bank position was problematic for the bank as it was subject to public pressure to keep the firms alive or else suffer the costs in terms of publicity or relations with political authorities.

How representative is this picture? The more recent study by Harhoff and Körting (1998), based on a more extensive survey of some fifteen hundred small and medium-sized firms, finds the same multiplicity of banking relations of firms; in contrast to Edwards and Fischer, they find that even with this multiplicity, there is significant concentration in loan provision. However, this concentration in loan provision seems to have no impact on the availability of funds or on the terms at which the money is lent. If there is any effect at all, a firm with a long and favorable credit history with its main bank may face a lower collateral requirement. The same conclusion is drawn by Machauer and Weber (1998) from their study of bank lending based on internal bank data from recent years.

The use of collateral provides a key for understanding bank lending to firms in Germany. In assessing the quality of bank lending decisions in Germany, Edwards and Fischer (1994) suggest that (i) main banks do not in general have a significant information advantage over other banks, at least not one that is reflected in firm behavior, firm performance, or even the bank's ability to foresee oncoming difficulties, and (ii) most bank lending in Germany is protected by wholesale collateralization, which implies that for the banks at least even bankruptcy is not an unmitigated disaster. According to the systematic study of Gessner et al. (1978), German banks collect an average of some 80 percent of their claims on collateralized loans in bankruptcy; this contrasts with 60 percent for suppliers' claims protected by reservation-of-title clauses and 3 percent for unprotected claims. Given such protection through collateralization, the banks do not have an incentive to spend many resources on monitoring and can perhaps do without much control over their borrowers' activities. More generally, the explicit specification of debtor obligations under loan finance may provide for financing relations in which control by the financiers plays only a subordinated role.

This picture is rather at odds with the myth of the German "main-bank system" as articulated initially by Jeidels (1905) and Riesser (1910) and taken up later, for example, by Gerschenkron (1962) and Mayer (1988). According to this myth, a firm in need of external funds obtains loan finance by committing itself to one bank, the main bank, providing this bank with a position of exclusivity that would enable it to control the firm and thereby assure itself of a return on its investment. For the overall allocation of resources, such a "main-bank relation" is said to be advantageous because it encourages the funding of projects with long gestation periods that might otherwise involve all sorts of abuse and suspicion in the interim (Mayer 1988, and von Thadden 1995). The main-bank relation is also seen as encouraging funding in situations involving inital uncertainty about firm quality: As the exclusivity of the relation discourages the borrower from going elsewhere if things turn out well, it enables the lender to share in the long-term rents from those initial financings that happen to be successful and therefore makes him more willing to accept the initial quality uncertainty (Mayer 1988; Fischer 1990; and Sharpe 1990).

Note, however, that Gerschenkron (1962), perhaps the most effective propagator[5] of the myth of the main-bank system, treated the use of banks to finance German industrialization as a sign of "economic backwardness." The "normal" source of funds in an advanced economy was taken to be internal finance. Indeed, this had been the main source of funds for fixed capital investment in the Industrial Revolution in England, some coming from "initial" wealth, family, and personal friends, most however from retained earnings. This was feasible because initial outlays required to achieve an efficient scale, as in textile production, were not all that large (Landes 1969; Mathias 1969; Crouzet 1972). A century later an efficient scale of investment in steel, power production, and chemicals, then the advanced sectors, transcended the means of an individual with family and friends and required either accumulated funds from earlier industrial activities or in the "backward economy," where such accumulated funds were unavailable, the mobilization of external finance through banks or the government (the latter in Russia in the 1890s). As he was sketching the role of the main bank controlling a firm and relying on this control to assure itself of a return on its investment, Gerschenkron emphasized that he considered this to be a transitory phenomenon, which was bound to disappear as the "backwardness" of

---

[5] As a treatment of the "main-bank system," Gerschenkron (1962) adds little to Jeidels (1905) and Riesser (1910), but this was not actually his concern. He was mainly concerned with the conclusion for development economics that "backward economies" can be competitive in the most advanced industries if they have suitable institutions like the German banks collecting funds through deposits or the Russian government collecting funds through taxation in the late nineteenth century.

the economy receded and firms had retained earnings on which to rely for further finance.

Aficionados of the repertory play "Banks versus Markets" have tended to cite Gerschenkron for his account of the main-bank system and to ignore his account of the tendency of firms to emancipate themselves from the dependence on external finance and on banks. Gerschenkron himself substantiates this account by an assessment of bank–firm relations in the German chemical industry after the turn of the century. Already the contemporary authors had observed that, following the crisis of 1903–4, the character of the main-bank relation was changing (Jeidels 1905; Riesser 1910). Modern historical research shares this assessment of bank-firm relations after 1900 (see, e.g., Edwards and Ogilvie 1996; Feldenkirchen 1979; Fohlin 1998b; Pohl 1983). Some authors even question whether in its putative heyday between the 1870s and the turn of the century, the main-bank system represented the "ideal type" of bank–firm relations in Germany.[6] For the 1920s, the recent study by Wixforth (1995) shows that even the steel industry had almost entirely rid itself of any controlling influence of banks.

As discussed in Hellwig (1991), such developments raise questions about the stability of governance systems based on exclusionary relations tying firms to their main banks. Whereas Mayer (1988) and apparently also Shleifer and Vishny (1997) regard the main-bank relation with significant power on the side of the bank as an internally stable system of governance, it seems that in fact this system is subject to erosion by firms desiring to emancipate themselves. Such emancipation is possible if retentions suffice to finance investments; it is also possible if accumulated retentions provide the firm with enough of a capital base for them to be able to play different banks off against each other in loan negotiations. Lending to large – and sometimes even to medium-sized – companies in Germany is viewed as being extremely competitive (Edwards and Fischer 1994).

So far in this discussion I have not considered the role of banks holding blocks of shares in their own portfolios, bank representatives sitting on company boards or banks voting at shareholder meetings as proxies for their clients. All these figure prominently in the myth of the German main-bank system (Jeidels 1905; Riesser 1910; Gerschenkron 1962), but their significance is far from clear. Somewhat contrary to the myth, Fohlin (1996) shows that these roles of banks only emerged in the second half of the 1890s, "well after the period considered pivotal for the

---

[6] The case studies of Wellhöner (1989) as well as the cliometric studies of Fohlin (1997, 1998a) suggest an extremely heterogeneous picture with bank–firm relations taking all sorts of different forms, including different degrees of dependence and independence.

development of heavy industry and after many firms had achieved financial self-sufficiency." Noting that the rise of interlocking directorates involved firm representation on supervisory boards of banks as well as bank representation on supervisory boards of firms, she accounts for the phenomenon in terms of networking effects rather than bank control over firms.

A similar interpretation is given by Ziegler (1998), who finds that in a sample of 78 German companies in 1927–8, 14 had no bankers, 12 had exactly one banker, and 52 had two or more bankers (from different institutions) on their supervisory boards. In his view, the multiplicity of banks represented on supervisory boards of industrial companies indicates the extent of competition between them rather than any significant power of control. Indeed the individual top banker sitting on 20 or more supervisory boards simultaneously would have found it difficult to have more than a distant involvement with any one of the companies in question. I shall return to this issue in Section 4.2. For the moment I merely note that bank representation on supervisory boards of firms does not seem to be closely related to bank finance of firms, let alone a surrender of control by firms to their banks in return for finance.

## 2.3. Are Promises of Control for Finance Credible?

To the extent that bank finance does involve an element of control by the main bank, this tends to be a matter of implicit rather than explicit contracting. For instance, the exclusivity of a main-bank relation can hardly be stipulated explicitly in a contract; a contractual clause restricting the firm to just its main bank would most likely not be enforceable in court. Exclusivity may however be the result of an implicit understanding, supported by (i) a threat of the bank to call in loans at short notice if the firm were to misbehave and (ii) a reluctance of other banks to step in as the information advantage of the main bank makes them fear the possibility that the client comes to them only because the main bank has decided to throw him off as a bad risk (Fischer 1990; Sharpe 1990). The power of the main bank then depends on the effectiveness of this mechanism.

However, the more effective the threats of the main bank are, the greater is the incentive for the firm to try to get out of the bank's hold. As discussed in Hellwig (1991), Rajan (1992), and von Thadden (1992), any device that strengthens the position of the bank over the firm will also raise the prospect of power abuse. This provides incentives for the firm to try to escape, e.g., by developing alternatives, if necessary in secret. On this point, Fischer (1990) gives the example of a medium-size company that started out with an exclusive main-bank relation and at some point went out of its way to cultivate "information relations" with a second bank, even without obtaining much finance from them. When some two years later the main bank tried to renegotiate its loan terms, the firm was very happy to have the second bank as an alternative, available because the intervening "information relations" had reduced their fear of a winner's curse problem.

If we start from the view of Gerschenkron (1962) or Mayer (1988) that exclusivity in bank finance may be advantageous because the power given the bank in an exclusive relation may be needed for the firm to obtain its initial funds at all, the behavior of the firm in Fischer's example amounts to a breach of the initial contract. However, regardless of what the initial contract actually was in this particular case, it seems clear that such a breach can hardly be prevented if the firm's management sets its mind to it.

To assess this issue further it will be interesting to see how bank–firm relations in Japan will continue to evolve. For the postwar period, Japan, even more than Germany let alone any other country of continental Europe, has been regarded as the epitome of a system built on the main-bank relation (Mayer 1988; Hoshi, Kashyap, and Scharfstein 1991), in which banks relied on their power over firms to collect rents (Weinstein and Yafeh 1998). Even in Japan, though some emancipation of firms from banks seems to have taken place, relying on newly developed bond markets as well as internal finance is an alternative to bank finance (Hoshi, Kashyap, and Scharfstein 1990). The effects of the ongoing recession-cum-banking crisis remain to be seen.

The notion that management has a tendency to rescind control rights and control powers of financiers applies to outside shares as well as to bank debt. With share finance, the problem of viability of promises of control arises in yet another way. In contrast to the creditor, the shareholder does not have a well-specified financial claim on the company. He only has the right to participate in future shareholder decision making concerning the distribution or retention of earnings or the election of certain officers of the company. Whereas the exclusivity of a main-bank relation provides the bank with an *implicit* provision of control, the outside shareholder is actually given an *explicit* control right in return for the finance he provides. However, with dispersed shareholdings, exertion of this control right is hampered by free-rider problems (see, e.g., Grossman and Hart 1980). In the usual process of affairs, management can therefore expect to proceed without interference from outside shareholders unless their "voice" is organized either through a third party collecting proxy votes or through the concentration of a large block of shares with a single party, in the most extreme case a hostile takeover.

Given this state of affairs, the management of a company with dispersed outside shareholders has a significant incentive to make sure that shareholders remain dispersed, that is, that there be no hostile takeover and no other concentration of a controlling block of shares outside of their own control. To the extent that this is legally permitted, incumbent management will therefore try to use its incumbency, including its power to manipulate or otherwise influence the shareholders' meeting, so as to make sure that the control rights associated with shares remain dispersed and therefore ineffective. The UBS case that I summarized in the introduction provides a rather striking instance of this.

Altogether the state of relations between dispersed shareholders and the company is very well characterized by the bon mot of the German banker Carl Fürstenberg (1850–1933): "Shareholders are stupid and impertinent – stupid because they give their money to somebody else without any effective control over what this person is doing with it and impertinent because they ask for a dividend as a reward for their stupidity." We should add that the peak of impertinence is reached when outside shareholders in opposition to management try to exert some control after all.

Statutes giving management discretion to register a new owner of a name share are specific to Switzerland, but, at least until very recently, statutes limiting voting by any one shareholder or coordinated group of shareholders to 3 percent or 5 percent have been common elsewhere as well (as well as statutes giving multiple voting rights to parties close to management). In the case of Germany limitations on voting rights have been supplemented by the device of cross-holdings of shares. Figure 3.1 illustrates this phenomenon with 1991 data for a group of public corporations centered around Allianz and Münchner Rück (Munich Reinsurance). The numbers next to the arrows indicate percentages of shareholdings, for example, Allianz having a holding 23 percent direct holding of Dresdner Bank and Dresdner Bank having a 10 percent direct holding of Allianz.[7] Whatever dealings the managers of the different

---

[7] The full extent of cross-holdings is not publicly known because they are frequently subdivided so as to remain below the threshold levels that would imply mandatory publication. For a systematic account of publicity requirements and their insufficiency for ensuring transparency of group structures, see Becht and Böhmer (1997). Using 1985 data at the Bank for International Settlements, Prowse (1994) suggests that 52% of German stock market capitalization is accounted for by cross-holdings, so that after netting the ratio of stock market capitalization to GNP drops from 29% to 14% (the corresponding numbers for the United States are 51% and 48%, for the United Kingdom 90% and 81%). Using publicly available 1994 data, Wenger (1996) shows that 27% of German stock market cap-

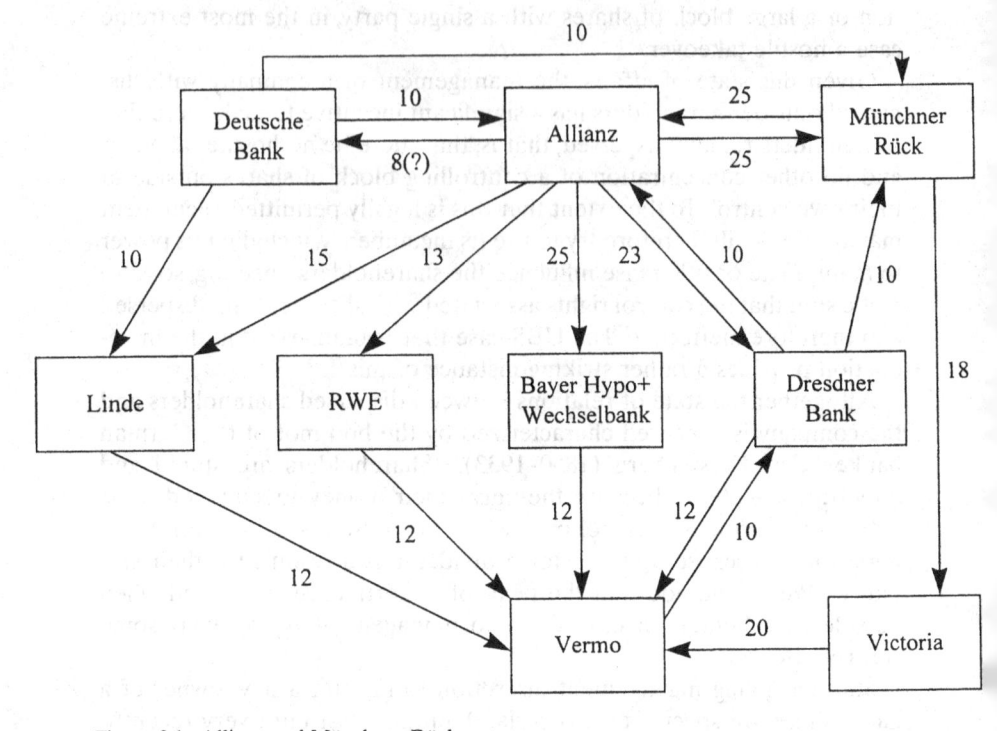

Figure 3.1. Allianz and Münchner Rück.

companies may have with each other, it seems clear that a system of cross-holdings like that presented in Figure 3.1 leaves no scope for outsiders to effectively use the "control rights" inherent in their shares, whether directly in voting or indirectly by tendering their shares to a potential raider. If Franks and Mayer (1995) point to the almost total absence of hostile takeovers in Germany, cross-holdings, as well as voting rights limitations, provide an explanation.

Are matters so different in the United States? According to the myths

italization is accounted for by known cross-holdings, but he emphasizes that this is a lower bound: Observed inconsistencies between the numbers available in different reporting routes lead him to suggest that the true number must be above 30% and that Prowse's estimate for 1985 may not be too high. In the case of Allianz, publication of the numbers used in Figure 1 has been forced through litigation by Wenger; in fact he had to go through the same litigation for 1991, 1992, . . . , repeatedly, because in any given year the company again tried to withhold the information that it had been told to provide by the court in the year before. Figure 1 gives only holdings exceeding 10%. The full picture, including smaller holdings, exhibits a significantly more intricate maze; see Adams (1994).

that underlie the "Banks versus Markets" discussion, corporate managers in the United States are disciplined by the market, more precisely, by the prospect of hostile takeovers taking place unless they run their companies efficiently in the interests of their shareholders. In this view, dispersed outside shareholders can exercise their residual control rights by selling the company and its assets to a third party who is then free to fire the managers and reorient the company (Manne 1965; Jensen and Ruback 1983). The market for corporate control is seen as an ongoing affair in which managers are continuously subject to takeover threats.

In fact, however, the American experience is more complex, involving active takeover markets in the twenties, the sixties, and the eighties, and practically no takeover markets at all in the intervening periods. After a pause, takeover and merger markets in the nineties have become very active again, but much of this activity seems to concern market power in product markets rather than corporate governance. The takeover phase of the eighties was tied to certain innovations in finance (junk bonds, S&L deregulation), tax rules, judicial rulings on state anti-takeover laws; its end in 1989 was not only due to adverse market developments but also to the installation of anti-takeover defenses and new judicial rulings on state anti-takeover laws (Roe 1994; see also Jensen 1991, 1993).

The implementation of anti-takeover measures in the late eighties, for example the introduction of "poison pills" or "shark repellants" or the reincorporation of the company in the State of Delaware, followed the same pattern and had the same purpose as the introduction of voting rights limitations in Germany and Switzerland or the introduction of management discretion in the registration of new owners of name shares previously in Switzerland. In each case, an incumbent management uses its sway over shareholders' meetings to obtain statute changes that protect them from outside interference. The judicial tools used are different, but this should not obscure the basic functional similarity. In each case, in the United States[8] as in continental Europe, ongoing changes of statutes are used to buttress management independence from outside control and to dilute or void the control rights of outside shareholders.

There is nothing surprising about this. The theory of the market for corporate control as a mechanism for disciplining managers starts from the observation that, with dispersed shareholdings, shareholders' meet-

---

[8] Anecdotal evidence as told, e.g., by Pickens (1987) suggests that the Fürstenberg attitude to shareholders is not unheard of in American boardrooms as well as German ones.

ings are dominated by management; shareholders find it simply too costly to organize an opposition against management. However, this observation applies to management proposing statute changes just as it applies to management proposing, for example, miserly dividend payments. This includes statute changes that dilute or void the control rights of outside shareholders. Given the stake that management has in such statutes, we should expect such changes to take place whenever management considers them convenient or necessary. This undermines the theory of the market for corporate control as a mechanism for disciplining managers; implicitly this theory assumes that the problem for which the takeover mechanism is to provide a remedy, namely the impotence of dispersed shareholders vis-à-vis management, does not arise when management proposes antitakeover amendments to the corporate charter. In the absence of legal restrictions this assumption is problematic.

Legal restrictions do make some difference for the ability of American as opposed to Continental European or Japanese managers to immunize themselves against the threat of outsiders taking control of their companies.[9] But this does not necessarily mean that American corporate managers are subject to *more* outside control than their European or Japanese counterparts. As in the case of the Japanese bond markets referred to above, organized stock markets provide companies with a device to reduce their dependence on particular financiers. In a system with arm's-length relations between market institutions and the company, going public provides an outside option to the entrepreneur or manager who feels threatened by bankers, venture capitalists, or not so silent partners meddling with his business (for a picturesque example see Pickens 1987). To the extent that legal restrictions protecting shareholders serve to make the market available for this purpose, they actually help incumbent management to emancipate itself from financiers who want to have an active say in company affairs.

### III. Allocative Implications of Management Autonomy

#### 3.1. Does Lack of Outside Control Lead to Underinvestment?

The preceding account of entrepreneurial and managerial attitudes and behaviors suggests that the exchange of control for outside finance plays

---

[9] For an exhaustive and systematic account of relevant differences see La Porta et al. (1998).

rather less of a role than the contract-theoretic approach to finance would seem to indicate. As indicated by the introductory quote from Shleifer and Vishny (1997), this should make outside financiers reluctant to provide funds to firms, at least to provide them on terms where control is important. Empirically we should therefore observe a prominence of internal finance in the financing of investment. We should also observe a dominance of debt finance, in particular secured debt finance (loans or bonds) over share finance. It would be nice to have precise numbers on this. Using a flow approach to disentangle sources of funds, Mayer (1988, 1990) reports that in terms of macroeconomic aggregates in a large number of developed countries in the period 1970–85 the share of real investment financed by retentions ranged between 50 percent and 100 percent, with some differences between countries, perhaps even between financial systems ("banks versus markets"!?), where, however, these differences seem less significant than the overall observation that retentions are important. Mayer lists credit instruments, loans and bonds, as the second most important source of funds, with shares ranging between 10 percent and 50 percent; in contrast the financing contribution of share issues is reported to be negligible in terms of aggregates – in the "market-oriented" systems of the United States and the United Kingdom as well as in the "bank-oriented" systems of Germany or Japan.

Unfortunately, there is an upward bias in Mayer's assessment of the role of retentions. His numbers for retentions include depreciation including the depreciation attributable to loan-financed investment (Wenger 1996; Hackethal and Schmidt 1999). Even so, his work contains two important lessons: (i) To assess the financing contribution of the stock market, one must look at flows and distinguish between retentions and new stock issues. To the extent that corporate investment is financed by retained earnings, large stock market capitalizations may reflect management discretion over retentions rather than the financing function of the stock market.[10] (ii) In terms of aggregate flows, the financing contribution of organized stock markets is relatively small: The bias from the treatment of depreciation affects the comparison of retentions with other sources of funds, but *not* the relative assessment of credit instruments and shares.

At the microeconomic level, the role of internal finance is reflected in the sensitivity of firm investment to cash flow as reported by Fazzari, Hubbard, and Peterson (1988) for the United States, by Elston (1997)

---

[10] This observation casts doubt upon the use of stock market capitalization as a measure of *external* share finance in La Porta et al. (1997) or Rajan and Zingales (1998). To be sure, La Porta et al. (1997) try to adjust for insider holdings of shares, but this does not correct for the part of market capitalization that is due to internal growth.

for Germany, and by Hoshi et al. (1991) and Hall and Weinstein (1996) for Japan. The cash flow sensitivity of investment tends to be the more pronounced the smaller the company is. This reflects the fact that the larger, more established corporations offer better security and therefore find it easier to get loans to bridge them over a cash flow shortfall. To the extent that cash flows shocks of small and large companies are correlated through the business cycle, it may also reflect changes in borrower quality requirements with the business cycle, that is, banks shifting funds in bad times from small, presumably risky firms to large highly rated companies.

How are we to assess the allocative impact of these findings? According to Myers and Majluf (1984), the dominance of internal finance in the "pecking order" reflects the fact that internal finance involves lower agency costs than any other form of finance suggesting that the pecking order is in fact quite efficient. In the interpretation given here, the dominance of internal finance reflects the convenience of internal finance for management; however, this in itself may be a way of treating shareholders à la Fürstenberg, that is, of not providing them with a suitable return on their investment. To the extent that this is the case, the agency costs of retentions cannot be deemed to be zero but instead must be linked to the difficulties of obtaining outside equity ex ante when investors less stupid than Fürstenberg's shareholders anticipate that ex post they will have little influence on the division of earnings between retentions and dividends. In this respect, Jensen's (1986) criticism of excessive retentions of "free cash flow" captures the agency problem of retentions better than the Myers–Majluf analysis, which fails to consider the conditions of prior issues of external equity.

The literature interprets the cash flow sensitivity of investment in terms of a *rationing* of funds (Fazzari et al. 1988; Hoshi et al. 1991; Gerke et al. 1995). Firms are deemed to have many profitable investment opportunities. However, their ability or their willingness to raise external finance is limited, and therefore they are constrained by their self-financing ability. Even where they have access to credit, credit lines will depend on their net wealth positions, so cash flow affects investment opportunities indirectly through credit lines as well as directly through the ability to self-finance. The inherent view seems to be that a substantial reliance on internal finance must give rise to insufficient investment as internal funds do not exhaust profitable investment opportunities. In terms of the statement from Shleifer and Vishny (1997) cited in the introduction to this essay, the inability or unwillingness of managers to commit to a credible transfer of control rights to outside financiers restricts the funds flowing into business investments.

I have difficulties with this assessment. *A system based on internal finance can exhibit overinvestment as well as underinvestment.* There is no a priori reason why internal financing capacity should always fall below profitable investment opportunities. If indeed cash flow exceeds a firm's profitable investment opportunities, retentions may lead to over-investment. The phenomenon is familiar from the American oil companies in the early eighties: High cash flow from known wells served to finance large-scale drilling activities with recognizably poor returns; this was continued until the takeover wave of the mid-eighties forced a reorganization of the industry. This sort of overinvestment phenomenon is at the heart of Jensen's (1986) "free cash flow" hypothesis: Management is prepared to invest "free cash flow" inefficiently if this serves to keep the funds in the firm rather than distribute them to shareholders.

From the perspective of Jensen's "free cash flow" hypothesis, the rationing interpretation of empirical results on the cash flow sensitivity of investment is unwarranted. If we assume that investment opportunities are *not* correlated with cash flows (as this literature does), the observed correlations of investment spending and cash flow can be due just as much to excessive investments by firms with large cash flows as to insufficient investment by firms with small cash flows.

In trying to evaluate over- and underinvestment effects of the predominance of internal finance, one has to distinguish between *aggregate effects* and *structural effects*. In terms of *aggregates*, I conjecture that in advanced economies the overinvestment effect from the "free cash flow" problem will dominate the underinvestment effect in the long run. To be sure, a less developed economy with little capital will at least temporarily have too little investment if investment is constrained by internal financing capacity. However, we know from standard growth theory that on efficient growth paths rates of return on capital will eventually exceed real growth rates, which implies that *aggregate returns to capital exceed aggregate investment*. This suggests that in the long run, aggregate earnings of the corporate sector should exceed efficient levels of aggregate investment, in which case "excessive" retentions may give rise to *overinvestment* on aggregate.

### 3.2. Structural Change and the Allocation of Funds for Investment

For mature economies, the availability of finance for *structural change* may be more important than the behavior of aggregates. An analysis that focuses on aggregates neglects the role of structural change in the economy. Different firms and different sectors have different cash flows

115

and different investment opportunities. In the cross-section of firms in the economy, cash flows and investment opportunities are not always correlated. This raises the possibility that one may have overinvestment and underinvestment phenomena at the same time, overinvestment phenomena at mature firms milking their cash cows, underinvestment phenomena at new firms that do not yet have enough profits from sales of established products to finance their development activities. The two effects, overinvestment at old firms and underinvestment at new firms, are then but two sides of the same coin, namely the imperfect correlation of cash flows and investment opportunities across firms.

If investment opportunities are particularly favorable in those firms and industries that also have high cash flows, there is not much of a problem. Consider the case of Germany in the fifties: Production capacity was scarce, consumer needs as well as production technologies were by and large known, and the main allocation problem was to direct funds into those lines where additional production capacity was most needed. In such a situation, current profits would seem to be good indicators of scarcity and hence of further investment needs. One suspects therefore that the reliance on internal funds in these years (retained earning and accelerated depreciation with significant tax subsidies) has not created too much of a distortion in the allocation of funds.[11]

Difficulties arise when cash flow is *not* a good signal of investment needs. However, even in this case we cannot simply assume that a system based on internal finance will *necessarily* impede the requisite structural change in the economy. Structural change often takes the form that an established large company buys up a small new company and implements their developments on a large scale. As yet we have little understanding of the economics of this process. On the one hand there are spectacular failures such as Daimler-Benz in the eighties trying to become a "technology conglomerate" by buying up an electrical-appliances producer (AEG) and three airplane and armaments producers (Dornier, MBB, and Fokker) and then financing their losses for a few years from profits in automobiles. On the other hand there have also been remarkable successes such as Swiss Bank Corporation buying up the derivatives firm O'Connor and using the occasion to revolutionize their entire asset allocation system relying on risk management techniques and personnel from their acquisition. Traditional chemical and

---

[11] This consideration has some relevance for transition policy in Eastern Europe. Given that the situation in Eastern Europe in the nineties has some similarity to that of Germany in the fifties, it may perhaps be less important to settle the "banks versus markets" discussion in Eastern Europe than to provide firms with (i) opportunities to earn profits and (ii) incentives to reinvest these profits at home rather than in Swiss or American bank accounts.

pharmaceutical companies buying up small biotech ventures might be another positive example.

These considerations suggest that we should reassess the task of the financial system. In a highly developed economy in which returns on capital exceed efficient investment, the task of the financial system may not so much be that of channeling funds from the household sector to firms as to channel funds from firms with an excess of cash flow over profitable investment opportunities to firms with a shortfall of cash flow below profitable investment opportunities. *One possibility* to fulfill this task is to distribute earnings to the household sector through interest payments, dividend payments, and takeover premia and then to have the household sector reinvest its funds in other firms. Another possibility is to have firms with "free cash flow" engage in mergers and acquisitions so as to finance new activities directly. The relative pros and cons of these two alternatives are not altogether clear.

To assess a financial system, one must go beyond the consideration of individual firms à la Fazzari et al. (1988) or the consideration of aggregates à la Mayer (1988) and look at the *mechanisms* of financing structural change. If Mayer (1988) suggests that in the United States in the years 1970–85 only 1.1 percent of investment was financed by net issues of shares, this aggregate is computed as the difference of positive share issues of new firms and "negative share issues" in the context of corporate takeovers and the like. In the United States, forced distributions to households through takeover premia went together with new share issues in new sectors such as biotechnology or software. This structural effect is overlooked if one only sees the 1.1 percent and compares it, for example, to the corresponding aggregate number of 0.6 percent for Germany.

As yet we do not have a good theoretical understanding of the different mechanisms of structural change and the role of finance in structural change. A few points seem obvious even without a sophisticated theory: First, a system involving more distributions of funds to households and reinvestments of funds by households will have more decentralized decisions. Such a system is likely to provide for more experimentation. Many experiments will be flops, but (i) there will be more reliance on the law of large numbers, and (ii) there will be less of a chance that some really good opportunity is missed simply because nobody bothers to look at it. Second, a system involving more distributions to households and reinvestments by households is likely to spread its funds more thinly; this may be disadvantageous in areas where there are significant economies of scale. In contrast to these considerations, a system relying on CEOs of established companies to reinvest significant

117

sums outside of their own fields of expertise is less able to exploit the law of large numbers but more able to exploit scale economies moving quickly once a success has been identified.[12]

Another effect to be considered is the difference between the functioning of a new organization as a company of its own and as a division of some established corporation. The biotechnology company that stands on its own is subject to different incentives, control, and financing prospects than one that has been taken over by a more traditional pharmaceutical company. Insights from the theory of vertical integration (see, e.g., Grossman and Hart 1986) should be useful for understanding this, but as yet I can do no more than point to the problem.

### 3.3. Agency Costs of "Free Cash Flow": Are There Any? What Are They?

Jensen (1986, 1993) emphasizes the agency costs of a system based on retentions and reinvestment of funds by incumbent management. He argues that investment decisions in such a system are likely to be inefficient because managers neglect the portion of the returns on investment that accrue to shareholders rather than themselves.

I find this argument unconvincing, at least in the form in which it is given. The notion that the marginal returns on investment accrue to shareholders rather than managers is somewhat at odds with the notion that managers have discretion over the use of "free cash flow." Presumably management's discretion over the use of free cash flow extends from the present into the future. This means that the marginal returns to today's investment decision will accrue to the future maneuvering mass of managers. In a world in which management has discretion over the use of free cash flow, management is in fact a kind of residual claimant. Shouldn't we then expect the reinvestment decisions taken by management to be efficient?

Absurd though it may seem, this question is not so easy to dispose of. Indeed the most obvious objections are invalid: First, the argument given above that anticipations of management control over retentions makes it hard to raise equity finance in the first place rests on the assumption that such equity finance is needed. In a world in which investment is

---

[12] One may of course wonder whether the scale economies are not simply in the savings on monitoring effort that comes from one huge as opposed to many small investments. If VW paid DM 1.4 billion for Rolls Royce, did they spend 1,000 times the effort they would have spent on a project costing DM 1.4 million? For a formal analysis of the underlying agency problem, see Hellwig (1998).

financed by retained earnings, either directly or indirectly through corporate acquisitions and subsequent intrafirm subsidization, such outside equity finance is not actually needed. Second, the argument that internal subsidization in the American oil industry in the early eighties was obviously inefficient neglects the significance of consumption on the job. If management got consumption value out of using its power to play with money in this particular way, what was so inefficient about that? Shocking though this question may seem, it highlights the point that many spontaneous reactions to such observations are driven by fairness rather than efficiency considerations. For fairness reasons, we may consider it outrageous if management expropriates shareholders and indulges in consumption on the job (Adams 1994; Wenger 1996); however, it is important to separate this from the assessment of efficiency.

To get at the efficiency implications of management discretion over the use of free cash flow, one has to start from the observation that money in the company till is not the same as money in the manager's pockets. Residual claimancy on money in the company is not the same as residual claimancy on money for private use. Given this difference, the following effects are likely to be relevant:

- The incumbency horizon of management is shorter than the horizon of the firm. A manager who becomes CEO at the age of 50 (or later) and expects to retire at 65 (or earlier) will try to follow strategies that he enjoys while he is there even if they may cause problems for the company thereafter (Noll and Bachmann 1988). From a price-theoretic perspective, the problem is that the transfer of control from one CEO to the next is not accompanied by any compensation that would correspond to the effective value of the company at the time of the transfer.

- To the extent that the manager's position is less than secure, he may have a tendency to use company resources to buttress it. For example, he may invest in assets that permit the easy accumulation and decumulation of hidden reserves, because this makes it more difficult to assess his true performance. If a company like Thyssen at the time of the Krupp takeover attempt in March 1997 was said to hold (mainly hidden) reserves of DM 4 billion in real estate (with a stock market capitalization of DM 12 billion; see below), the rationale would seem to be that such reserves provide for smoothing and presumably for protection from altogether too drastic consequences of cash flow fluctuations. To the extent that such protection is intended to preempt nasty questions about profit shortfalls, one may expect investment in such assets to be excessive. If strategy changes are thereby precluded or delayed, this is a further source of distortions.

Our thinking about these issues is impeded by the fiction, which is implicit in most discussions of corporate finance and corporate control, that "management" consists of a single person. The notion that the "market for corporate control" takes place on Wall Street (if at all) overlooks the fact that career competition, boardroom infighting, and decisions on CEO succession provide an internal market for corporate control, which in many cases is just as competitive as any external market. Managers may be unanimous in keeping the outsiders out, but this does not mean that they are unanimous in anything else, especially if the matter at issue may be used to eliminate potential rivals. Agency problems of the Jensen-Meckling (1976) laziness type are perhaps more effectively controlled by rivals trying to expose each other's weaknesses than by any outsider monitoring.

Before we proceed to name the effects discussed above as obvious sources of inefficiencies from excessive management discretion, we therefore need to check whether these inefficiencies may not be curbed by internal control mechanisms. As yet we know very little about these. Jensen (1993) claims that internal control mechanisms in large American corporations are ineffective, but the theoretical status of his argument is unclear. As indicated by the juxtaposition of the Daimler-Benz and Swiss Bank Corporation examples above, it is not enough to show that a given system leaves room for mistakes; one has to compare the distribution of such mistakes to the distribution one would have under an alternative system.

In this context, it is of interest to recall the empirical findings of Kaplan (1994a, b), whereby the effects of poor performance of a company on management turnover in the United States, Japan, and Germany are roughly comparable, that is, the differences of systems that are stressed in the "banks versus markets" literature are not obviously of great importance. If we think of corporate governance in Germany in terms of networks of insiders along the lines suggested by Figure 3.1, Kaplan's findings suggest that these insiders provide each other with mutual control as well as mutual protection against interference from outsiders, and moreover, the control policies implemented are not all that different from those in the United States.

In terms of the brute mechanics of control, Kaplan's findings are not all that surprising. On the one hand, a person's being appointed to do a job implies that mere professionalism will provide this person with a certain leeway in how to handle the job – at least as long as things do not go badly. Excessive interference would endanger the division of labor which is the rationale for the person's appointment in the first place. A striking example of this consideration is provided by Daimler-Benz in the eighties. The diversification strategy was pursued by the chairman of Daimler-Benz over the opposition of chairman of the Daimler-Benz supervisory board, who at the same time was the chairman of Deutsche Bank, in control – directly or indirectly – of roughly 50 percent of Daimler-Benz's outstanding stock. Given that Daimler-Benz at the time was very profitable and did not need external funds for its acquisitions, the chairman of Deutsche Bank preferred to be overruled rather than interfere with the job of the chairman of Daimler-Benz.

On the other hand, if things turn out badly, the other members of the network have an incentive to interfere before the damage spills over to them. Given that downturns in profits or market values provide the same sort of signal as in the American environment, the dependence of this sort of interference on such information should not be all that different.

This being said, in any such system of insiders mutually controlling and mutually protecting each other, *incumbency* is likely to be a significant source of distortions. People who have been there for a while tend to pursue their own activities and to neglect new opportunities, sometimes because their perceptions are biased toward the things they know, sometimes because they do not want to nurture future rivals. A well-known example of this bias is provided by IBM's decision in the early eighties to give priority to mainframe development over personal computers. A parallel example is provided by the relative slowness of continental Europe in biotechnology: Here the traditional chemists who dominated the large chemical and pharmaceutical corporations found it difficult to appreciate the new paradigm for pharmaceutical research that underlay the development of biotechnology; now of course everybody is trying to catch up.

In this context, the example of successful structural change within a given institution that I gave above, namely the comprehensive introduction of modern risk management techniques at Swiss Bank Corporation, seems to be an exception that proves the rule. According to Schütz (1998), the wholesale transformation of SBC following the O'Connor acquisition could take place because (i) this happened to be convenient for the career aspirations of the person in charge, and, just as importantly, (ii) the potential opposition to this transformation happened to be politically weak, a few spectacular losses on commercial loans in the late eighties having discredited the more traditionalist loans department. In

121

this case too, the internal politics of the organization seem to have been at least as important as the consideration of merit of the route that was taken.

## IV. The Politics of Corporate Control

### 4.1. The Natural Alliance of "Stakeholder Interests" and Incumbent Management

In March 1997, Krupp, with the assistance of Deutsche Bank, made a hostile tender offer for Thyssen AG. Prior to the offer, the stock market capitalization of Thyssen was about DM 12 billion. The offer amounted to DM 15 billion. Thyssen management started a public campaign arguing (i) that Krupp was trying to hurt shareholders by bidding DM 15 billion when in fact the company was worth DM 18 billion and (ii) that Krupp was threatening "the company," its workers, managers, by proposing to plunder its assets in order to pay the shareholders. The second argument was very successful. Politicians from left to right, from state government to federal government, union leaders, the media, all protested against the Krupp move and clamored to have the tender offer withdrawn. After a week's negotiations under the "mediation" of the state government, Krupp indeed withdrew its offer in return for an agreement to merge the two companies' steel operations. The stock market capitalization of Thyssen returned to the level of DM 12 billion, where it had been before the tempest started. No complaint was raised in public that this deprived shareholders of DM 3 billion, nor had there been any further complaint about the fact that the German economic and financial system was not competitive enough to force Krupp to raise its bid to the "true" (?) value of DM 18 billion.

This episode illustrates a common phenomenon: Incumbent managers who try to buttress their positions will regularly find allies in the political system, labor, the media, the judiciary, and even the universities.[13] In the United States, the mechanism can be observed in the reactions of the political system and the judiciary to the takeover movement of the eighties (Jensen 1991; Roe 1994). In Switzerland, one may point to the political system's and the judiciary's long-lasting acceptance of statutes giving managers the right to refuse new holders of name shares without giving reasons, or to the legal provision requiring banks to use proxy votes in favor of corporate management unless they have explicit

---

[13] Historically, partisan expertise has been considered to be part of the university professor's job much earlier than research.

instructions to the contrary. In Germany, the Krupp–Thyssen affair is not an isolated episode but part of a long tradition ranging from legally mandated limits on dividend payments in the thirties to the present-day unfavorable treatment of minority shareholders by the legislature and the judiciary or the rules governing cross-holdings (Wenger 1996). In each country the details are different, but the overall mechanism is the same.

Jensen (1991) seems to regard the treatment of corporate control by the political system and the judiciary as the result of a misunderstanding, a mistaken reaction to populist rhetoric about "plundering assets," without understanding for the systemic implications. In contrast I share the view of Roe (1994) whereby the alignment of politicians, judges, and so forth with corporate management reflects systematic effects rather than misunderstanding. In the Krupp–Thyssen affair, the two companies have by now been merged after all – without any cash payment to shareholders. The sums that were thereby saved are available for others, workers who get a sweetening for the downsizing that will occur, politicians who need to put a costly problem into somebody else's purse, representatives of "culture" in search of a sponsor, and of course the management of the merged company that decides over their use.

The regulation of corporate governance has important distributional implications: Funds that are distributed to shareholders are not available to anybody else. Anybody with an eye on a firm's funds will therefore be opposed to these funds being paid out to shareholders, whether as dividends or as takeover premia. This distributional conflict is an important element of the discussion about "stakeholder interests versus shareholder value" in public corporations. It is particularly pronounced in mature companies when cash flows exceed investment needs within the company's area of competence. In such companies, for example, workers and their representatives as "stakeholders" have a natural interest in retentions contributing to the building of reserves that may help the company to avoid, delay, or at least financially sweeten layoffs if ever the company were to fall upon hard times. This "stakeholder interest" is directly opposed to the outside financier's interest in getting his money back and deciding for himself what is the most suitable reinvestment opportunity.

The political system may be seen as a stakeholder in its own right. At one level, there is an immediate financial interest, ranging from a concern about corporate income taxes[14] to campaign contributions and, more

[14] In the Krupp–Thyssen episode, the success of Thyssen's defense was partly due to the fact that through an illegal indiscretion the Krupp offer was prematurely disclosed. As yet the source of the indiscretion has not been established, but some of the evidence seems to

generally, the ability to induce corporations to finance activities that the politician wants to get off the government budget. In the Daimler-Benz case mentioned above, the company's diversification into a "technology conglomerate," more precisely its acquisition of the ailing airplane producer MBB, enabled the government to shift expenses of the Airbus off the public purse and onto the shareholders of Daimler-Benz who \got to enjoy rather less of the profits the company earned in automobiles. Surely the government was not unhappy to be freed of this burden!

At another level, the political system – and the media – reflect the stakeholder interests of their constituencies. Local politics in particular will reflect the workers' interests in having their companies hold reserves to smooth over potential future difficulties and delay or sweeten needed adjustments. To the extent that, for example, layoffs affect not just the workers, but the entire community, shopkeepers, real estate owners, and the government itself, this interest is actually shared by all of "Main Street." As discussed in detail by Roe (1994), the proprietary attitude of Main Street toward "its" company provides the basis for a certain deference toward the company's management and for hostility against the claims of outsiders, in particular financiers, against the company.

Stakeholders have the advantage that they are easy to identify. They tend to be concentrated in certain locations, with little intention to move if they can help it. Outside shareholders in contrast are difficult to identify and to see as actual people. They tend to be dispersed. Their identities and locations change with every stock market transaction. Therefore, politicians, in particular local politicians, tend to align with stakeholders rather than shareholders: Stakeholders vote in well-defined constituencies, shareholders do not. Stakeholders also buy newspapers in well-defined constituencies; so for journalists as well they provide an easily identified clientele with a significant element of human interest. This explains why so often we observe the media as well as leading politicians rallying on the side of incumbent management when the latter asserts its "responsibility for the overall economy"[15] as a way of rebutting shareholder interference.

From a theoretical perspective, the assertion of stakeholder interests involves a valid point. The decisions of corporate management do affect the company's stakeholders, some of them directly, some of them indi-

---

point to the state government, represented on the board of Krupp and perhaps afraid of a loss in corporate income taxes in the wake of a highly leveraged takeover.

[15] This was the formulation of UBS in its 1994 dispute with a large blockholder.

124

rectly through pecuniary and nonpecuniary externalities (Shleifer and Summers 1988). In the absence of explicit contracts regulating these effects, this may justify some consideration of stakeholder interests in corporate governance.

However, the argument carries less far than may appear at first sight. It involves two important biases. First, it neglects all the stakeholders of companies that are yet to be created, that would find it easier to obtain external share finance if "free cash flow" at mature companies was distributed to shareholders and then reinvested through the market. Characteristically, when Shleifer and Summers (1988) talk about shopkeepers and real estate owners in a depressed company town after a closure decision, they neglect to talk about the shopkeepers and real estate owners in the thriving new company town where funds have gone instead. This is akin to the incumbency bias we observe in decision making within companies: Stakeholders from past and present activities are in a good position to make their case known; stakeholders from potential future activities are not yet known, and their interests cannot yet be articulated. This point is directly related to the discussion of allocative distortions in Section 3. If one thinks of reinvestments of retentions through mergers and acquisitions as a vehicle for structural change in an otherwise closed corporate system, presumably the candidates that one is looking for should not be problem cases in search of someone with cash to pay for their difficulties; in fact this was the common feature of *all* the major acquisitions in the diversification strategy of Daimler-Benz in the eighties.

Second, the argument for the consideration of stakeholders in corporate governance neglects the fact that among all the parties that are involved with a firm, the outside shareholder is the one whose contractual protection is weakest. He has provided funds to the company in return for a piece of paper that entitles him to little more than a vote in future decisions of shareholder meetings. As noted by Shleifer and Vishny (1997), any financier has the problem that once he has provided his funds, he becomes a nuisance as his only remaining function is to be paid off. With nothing else to be expected from the financier, his debtor would like to get out of his obligation if he could. Given that he sits on the cake that is to be distributed, it is not hard for him to find political allies who will join in disputing the financier's claims if only they can get a piece of the cake. When the financier is an outside shareholder whose claim is not even well defined, the result seems a foregone conclusion. The "residual power" of management to disenfranchise outside shareholders is significantly related to its ability to rally stakeholder interests to its support in political and judicial controversy.

## 4.2. Corporate Control and Banks: A Second Look

In discussing the politics of corporate control, Roe (1994) points to differences between the United States on the one hand and Japan or Germany on the other, and suggests that in the United States control of corporate managers is weaker because the support of Main Street against Wall Street has enabled management to induce the political system to weaken the power of the financial sector. This is contrasted with Japan or Germany, where there are fewer regulatory constraints on financial institutions and therefore the control of corporate managers by banks is said to be more effective.

I am not convinced that this interpretation of cross-country differences is appropriate. Implicitly it assumes that banks in Germany or Japan act as the representatives of final investors – delegated monitors à la Diamond (1984). This is questionable. The orthodox view of banks as delegated monitors and controllers of firms presumes not only that firms are willing to submit to such control but also that banks are eager to engage in it. Leaving aside the question discussed before whether firms are willing to accept control by banks, one may also doubt the latter presumption. Firms with ample funds for investment make interesting clients for a bank's mergers and acquisitions department. *In a financial system that is channeling funds from firms with surplus cash to firms with insufficient cash, financial institutions will offer their services and obtain appropriate fees.* Such institutions have a vested interest in protecting management autonomy vis-à-vis shareholders, more precisely, in protecting management discretion over retentions, which provide the financial basis for mergers and acquisitions. Fürstenberg after all was a banker!

This consideration would explain why in large German corporations the banks' proxy votes on behalf of their depositors seem to be used more as a tool to protect management than as a tool to impose the bank's will on the company (Baums and Fraune 1995; Wenger 1996). Whereas empirical research on the effects of bank proxy voting on firm performance is inconclusive,[16] Baums and Fraune (1995) find that prominence

---

[16] The impact of bank relations on firm performance is controversial. For Germany, Cable (1985) as well as Gorton and Schmid (1996) argue that main-bank relations supported by the bank's holding a significant block of shares have a positive impact on firm profitability. Perlitz and Seger (1994) claim the opposite. Chirinko and Elston (1996) argue that the data do not contain enough information to settle this question. The same applies to the effects of banks' controlling large blocks of proxy votes. In any case, as pointed out by Edwards and Fischer (1994), a study focusing on banking relations when banks own large blocks of shares will not distinguish between the performance effects of having a large shareholder at all and the effects of having the shareholder be a bank.

126

in proxy voting at a company's shareholders' meeting is correlated with prominence in underwriting the company's securities offerings, suggesting that in fact there is a trade of protection against fees for services. Given the small number of observations they have, it is too early to assess the validity of this conjecture. It does however suggest that the concentration of the literature, for example, Edwards and Fischer (1994), on the *financing* role of financial institutions may be misplaced. The services provided by financial institutions may be as important in shaping bank–firm relations. Moreover the lesser transparency of quality–price tradeoffs in services may make it easier to maintain special relations in these markets.

Similar roles have been played by investment banks such as J. P. Morgan in the United States until the early eighties or Mediobanca in Italy. Quite generally, banks should perhaps be seen as one set of players in the network of insiders. As such they will not be averse to interfering with a firm in order to obtain a profit for themselves, but as a general rule they will contribute to the protection of the system against outsiders. A remarkable illustration of this is provided by Penati and Zingales (1998), who report that in the restructuring of the Ferruzzi Group in Italy, the investment bank Mediobanca used its sway over the restructuring process to even get the priority of creditors over shareholders reversed; the creditors in question were outsiders, the shareholders insiders of the system.

If we regard banks – more precisely, bankers – as one set of players in a system of insiders, we find that the distinction between Wall Street and Main Street, between finance and production, is rather less important than the distinction between outsiders and insiders. If Deutsche Bank in its relations to an industrial company is subject to less regulatory constraint than a financial institution in the United States, this does *not* mean that in Germany the club of insiders as a whole is less protected by the political system than in the United States. Indeed the contrary is true. As documented most extensively by Wenger (1996), protection of insider control by the political system and the judiciary is significantly more effective in Germany than the United States. Outsiders have practically no scope whatever for exerting control. The United States in contrast does have these phases once every few decades when financial innovation activates the "market for corporate control" and it takes a few years before new anti-takeover measures are installed. Even outside of such takeover waves, regulation of corporate governance in the United States seems to be rather more friendly toward outside shareholders than in any continental European country (La Porta et al. 1998).

I wonder whether the difference may be related to the different forms of organization of the financial sector. In the fragmented financial system of the United States, brokerage firms and investment banks do provide a lobby that is interested in an active market for corporate control. Their influence is notable at the level of federal politics as well as the Securities and Exchange Commission (SEC). In contrast, in a universal-banking system this interest is only one of many concerns of a given institution. If a universal bank is interested in safeguarding its cheap deposit base or in having lucrative fees for services from firms, they may find that these concerns outweigh whatever they might gain from a functioning market for corporate control. Whereas Roe (1994) regards the fragmentation of the American financial system as a source of its weakness in exerting control over firms, the argument here would suggest that this very fragmentation may help explain why the American political and regulatory system is somewhat less hostile to outsiders than others. In this context it should also be noted that, as discussed in Section 2.3 above, the more shareholder-friendly regulatory structure in the United States may actually be in the interest of a management that relies on the market as a mechanism to emancipate itself from the influence of financiers who want to have a direct say in the firm's affairs.

### 4.3. The Interplay of the Corporate Sector and the Political System

Debates about "stakeholder interests versus shareholder value" tend to have two rather peculiar features:

- They rarely address the role of management as a stakeholder of its own.
- They rarely address the procedural question of how one is to check whether management is living up to its responsibilities on either account.

These omissions are not coincidental. They serve to divert attention away from the fact that management is a player in its own right, interested in keeping control over the company's assets and wanting to remain in charge. The chief executive officer of a corporation may defend himself in one year against shareholder interference by citing stakeholder interest, and in the next year announce layoffs in the name of shareholder value. On both occasions he really means the same thing, namely his decisions are nobody else's business. By focusing on the substance of what interests "the firm" should cater to, the debate on stakeholders versus shareholders diverts attention from this role of management itself.

Interestingly, professed concerns for stakeholders have rarely had implications for governance. Codetermination of labor in Germany is the major exception. Given the prominence of rhetoric on the public responsibilities of large corporations, one may wonder why we do not observe more attempts to institutionalize the consideration of "stakeholder interests" in corporate governance.

I see several answers to this question. First, the polity may be too weak to impose governance structures against the wishes of corporate management. This would, for example, be the case when different jurisdictions are competing to be the seats of corporate headquarters and try to attract companies by offering a management-friendly regulatory environment. The role of the State of Delaware and its success with this strategy have been much discussed in this context (Jensen 1991; Roe 1994); incorporation in this state seems to be one of the moves available to managers trying to change the rules of the game they play with their shareholders.

Second, politicians and other stakeholder representatives may be reluctant to be visibly drawn into firm decision making, assuming a coresponsibility for policy choices that will to some extent lie outside their areas of expertise and over which sometimes they have no control after all. In terms of their own accountability to their constituents such coresponsibility would seem to put them into an awkward position.

Third, it may actually be quite nice for politicians and other stakeholders to know that there is a party with control over resources to whom they can turn when they need to unload a costly problem. Daimler-Benz taking MBB and the further costs of the Airbus off the German government's budget provided a nice escape from awkward discussions about the costs of industrial policy. On a more regular, day-to-day basis we do observe large corporations accepting "obligations to the community" that are not in any sense legal obligations, but simply part of an informal give-and-take with the political system. The informality of such give-and-take is one of its charms for politicians as it reduces transparency and allows them to reduce accountability for at least some of the costs they generate.

In terms of the functioning of the overall economic and political system, informal give-and-take has the advantage that it saves on transactions costs. One can exploit the gains from cooperation in a long-term relation with repeated interactions. This permits, for example, the functioning of the German apprenticeship system in which companies train people without any guarantee that they will stay with them, largely as a result of political pressure and peer pressure, without any need for formal legislation. At the same time though the lack of transparency about such dealings makes it difficult to hold anybody responsible for

129

costs. Presumably the German corporate sector's acceptance of the apprenticeship system is rewarded by the taxpayer somehow – but it is not clear how and at what cost.

An even more important concern may be in the entire system closing itself against innovation. Informal mechanisms of coordination between the political system, the corporate sector, and so forth can work well if one is in a situation where everybody knows everybody else, no untoward surprises occur, and everyone knows what measures will be effective in punishing untoward behavior. Outsiders naturally generate mistrust – one does not know how to deal with them through informal mechanisms. This makes it tempting to exclude them from any significant influence. Indeed the natural alliance of the political system, the judiciary, the unions, and so on against the assumption of control by outsiders is very much related to the fact that outsiders are difficult to fit into informal mechanisms of give-and-take. But if all control and coordination mechanisms are designed to exclude outsiders, this poses a serious danger for the overall political and social system, carrying the incumbency bias toward known activities one level further to the assessment of legitimacy on the basis of incumbency.

## References

Adams, M. (1994). Die Usurpation von Aktionärsbefugnissen mittels Ringverflechtung in der Deutschland AG. *Die Aktiengesellschaft* 4: 148–59.

Admati, A., P. Pfleiderer, and J. Zechner. (1994). Large Shareholder Activism, Risk Sharing and Financial Market Equilibrium. *Journal of Political Economy* 102: 1097–1130.

Aghion, P., and P. Bolton. (1992). An "Incomplete Contracts" Approach to Financial Contracting. *Review of Economic Studies* 59: 473–94.

Barca, F. (1995). On Corporate Governance in Italy: Issues, Facts, and Agency. Mimeo, Bank of Italy, Rome.

Baums, T., and C. Fraune. (1995). Institutionelle Anleger und Publikumsaktiengesellschaft: Eine empirische Untersuchung. *Die Aktiengesellschaft* 40: 97–112.

Becht, M., and E. Böhmer. (1997). Transparency of Ownership and Control in Germany. Discussion Paper No. 1997–91, Sonderforschungsbereich 373, Humboldt-Universität, Berlin.

Bhide, A. (1993). The Hidden Costs of Stock Market Liquidity. *Journal of Financial Economics* 34: 31–52.

Bolton, P., and E. L. von Thadden. (1998). Blocks, Liquidity and Corporate Control. *Journal of Finance* 53: 1–25.

Cable, J. (1985). Capital Market Information and Industrial Performance. *Economic Journal* 95: 118–32.

130

Chirinko, R. S., and J. A. Elston. (1996). Finance, Control, and Profitability. An Evaluation of German Bank Influence. Mimeo, California Institute of Technology.

Crouzet, F. (Ed.) (1972). *Capital Formation in the Industrial Revolution*. London: Methuen.

Dewatripont, M., and J. Tirole. (1994). A Theory of Debt and Equity: Diversity of Securities and Manager-Shareholder Congruence. *Quarterly Journal of Economics* 109: 1027–54.

Diamond, D. (1984). Financial Intermediation as Delegated Monitoring. *Review of Economic Studies* 51: 393–414.

Edwards, J., and K. Fischer. (1994). *Banks, Finance and Investment in Germany*. Cambridge: Cambridge University Press.

Edwards, J., and S. Ogilvie. (1996). Universal Banks and German Industrialization: A Reappraisal. *Economic History Review* 49: 427–46.

Elston, J. (1997). Investment, Liquidity Constraints and Bank Relationships: Evidence from German Manufacturing Firms. Mimeo, California Institute of Technology.

Fazzari, S., G. Hubbard, and R. Petersen. (1988). Financing Constraints and Corporate Borrowing. *Brookings Papers on Economic Activity*, pp. 141–95.

Feldenkirchen, W. (1979). Banken und Stahlindustrie im Ruhrgebiet – Zur Entwicklung ihrer Beziehungen 1873–1914. *Bankhistorisches Archiv* 5: 26–52.

Fischer, K. (1990). Hausbankbeziehungen als Instrument der Bindung zwischen Banken und Unternehmen: Eine theoretische und empirische Analyse. Doctoral Dissertation, University of Bonn.

Fohlin, C. (1996). The Rise of Interlocking Directorates in Imperial Germany. California Institute of Technology, Social Science Working Paper No. 931, Revised Version, Pasadena, Calif.

(1997). Universal Banking Networks in Pre-War Germany: New Evidence from Company Financial Data. *Ricerche Economiche* 51: 201–25.

(1998a). Relationship Banking, Liquidity and Investment in German Industrialization. *Journal of Finance* 53.

(1998b). Financial System Structure and Industrialization: Reassessing the German Experience before World War I. California Institute of Technology, Social Science Working Paper 1208, Pasadena, Calif.

Franks, J., and C. Mayer. (1995). Ownership and Control. In H. Siebert (Ed.), *Trends in Business Organization: Do Participation and Cooperation Increase Competitiveness?*, Tübingen: Mohr(Siebeck), pp. 171–95.

(1998). Bank Control, Takeovers and Corporate Governance in Germany. *Journal of Banking and Finance* 22: 1441–56.

Gerke, W. et al. (1995). *Probleme mittelständischer Unternehmen beim Zugang zum Kapitalmarkt*. Baden-Baden: Nomos.

Gerschenkron, A. (1962). *Economic Backwardness in Historical Perspective*. Cambridge, Mass.: Harvard University Press.

Gessner, V. et al. (1978). *Die Praxis der Konkursabwicklung in der Bundesrepublik Deutschland.* Cologne. Bundesverlag.

Gorton, G., and F. A. Schmid. (1996). Universal Banking and the Performance of German Firms. Mimeo, Wharton School, University of Pennsylvania.

Grossman, S., and O. D. Hart. (1980). Takeover Bids, the Free-Rider Problem, and the Theory of the Corporation. *Bell Journal of Economics* 11: 42–64.

——— (1986). The Costs and Benefits of Ownership: A Theory of Vertical and Lateral Integration. *Journal of Political Economy* 94: 691–719.

Hackethal, A., and R. H. Schmidt. (1999). Financing Patterns: Measurement Concepts and Empirical Results. Discussion Paper No. 33, Working Paper Series: Finance and Accounting, University of Frankfurt.

Hall, B., and D. Weinstein. (1996). The Myth of the Patient Japanese: Corporate Myopia and Financial Distress in Japan and the United States. NBER Discussion Paper, National Buearu of Economic Research, Cambridge, Mass.

Harhoff, D. (1998). Die Finanzierung von Innovationsprojekten. In N. Franke and C. F. von Braun (Eds.), *Innovationsforschung und Technologiemanagement.* Berlin: Springer.

Harhoff, D., and T. Körting. (1998). How Many Does It Take to Tango? Discussion Paper, ZEW Mannheim.

Hart, O. D. (1995). *Firms, Contracts, and Financial Structure.* Oxford: Oxford University Press.

Hellwig, M. (1991). Banking, Financial Intermediation and Corporate Finance. In A. Giovannini and C. Mayer (Eds.), *European Financial Integration.* Cambridge: Cambridge University Press, pp. 33–63.

——— (1998). Allowing for Risk Choices in Diamond's "Financial Intermediation as Delegated Monitoring." Mimeo, University of Mannheim.

Hoshi, T., A. Kashyap, and D. Scharfstein. (1990). Bank Monitoring and Investment: Evidence from the Changing Structure of Japanese Corporate Banking Relationships. In R. G. Hubbard (Ed.), *Asymmetric Information, Corporate Finance, and Investment.* Chicago: University of Chicago Press, pp. 105–26.

——— (1991). Corporate Structure, Liquidity and Investment. *Quarterly Journal of Economics* 106: 33–60.

Jarrell, G., J. A. Brickley, and J. M. Netter. (1988). The Market for Corporate Control: The Empirical Evidence since 1980. *Journal of Economic Perspectives* 2: 49–68.

Jeidels, O. (1905). *Das Verhältnis der Deutschen Grossbanken zur Industrie.* Duncker & Humblot, Leipzig.

Jensen, M. (1986). Agency Costs of Free Cash Flow, Corporate Finance and Takeovers. *American Economic Review, Papers and Proceedings* 76: 323–9.

——— (1991). Corporate Control and the Politics of Finance. *Journal of Applied Corporate Finance* 4: 13–33.

——— (1993). The Modern Industrial Revolution, Exit, and the Failure of Internal Control Systems. *Journal of Finance* 48: 831–80.

Jensen, M., and W. H. Meckling. (1976). Theory of the Firm: Managerial Behavior, Agency Costs and Capital Structure. *Journal of Financial Economics* 3: 305–60.

Jensen, M., and R. Ruback. (1983). The Market for Corporate Control: The Scientific Evidence. *Journal of Financial Economics* 11: 5–50.

Kaplan, S. (1994a). Top Executive Rewards and Firm Performance: A Comparison of Japan and the United States. *Journal of Political Economy* 102: 510–46.

(1994b). Top Executives, Turnover, and Firm Performance in Germany. *Journal of Law, Economics and Organization* 10: 142–59.

La Porta, R., F. López-de-Silanes, A. Shleifer, and R. Vishny. (1997). Legal Determinants of External Finance. *Journal of Finance* 52: 1131–50.

(1998). Law and Finance. *Journal of Political Economy* 106: 1113–55.

La Porta, R., F. López-de-Silanes, and A. Shleifer. (1999a). Corporate Ownership around the World. *Journal of Finance* 54: 471–517.

La Porta, R., F. López-de-Silanes, A. Shleifer, and R. Vishny. (1999b). Agency Problems and Dividend Policies around the World. Mimeo, Cambridge, Mass.: Harvard University.

Landes, D. (1969). *The Unbound Prometheus*. Cambridge: Cambridge University Press.

Machauer, A., and M. Weber. (1998). Bank Behavior Based on Internal Credit Ratings of Borrowers. *Journal of Banking and Finance* 22: 1355–83.

Manne, A. (1965). Mergers and the Market for Corporate Control. *Journal of Political Economy* 73: 110–20.

Mathias, P. (1969). *The First Industrial Nation*. London: Methuen.

Mayer, C. (1988). New Issues in Corporate Finance. *European Economic Review* 32: 1167–88.

(1990). Financial Systems, Corporate Finance and Economic Development. In R. G. Hubbard (Ed.), *Asymmetric Information, Corporate Finance, and Investment*. Chicago: University of Chicago Press, pp. 307–32.

Myers, S., and N. S. Majluf. (1984). Corporate Finance and Investment Decisions When Firms Have Information That Investors Do Not Have. *Journal of Financial Economics* 13: 187–222.

Noll, P., and H. R. Bachmann. (1988). *Der kleine Machiavelli*. Zürich: Pendo.

Penati, A., and L. Zingales. (1998). Efficiency and Distribution in Financial Restructuring: The Case of the Ferruzzi Group. Mimeo, University of Chicago, Graduate School of Business, Chicago.

Perlitz, M., and F. Seger. (1994). The Role of Universal Banks in German Corporate Governance. *Business and the Contemporary World* 6: 49–67.

Pickens, T. B. (1987). *Boone*. Boston: Houghton Mifflin.

Pohl, H. (1983). Formen und Phasen der Industriefinanzierung bis zum 2. Weltkrieg. *Bankhistorisches Archiv* 9: 13–33.

Prowse, S. (1994). Corporate Governance in an International Perspective: A Survey of Corporate Control Mechanisms among Large Firms in the United States, the United Kingdom, Japan and Germany. BIS Economic Papers No. 41. Bank for International Settlements, Basle.

Rajan, R. (1992). Insiders and Outsiders: The Choice between Relationship and Arm's Length Debt. *Journal of Finance* 47: 1367–400.

Rajan, R., and L. Zingales. (1998). Financial Dependence and Growth. *American Economic Review* 88: 559–86.

Riesser, J. (1910). *Die Deutschen Grossbanken und ihre Konzentration im Zusammenhang mit der Entwicklung der Gesamtwirtschaft in Deutschland.* Jena: Gustav Fischer.

Roe, M. J. (1994). *Strong Managers, Weak Owners: The Political Roots of American Corporate Finance.* Princeton, N.J.: Princeton University Press.

Schütz, D. (1998). *Der Fall der UBS.* Zürich: Bilanz: Weltwoche-Verlag.

Sharpe, S. (1990). Asymmetric Information, Bank Lending, and Implicit Contracts: A Stylized Model of Customer Relationships. *Journal of Finance* 45: 1069–87.

Shleifer, A., and L. Summers. (1988). Breach of Trust in Hostile Takeovers. In A. Auerbach (Ed.), *Corporate Takeovers, Causes and Consequences.* Chicago: University of Chicago Press, pp. 33–56.

Shleifer, A., and R. Vishny. (1986). Large Shareholders and Corporate Control. *Journal of Political Economy* 94: 461–88.

——— (1997). A Survey of Corporate Governance. *Journal of Finance* 52: 737–83.

Tirole, J. (1998). Corporate Governance. Mimeo, Institut d'Economie Industrielle, Toulouse.

von Thadden, E. L. (1992). The Commitment of Finance, Duplicated Monitoring, and the Investment Horizon, CEPR Network in Financial Markets. Working Paper 27. London.

Weinstein, D., and Y. Yafeh. (1998). On the Costs of a Bank-Centered Financial System: Evidence from the Changing Main Bank Relations in Japan. *Journal of Finance* 53: 635–72.

Wellhöner, V. (1989). *Grossbanken und Grossindustrie im Kaiserreich.* Göttingen: Vandenhoek & Ruprecht.

Wenger, E. (1996). Institutionelle Defizite am deutschen Kapitalmarkt. Report for the German Monopolkommission, Würzburg.

Wixforth, H. (1995). *Banken und Schwerindustrie in der Weimarer Republik.* Cologne: Böhlau.

Ziegler, D. (1998). Die Aufsichtsräte der deutschen Aktiengesellschaften in den zwanziger Jahren: Eine empirische Untersuchung zum Problem der "Bankenmacht." *Zeitschrift für Unternehmensgeschichte* 43: 194–215.

## Discussion

### Comments on Hellwig, "On the Economics and Politics of Corporate Finance and Corporate Control"

*Andrei Shleifer*

Martin Hellwig has written a characteristically insightful paper on the economics and politics of corporate governance in Europe. The essentials of the picture seem to be as follows. Continental European firms are typically controlled either by families or by the State. Outside shareholders of these firms are typically poorly protected against expropriation by the insiders, and as a consequence firms have trouble raising equity funds, and stock markets are relatively small. In some countries, such as Germany, creditors are better protected, and hence firms can finance their investment with bank credit. In other countries, creditors are also poorly protected, and hence credit is not easily available to firms either, and debt markets are as undeveloped as equity markets. When private external capital is unavailable, non-State firms in countries such as Belgium, Spain, Italy, and to some extent France, are relatively small.

The question is how this unfortunate state of corporate governance can be improved. Hellwig is skeptical about the top-down legal and corporate governance reform, and for a good reason. The first-order effect of such a reform is to redistribute wealth from the controlling families (and in some cases banks) to minority shareholders and creditors of public firms, since the private benefits of control (that is, expropriation) are likely to diminish. Not surprisingly, the controlling shareholders do not welcome such reforms, and hence their political prospects are relatively dim. In contrast, principal beneficiaries of corporate governance reforms, who are the owners of private companies that are thinking of going public as well as the would-be entrepreneurs, do not have nearly as much political influence as the controlling shareholders of the major public firms, and hence their voice is nowhere near as loud.

There are of course other ways for firms to improve their corporate governance, and thus to enhance their access to external finance. Among the most important strategies is to opt into a legal regime more supportive of outside investors, for example by listing the stock in New York or London. Some Continental European and emerging markets companies have in fact followed this strategy, and I expect that this trend will continue.

An alternative way to opt into a better legal regime is to be acquired by a company operating in such a regime (or, more generally, by a company that has better access to external finance). It is easy to show that if private benefits of control result from an inefficient conversion of cash flows into personal perquisites and wealth, then a company is worth more overall when it operates in a good legal regime than if it operates in an unprotective regime. Suppose for example that a company makes profits of 500, of which 300 accrues as dividends to all shareholders, and 200 is diverted by the controlling shareholders and yields them the benefit of 100. In this case, this company is worth 400 in an unprotective legal regime, and 500 in a protective legal regime. Moreover, the controlling shareholder would happily sell it for a price above 400, that is, there are gains from trade because diversion is inefficient.

In fact, such acquisitions are becoming extremely common in Western Europe, and I believe the trend will continue unless there is extensive anti-acquisition legislation. In a decade, we may see relatively few valuable companies operating in a legal regime that is not protective of outside shareholders and creditors. All is not lost for the future of continental corporate governance.

# CHAPTER 4

# How Do Financial Systems Affect Economic Performance?

WENDY CARLIN AND COLIN MAYER

## I. Introduction

There have been debates about the role of financial systems in corporate activity for the best part of a century. A consensus view is yet to emerge as to whether cross-country differences in the structure of financial, corporate, and legal systems have any causal influence on cross-country economic performance. But interest in this question has stimulated attempts to assemble data banks on financial and corporate systems that allow international comparisons to be performed. The objective of this essay is to review these debates, to present additional empirical evidence, and to put forward some new interpretations of this evidence.

We begin in Section 2 with the debates about the comparative merits of different financial, corporate, and legal systems for economic performance. These debates have a long history. Until recently, they primarily took the form of bilateral country comparisons on, for example, the role of banks in comparative British and German industrial performance since the late nineteenth century. The positive role of the German banking system in promoting German industrialization through the provision of external finance frequently acquired the status of a "stylized fact" in the discussion of comparative performance. The influence of "bank" versus "market"-based financial systems was revisited in the examination of the postwar "Golden Age" growth of the West European and Japanese economies. But more detailed empirical work, using individual firm and institution data, has frequently failed to identify the source of advantage of the German and Japanese systems. Skepticism has been heightened by the comparative performance of Anglo-American and Continental European/Japanese systems during the 1990s.

The debate about the merits of different systems has been widened to include cross-country differences in ownership structures. Only recently

The research for this project was funded from a donation from the Peter Moores Foundation to the Said Business School. We are very grateful to Esra Erdem for excellent research assistance on this and related projects and to Marco Becht, Vicente Salas, and Xavier Vives for comments on a previous version of this essay.

has there been a systematic attempt to document differences in owner-ship structures across countries. The finding that the classic Berle–Means corporation with widely dispersed ownership is not typical of large firms in most countries has encouraged studies of the impact of ownership concentration on performance. As in the "bank versus market" debates, analysis has been conducted at the level of countries and individual firms and institutions. In the former, the question is whether concentrated ownership contributes to or detracts from country performance. In the latter, the variation in ownership concentration across firms within a country is exploited to identify the mechanisms through which owner-ship structure affects performance. The final aspect of comparative struc-tures that is examined in Section 2 is that of legal codes. The significance of legal codes for corporate performance derives from the observation that investor and creditor protection varies appreciably across countries depending on the nature and origin of legal codes, and in particular whether they derive from common law (essentially English-speaking) or civil law (Continental European) systems.

The evaluation of the debates on comparative financial, corporate, and legal systems in Section 2 indicates that while there are clear differences in structures, the impact of these differences on performance is much harder to establish. In particular, the mechanisms that are often hypoth-esized to provide the link from structural differences to performance are rarely present in firm-level data sets.

In Section 3, we move from the comparative systems to the growth lit-erature, where there is a well-developed body of analysis focusing on the role of financial *development* in comparative growth. The aim is to dis-entangle the question of whether economic growth leads to the devel-opment of a more mature financial system or whether the maturity of the financial system promotes economic growth. Such studies use large samples of countries at widely differing levels of per capita gross domes-tic product (GDP). They invariably record that financial development measured by the size and depth of banking sectors and securities markets promotes economic growth.

While there is therefore considerable evidence that financial develop-ment – bank or market based – is good for economic growth, there is no clear evidence from studies of advanced countries that one kind of finan-cial or corporate system is better for growth than another. Institutional differences between advanced countries appear to be very persistent over the last century during which performance measured by GDP per capita first diverged and then converged. This opens up the question of whether institutional differences in financial systems, ownership structure, and legal systems may create a form of comparative rather than absolute advantage, that is, whether they influence the *type* of activity in which a country specializes, rather than its aggregate performance.

This possibility is explored from a theoretical perspective in Section 4 and empirically in Section 5. Why might financial or ownership structure be related to the type of economic activity? The reason is that different forms of economic activity may have quite different characteristics associated with them that make the provision of particular forms of finance or certain types of governance arrangements desirable. For example, activities may differ in their degree of uncertainty or in the extent to which cooperation from stakeholders in the firm (employees, suppliers, and purchasers) is required for successful performance. Section 4 describes theoretical models in which stock markets support activities where there is a high degree of uncertainty in production. By contrast, banks may be beneficial for activities in which uncertainty is low (because, for example, technology is relatively stable and well understood) but gestation periods are long. In addition, only concentrated owners may be able to offer the commitments required for stakeholders to invest in training or dedicated plant and machinery.

The models discussed in Section 4 suggest that there is a matching of institutional structure with the characteristics of different economic activities. In Section 5, we provide empirical support for this from an empirical study of 14 OECD countries: we record a strong interrelation between type of financial and corporate system, the characteristics of different industries and their growth rates in different countries. In addition, we report that the channel through which this effect occurs is expenditures on research and development rather than fixed capital formation. We also report that the interaction between country structures and industrial activity is sensitive to stages of economic development. In the conclusion, we discuss the implications for economic policy of the view that there may be an interrelation between institutional structure and type of activity.

## II. Financial and Corporate
## Systems and Economic Performance

In 1912, Joseph Schumpeter described how the granting of credit was central to entrepreneurship and innovation: "While granting credit is not essential in the normal circular flow ... it is certain that there is such a gap to bridge in the carrying out of new combinations. To bridge it is the function of the lender, and he fulfills it by placing purchasing power created ad hoc at the disposal of the entrepreneur." Thorstein Veblen saw the process of judging firms as being a matter of "standardized bureaucratic routine" undertaken by the intermediaries that he dubbed "the lieutenants of finance" while "the captaincy has been taken over by the syndicated bankers" (Veblen 1919, p. 81). However, others, most notably Robert Lucas, argue that economists "badly over-stress" the significance of financial considerations in economic performance (Lucas 1988, p. 6).

While the role of financial systems is debated, the performance of different types of financial systems is even more heavily disputed. Clapham (1936) approvingly quoted a principal officer of one of the German Great Banks when he said: "In Germany our banks are largely responsible for the development of the Empire, having fostered and built up its industries. . . . To them, more than any other agency may be credited the splendid results thus far realized." "If his historical summary was not literally accurate," Clapham said, "it was accurate in substance" (Clapham 1936, p. 118). Kennedy (1987) talks in somewhat more measured but still supportive tones about the role of German banks: "With all their documented imperfections (capital markets in Germany), by making resources available to a large group of technologically progressive industries on a scale unequalled in Britain, account for much of the difference in the economic growth performance between Germany and Britain in the half century after 1865" (p. 120). The withdrawal of British banks in the second half of the 19th century was prompted by a series of bank failures: "the banks were by the 'eighties no longer showing such a readiness to act as partners in industrial concerns. They were moving further and further away from the concept of long term loans and were concentrating on an efficient national short term credit system" (Jefferys 1938, p. 119).

But others question this interpretation of German banking. Edwards and Fischer (1994) find that "the commonly-held view of the merits of the German system of finance for investment, in terms of the supply of external finance to firms and corporate control, receives no support from the analysis of the available evidence" (Edwards and Fischer 1994, p. 240). Edwards and Ogilvie (1996) go on to argue that, not only is the current role of German universal banking overstated, it probably never was as significant as suggested, even at its zenith at the turn of the century. "The picture which emerges is not consistent with the claim that German universal banks exerted substantial control over industrial companies and provided significant amounts of finance. Although there were some cases of this, these were the exceptions to the general rule, which was for companies to finance themselves internally to a very great extent" (Edwards and Ogilvie 1996, p. 441).

There have been similar debates about Japanese banks. Hoshi, Kashyap, and Scharfstein (1990) find that "firms with financial structures in which free-rider and information problems are small perform better than other firms after the onset of distress. In particular, we show that firms in industrial groups – those with close financial relationships to their banks, suppliers, and customers – invest more and sell more after the onset of distress than non-group firms." But this view has been challenged. Weinstein and Yafeh (1998) find that, even prior to the liberalization of financial markets in Japan, main-bank clients did not exhibit higher profitability or growth than their industry peers. Moreover, banks could use their monopoly power to squeeze their clients' profits and inhibit their growth through conservative investment policies.[1]

The negative impression of banking systems has been reinforced by recent experience of financial distress in the Far East. Instead of performing the active monitoring and governance function that financial intermediation theory ascribes to them, banks are perceived to have been at the center of corrupt, crony systems. General perceptions have swung markedly from admiration for systems that have been associated with sustained high levels of investment and growth rates to severe criticism for their lack of openness and transparency.

In the last decade, the debate in the comparative systems and finance literature has widened to include other cross-country differences. Franks and Mayer (1998a) reported marked differences across countries in concentration of ownership. "The United Kingdom and the United States have large quoted sectors, with share ownership dispersed across a large number of investors. In the case of the United Kingdom, the dominant shareholding group is institutional investors; in the United States, it is individual investors. In contrast, France and Germany have small quoted sectors. More significantly, even the largest quoted companies in general have at least one shareholder owning more than 25 percent of the equity and frequently a majority shareholding. These large shareholdings are in particular associated with family and other corporate investors" (p. 730).

These differences have recently been confirmed in two sets of studies that investigate concentration of both share ownership and voting power. The first, a large international comparison of ownership in 27 countries, "finds that the Berle and Means corporation is far from universal, and is quite rare on some definitions of control. Similarly, the so-called German model of bank control through equity is uncommon. Instead, controlling shareholders – usually the State or families –

---

[1] See also Caves and Uekusa (1976) and Nakatani (1984).

141

are present in most large companies. These shareholders have control rights in firms in excess of their cash flow rights, largely through the use of pyramids, but they also participate in management" (La Porta, López-de-Silanes, and Shleifer 1998, p. 5). The second is a more detailed study of nine European countries, which concludes, "the most striking fact about blockholdings in Europe is that they are so much higher than in the U.S.A. . . . Within Europe, the level of concentration of voting power is by no means uniform; and these differences are rooted in differences in customs and the legal environment. . . . In the UK, the largest 250 listed companies report a very modest median value (of size of share blocks) of 9.9%; while at the other extreme, Germany, Austria and Italy all exceed 50%" (Becht and Roell 1999).

Ownership may affect corporate performance in several ways. First, principal–agent models emphasize the significance of equity ownership for incentives. Higher powered incentive arrangements for managerial remuneration might be expected in the dispersed stock market economies of the United Kingdom and United States because of the weak incentive for any individual shareholder to incur the costs of monitoring management. Large owners in Continental Europe may have more incentive and capacity to monitor corporate performance directly instead of using schemes relating pay to stock market performance to align managers' incentives with those of owners. However, to the extent that there is evidence on executive pay in different countries, it fails to reveal pronounced differences. In a comparison of the response of executive remuneration to performance (share price, earnings, changes in earnings, and sales growth) in Japan and the United States, Kaplan (1994) concludes that Japanese "compensation responds to all four performance measures, and the responses are generally similar to those in the United States. . . . Cash compensation is positively related to earnings, stock and sales performance. In most cases, the sensitivities in the two countries are not statistically different" (p. 512).

Concentrations of ownership are likely to affect corporate control. The separation of ownership and control in the United Kingdom and United States has created free-rider problems of corporate control and passive (in particular, institutional) investors. Concentrations of ownership may overcome free-rider problems (Shleifer and Vishny 1986) but may worsen incentives and create conflicts between majority and minority investors (Burkhart, Gromb, and Panunzi 1996; Shleifer and Vishny 1997). Conflicts between majority and minority shareholders would arise, for example, in the case in which the majority owner derived benefits from control of the firm other than those associated with value maximization.

142

It is therefore an empirical matter whether concentrations improve corporate control and performance. In a comparison of relations between executive board turnover and performance in Japanese and U.S. firms, Kaplan (1994) concludes,

To a large extent, the turnover-performance relations are economically and statistically similar in Japan and the United States. The results are not consistent with Japanese managers being more highly penalized for poor sales growth. At the level of the top several executives, the results are also not consistent with Japanese managers being less highly penalized for poor stock performance than are U.S. managers. Because boards of directors (or the entities that control them) are responsible for hiring and firing top executives, these results suggest that boards in both countries focus on similar performance objectives. (p. 528)

In a similar vein, in a study of ownership and control in Germany, Franks and Mayer (1998b) conclude that there is "little relation between concentration of ownership and the disciplining of management of poorly performing firms and little relation between the type of concentrated owner and board turnover. The pronounced influence which might have been expected from the very high levels of concentration of ownership in Germany and the distinctive forms in which shares are held through banks and pyramids is not in evidence" (p. 28).

Whatever is the significance of the pronounced international differences in concentrated ownership, it does not appear to be associated with managerial incentives and disciplining. In fact, a common theme of many of the essays in this book is that the standard principal–agent view of the firm is not applicable to most countries' financial and corporate systems. The standard view sees the central problem of firm organization as aligning the interests of managers with those of the investors supplying external finance. Hellwig disputes the notion that outside financiers control firms and instead argues that concern about retaining control is a dominant influence on the way in which managers structure financial and ownership policies. Alliances between bankers, lawyers, managers, and politicians help to cement insider systems of corporate control and, far from providing external investor monitoring and control, banks in Germany reinforce managerial autonomy. Allen and Gale note that the question of how managers can be best motivated to act in the interests of shareholders simply does not apply in many countries' corporate systems and, even in the United Kingdom and United States, is not relevant to many legal forms, including not-for-profit organizations and mutuals.

Recently, a third factor has been introduced into international comparisons of finance and control: the variation in legal systems across

143

countries. La Porta, López-de-Silanes, Shleifer and Vishny (1997) argue that the nature and operation of financial systems are related to differences in the degree of investor protection across countries, that is, the extent of protection of minorities. Legal rules vary systematically across countries depending on whether they are of English, French, German, or Scandinavian origin. Common law countries of the English tradition protect both shareholders and creditors the most, French civil law countries the least, and German and Scandinavian civil law countries somewhere in the middle. They find that "civil law, and particularly French civil law, countries, have both the weakest investor protections and the least developed capital markets, especially as compared to common law countries" (La Porta et al. 1997, p. 1149). They argue that greater legal protection of minority owners implies less need for ownership concentration, which increases access of companies to external finance and reduces capital costs.

The aforementioned studies from the comparative governance and finance literature have documented substantial and persistent differences in the extent of bank involvement in the corporate sector, in the extent of ownership concentration and in the legal protection of investors. Yet attempts to pin down the mechanisms linking differences in structure to performance outcomes have been less successful.

### III. Financial Development and Economic Growth

Over the past few years, a literature has begun to emerge that attempts to use data from a large number of countries to establish the relevance of financial and legal systems for economic growth. The work has its origins in Goldsmith (1969), who correlated the relation between the size of financial systems, as measured by the ratio of the value of intermediary assets to gross national product, and economic growth in 35 countries over the period 1860 to 1963. He reports a positive association, but there are several obvious problems with Goldsmith's analysis. First, while the period of study is long, the sample size is small; second, the direction of causation is unclear; and, third, there is no control for other factors that might influence growth. In a series of studies, King and Levine have attempted to address these problems.

King and Levine (1993a–c) examine the growth of 80 countries over the period 1960 to 1989. They use four measures of financial development. The first is the ratio of liquid liabilities to GDP, which measures the scale of financial intermediation in different countries. The second is the proportion of domestic credit outside of the central bank, which captures the development of a financial system beyond a central banking function. The third and fourth variables measure the allocation of credit to the private rather than the public sector (the ratio of claims on the nonfinancial private sector to domestic credit control and the ratio of gross claims on the private sector to GDP). In separate equations, three measures of growth (real per capita GDP growth, growth in capital stock per person, and total factor productivity growth) are regressed on the average values of these variables over the period 1960 to 1989. The equations control for a range of other influences on growth, including initial income, education, government expenditure, inflation, and trade propensities.

King and Levine report a strong positive relation between the three measures of growth and the four measures of financial development. They also examine the extent to which financial development at the start of the period in 1960 predicts growth in the subsequent thirty years. They conclude, "the initial level of financial development is a good predictor of subsequent rates of economic growth, physical capital accumulation and economic efficiency improvements over the next thirty years" (Levine 1997, p. 707).

There have been two studies that have looked at the significance of securities markets as well as bank development on economic growth. Levine and Zervos (1998) report the influence of stock markets as measured by their size (ratio of market capitalization to GDP) and value traded (as a proportion of GDP) as well as bank credit on economic growth across more than 40 countries over the period 1976 to 1993. They find that value traded is positively and significantly related to growth even when market capitalization is included in the equation. They conclude that "stock market liquidity and banking development are both positively and robustly correlated with contemporaneous and future rates of economic growth ... and since measures of stock market liquidity and banking development both enter the growth regressions significantly, the findings suggest that banks provide different financial services from those provided by stock markets" (Levine and Zervos 1998, p. 554).

Rajan and Zingales (1998) argue that despite the inclusion of other variables, there may be a problem of controlling for omitted variables, such as saving rates, in the regressions mentioned above. Instead, they focus on one way in which financial development may affect economic growth: via external finance. They argue that financial development should be most relevant to industries that are dependent on external finance and that these industries should grow fastest in countries with well-developed financial systems. They therefore look at 36 individual industries in 41 different countries and examine the influence of the interaction between the external financial dependence of those industries and the financial development of the countries on the growth rates of those industries in the different countries over the period 1980 to 1990.

Rajan and Zingales use three measures of financial development of a country: the ratio of market capitalization to GDP, domestic credit to the private sector over GDP, and accounting standards. They measure financial dependence of an industry by the amount of external finance raised by firms in different industries in the United States. They use the United States on the grounds that it has the best-developed capital markets in the world and that its firms face the least friction in raising finance. The United States therefore provides the purest measure of the true financing needs of industries.

Controlling for other influences on economic growth by including dummy variables for industries and countries, Rajan and Zingales report a strong relation between economic growth in different industries and countries and the interaction of financial development of countries and the financial dependence of industries. There is a particularly strong relation when accounting standards are used as the measure of financial development of countries. They conclude that their results "suggest that financial development has a substantial supportive influence on the rate of economic growth and this works, at least partly, by reducing the cost of external finance to financially dependent firms" (Rajan and Zingales 1998, p. 584).

Demirguc-Kunt and Maksimovic (1998) use firm-level data to evaluate the influence of financial systems on growth. They estimate the excess growth of a firm over and above that which can be internally financed (with a zero dividend distribution) and from short-term finance (assuming that the firm maintains its current ratio of short-term debt to assets). They examine the influence of market capitalization to GDP ratios, stock market turnover, and bank deposits to GDP in 30 countries over the period 1980 to 1995 on the excess growth of firms in those countries over the period 1986 to 1991. They find that both stock market turnover and the size of the banking system are positively related to excess growth. They also include a measure of law and order (the extent to which the legal system of a country allows disputes to be mediated and contracts to be enforced) and find that this variable is also positively associated with excess growth. They conclude, "an active stock market and a well-developed legal system are important in facilitating firm growth. Firms in countries that have active stock markets and high ratings for compliance with legal norms are able to obtain external funds and grow faster" (Demirguc-Kunt and Maksimovic 1998, p. 2134).

Demirguc-Kunt and Maksimovic (1999) provide support for Rajan and Zingales' (1998) argument that financial development may influence economic growth through external financing. They examine the amount and maturity of debt of firms in 30 countries over the period 1980 to 1991 and relate these to turnover on stock markets, bank assets to GDP ratios, the same law-and-order variable described in the previous paragraph, and measures of shareholder and creditor rights. They find that stock market turnover is associated with more long-term debt among large but not small firms and that larger banking sectors are associated with more long-term debt of small but not large firms. Banks therefore appear to be particularly important in the financing of small firms and stock markets in the financing of large firms.

La Porta, López-de-Silanes, Shleifer, and Vishny (1998) report that the better investor protection in common law countries is reflected in higher dividend payouts than in civil law countries and lower dividend payouts by high- than low-growth companies in common but not civil law countries. Better investor protection therefore makes dividends more responsive to the investment needs of companies.

In sum, large-sample cross-country analyses that include developing as well as developed countries record a strong relation between financial development and economic growth. The Demirguc-Kunt and Maksimovic (1999) and La Porta et al. (1998) studies suggest that financial and legal systems may affect different types of firms in different ways – an issue that we will address in the next section.

## IV. Financial Systems, Corporate Systems, and Types of Economic Activity: Theory

### 4.1. Financial Systems

As noted in Section 2, a distinction is commonly drawn between bank- and market-oriented financial systems. Economic theory attributes a particular function to banks in monitoring corporate activities. Economies of scale in monitoring make banks more efficient monitors than individual market participants. As Allen (1993) notes, however, securities markets have the advantage of aggregating diverse views of a large number of market participants. Securities markets are therefore superior at promoting investment where there are legitimate grounds for differences in views. However, they are inefficient where good investment decisions require the costly accumulation of available information on, for example, the quality and performance of borrowers. This is an example of the way in which a bank-based system would be expected to benefit different kinds of activity from those promoted by a stock-market–oriented system.

Dewatripont and Maskin (1995) develop a model in which the structure of financial systems affects the degree of financial discipline imposed on firms. The structural difference that they have in mind is between a decentralized banking system with many small banks and a centralized system with one or a small number of banks. We will refer to the first as a multibank system and to the second as a single-bank system.

There are "good" and "bad" entrepreneurs, and the former can choose either a fast project that is completed in one period or a slow project that takes two. The bad entrepreneur's project takes two periods to complete and is assumed to be poor. The type of project is only revealed in the period in which it is completed. In a decentralized banking system, an individual bank lacks the funds to refinance the project in the second period. In this case, Dewatripont and Maskin show that there is a credible mechanism through which banks can commit not to refinance poor projects even though refinancing would be worthwhile once the fixed costs of the project have been incurred. If a second bank is required to provide refinancing, and if costly monitoring of borrowers is necessary, then the first bank will anticipate that the returns to monitoring will have to be shared with the second bank and, hence, will have little incentive to monitor in the first place. This undermines the viability of a project requiring refinance and creates an incentive for entrepreneurs to choose only fast projects. Thus a multibank system will impose hard budget constraints and exclude poor projects – but at the cost of also excluding efficient projects that are slow to generate revenues and require refinancing.

Multibank systems are therefore superior in imposing tough budget constraints on inefficient projects but are too short-termist in failing to sustain efficient long-term projects. It is plausible that industries differ in terms of the balance between short- and long-term projects. If so, then the Dewatripont–Maskin model suggests that an economy with many small banks will be one in which industries with more short-term projects will be fostered, whereas industries characterized by longer term investment projects will fare better in an economy with a few large banks.

Huang and Xu (1998b) describe a similar model, but in this case activities differ not in the gestation of investment projects (all of which are "slow" in the Dewatripont–Maskin sense) but in the extent of uncertainty attached to the success of projects. In their model, there are good and bad projects, the quality of which can be ascertained only by investors ex post. Projects can be financed by one or more banks. Huang and Xu assume that there is a choice of reorganization strategies available following a poor outcome for the project after the first period. As in the Dewatripont–Maskin model, the type of activity favored by a multibank system hinges on the commitment not to refinance projects that turn out to be poor after the first period but which, ignoring the sunk cost, would be worth continuing. This occurs in the Huang and Xu model because each bank has access to private information that on its own is inadequate to come to a correct decision about how to reorganize a firm and where there are conflicts that discourage banks from sharing information with each other.[2] As a consequence, multibanks prefer to liquidate projects seeking refinancing. Since information sharing and conflicts of interest are eliminated by a single-bank system, there will be no such commitment to liquidate projects that need refinance.

Where there is considerable uncertainty about returns from projects (that is, there is a high proportion of bad projects), then the commitment to terminate projects is valuable and multibank systems invest more than do those with single lenders. Where uncertainty is low, then single banks have more information with which to make ex ante investment decisions and they invest more. Multibank systems are therefore associated with industries characterized by intensive research and development (R&D), particularly when companies are young and uncertainty is high, and single-bank systems with lower uncertainty, imitative investments.

In all of the aforementioned models, financial systems are associated with different *types* of corporate activities and investments. In Allen (1993), new technologies, where there are legitimate grounds for diverse expectations, benefit from securities markets or require information pooling through venture capitalists. More traditional investments, where uncertainty primarily relates to the borrower and the quality of management benefit from the economies of monitoring that banks can provide. In Dewatripont and Maskin (1995), fragmented banking systems are associated with short-term investments and single-bank systems with long-term investments. In Huang and Xu (1998), multibank systems promote high-risk R&D investments and single banks lower risk, imitative investments.

---

[2] In contrast, Aoki in this book argues that venture capitalists in Silicon Valley play a crucial information collection and dissemination function. By running tournaments between aspiring entrepreneurs, venture capitalists can configure product systems and guide entrepreneurs in response to information about newly emerging technologies.

## 4.2. Corporate Ownership and Control

The structure of corporate sectors, in particular the ownership and control of corporations, as well as the structure of financial systems may influence patterns of corporate activities. Using a model with many similarities to that discussed here for the financial system, Huang and Xu (1998a) present a theory in which they argue that multi-investor financing dominates single-investor financing of R&D when there is high uncertainty. Conversely, when investment is directed to more routine, incremental innovation, their model predicts the superiority of single-investor or internal financing. The central idea in the model is the trade-off between the costs and benefits of finance from multiple external independent investors as compared with a single external investor or internal financing.

Huang and Xu focus on the benefits that come from having multiple independent investors financing the project because of their ability to commit not to refinance a project that is revealed ex post to be poor. It is assumed that conflicts of interest between the external investors prevent sharing of information that would make reorganization of a project revealed to be poor preferable to its liquidation. They assume that the entrepreneur learns the outcome of the R&D project earlier than those supplying the finance and will terminate the project if he knows that refinancing will not occur. The hard budget constraint that comes from multiple investors may therefore produce superior project selection because entrepreneurs terminate poor projects in a timely fashion. Just as in the single-bank case described here, where there is no conflict of interest between investors (which is true if there is a single investor or the project is internally financed), information about the optimal reorganization strategy in the event of project failure will be shared, implying that entrepreneurs face a soft budget constraint. If there is little riskiness associated with the R&D project, this source of inefficiency may be outweighed by the lower costs of internal or single-investor finance.

It is clear that the model closely parallels the one described here for multi- and single banks. Multiple investors will assist in the financing of high-risk projects where there is considerable uncertainty about quality, and a significant fraction of projects will need to be terminated. Where risks are small, then single investors can offer lower cost sources of finance. Huang and Xu therefore predict that single-investor financing will be observed during catch-up stages of development, when R&D primarily takes the form of imitation but that multi-investor finance will dominate in economies at advanced stages of development which are undertaking higher risk R&D.

Concentration of ownership and of voting rights also affects the balance between preserving and transferring control rights. Large block-holders can preserve their control over firms, while markets in control are possible when ownership is dispersed. Incentives for owners to monitor and control are greater where ownership is concentrated, and concentrated owners can display a greater degree of commitment to other stakeholders than dispersed shareholders. Unlike dispersed share-holders, large block-holders cannot anonymously withdraw from past commitments (see Franks and Mayer 1998a). Activities that require a high level of irreversible investment by other stakeholders, in, for example, human skill formation and knowledge about customer markets, therefore benefit from having large committed rather than dispersed anonymous shareholders.

Rajan and Zingales argue in this volume that the "new corporations" which rely heavily on high-level human capital skills require different governance and control structures from traditional corporations that primarily employ physical assets. For example, restrictions on control by outside shareholders may be required to encourage investments by managers that shareholders would reject in favor of other options. But they also provide other examples in which the holders of human capital in the firm are so powerful that ownership by outsiders with no specific investments in the company is required for efficiency.

Flexibility in the implementation of new technologies without commitments to those associated with past production processes can be more easily implemented by dispersed anonymous shareholders than identifiable large shareholders. Stock markets will therefore be well suited to activities for which changes in control are warranted because, for instance, the qualities required for good management of established activities are quite different from those of an entrepreneurial company. The scientific knowledge required to start up a high-tech firm may, for example, be quite different from the management skill needed to run the same firm at a later date.

The arguments presented in this section suggest that there will be an association between financial systems, corporate systems, and corporate activities (Table 4.1). Where active involvement and high levels of commitment of owners in corporate governance are required, then private benefits of control can be preserved through concentrated ownership or single-bank systems. Where activities benefit from the diverse assessments of many investors, the imposition of hard budget constraints and flexibility in changing control, then market finance, a fragmented multi-bank system and dispersed ownership will be observed. The former is particularly associated with long-term investments in relatively low-risk,

Table 4.1. *The Association of Different Financial and Corporate Systems with Corporate Activities*

| Financial and Corporate Systems | Benefit Activities That Require |
| --- | --- |
| Market systems | Diverse assessments and hard budget constraints |
| Banking systems | Monitoring by single party |
| Dispersed ownership | Hard budget constraints, flexibility in control |
| Concentrated ownership | Active governance and commitment |

well-established activities and with R&D focused on incremental innovation. It is therefore best suited to more traditional manufacturing activities. The latter is better suited to shorter term investments and to high-risk activities where R&D is directed toward more radical innovation.

Legal systems reinforce these effects. Those with the greatest degree of investor protection promote activities that are funded and controlled through the market; those with lesser investor protection encourage activities that require active corporate governance and bank finance.

## V. Financial Systems, Corporate Systems, and Types of Economic Activity: Empirical Evidence

In Carlin and Mayer (1999), we perform the first empirical analysis of the relation between the composition of economic activity and financial, corporate, and legal systems. To pursue the hypothesis that different systems might favor industries with different kinds of characteristics, they examine the interrelation between types of systems, the nature of different industries, and the levels of activity in those industries in different countries.

Building on the theories described in Section 4, we evaluate whether there is a relationship between the growth rates of industries in different countries and the interaction between country structures (such as the degree of market and bank orientation of their financial systems) and industry characteristics (the dependence of industries on external equity or bank debt sources of finance and inputs of skilled labor). For example, we suggested above that firms that are dependent on high levels of skilled labor would benefit from the commitment provided by concentrated ownership. In a cross-country context, we therefore ask whether industries identified as skill intensive flourish in countries where owner-

152

ship structures are concentrated, relative to the same industries in countries with dispersed ownership structures and relative to other industries that do not depend on high-level skills.

Specifically we define:

$\mathbf{Y} = k \times i$ matrix of $i$ industrial growth rates in $k$ countries
$\mathbf{X} = s \times k$ matrix of $s$ country structural features in $k$ countries
$\mathbf{Z} = c \times i$ matrix of $c$ industry characteristics in $i$ industries

We estimate $\mathbf{B}$, the $s \times c$ matrix, which relates country structural characteristics and industry financing variables to industry growth rates in particular countries in the equation

$$\mathbf{Y} = \mathbf{X'BZ} + \varepsilon$$

where $\varepsilon$ is the error term in the regression. The basic sample comprises 14 OECD countries and 27 three-digit industries over the period from 1970 to 1995.

The structure of different countries' financial systems (matrix $\mathbf{X}$) is measured by the size of their stock markets, accounting standards, the ratio of bank credit to GDP, and the degree of bank ownership of corporate equity. The structure of corporate systems is captured by the degree of concentration of ownership and by the extent of pyramid ownership. The characteristics of legal systems are measured in two ways: first, by indicators of legal protection of investors or creditors and second, by the common or civil law origin of the legal system as indicated by its source in English, German, Scandinavian, or French law.

There are positive correlations between the market capitalization/GDP ratio and a measure of accounting standards (0.29), between bank–firm ties (as measured by bank ownership of nonfinancial firms) and the ratio of credit to GDP (0.68), and between ownership concentration and a measure of the presence of pyramidal ownership structures (0.52). By contrast, there are negative correlations between accounting standards and the credit/GDP ratio (–0.46) and between accounting standards and ownership concentration (–0.20). There is a very low correlation between ownership concentration and the size of the banking sector (–0.04). These correlations are broadly consistent with the view that some clusters of institutional characteristics are found together in some countries and other clusters in other countries.

The characteristics of industries (matrix $\mathbf{Z}$) are captured by the amount of external equity and bank finance and investment in skills in different industries. In line with the ideas discussed in Section 4, industries may differ in their underlying characteristics such as the uncertainty

153

associated with R&D or the tendency for investment projects to be short- or long-lived or their reliance on human capital. We use as proxies for the different characteristics of industries the role of equity finance and bank loans as sources of investment finance and the use of skills (measured by the proportion of employees with off- and on-the-job training), where these characteristics are measured in countries where institutional structures are thought to be most conducive to their elastic supply. In principle, one wants to establish the extent to which industries that face no institutional constraints use external sources of finance and invest in skills. In practice, one cannot observe these. Instead, we measure these variables in those countries in which institutional constraints are likely to be least binding: Firms are thought to have easiest access to market sources of external finance in the United States, to bank loans in Japan, and to skilled labor in Germany. The scale of external finance and skills in different industries is therefore measured in these three countries. For the 27 industries, the correlation between equity-dependent and bank-financed industries is 0.07, between equity-dependent and skill-intensive industries is 0.17, and between bank-financed and skill-intensive industries is −0.46.

By creating interactive variables between the country structures and industry characteristics, this essay examines whether there is any interrelation between these variables and performance, as measured by the growth rates of industries in different countries over the period 1970 to 1995. Growth rates in 27 industries in 14 countries that are members of the Organization for Economic Cooperation and Development (OECD) are regressed on the product of interactive variables between country structures and industry characteristics. The initial shares of industries in different countries are included in the growth regressions to account for catch-up and regression to the mean effects. Controls are provided for other variables by taking the difference of all of the variables from their respective means across the entire samples.

In Carlin and Mayer (1999) we report strong evidence of a relation between industry growth rates in different countries and the interaction of country structures with industry characteristics. There is a particularly strong interactive effect of the country variables accounting standards and concentration of ownership with two industry characteristics – equity finance and skills. This means that industries that are dependent on equity finance and are skill intensive grow particularly rapidly in countries with a large number of accounting standards and high levels of concentration of ownership. Information disclosure and ownership concentrations are associated with high growth rates of industries that are dependent on market finance and skill-intensive labor forces. These

154

results are consistent with the thesis that market-based financial systems are suited to activities in which there is a need for forms of finance that involve diverse assessments by a large number of participants. It is also consistent with concentrations of ownership-benefiting activities that require investments to be made by other stakeholders, in this case employees.

In Carlin and Mayer (1999) we then perform similar analyses of the determinants of fixed investment shares and R&D shares (as a proportion of value added) in the 27 different industries (15 for R&D) and 14 OECD countries. The interactions between country structure and industry characteristic variables account for a far higher proportion of the variation in R&D than in fixed investment across industries and countries. The influence of country structures on industry growth rates therefore appears to come via R&D rather than fixed capital formation (FCF) expenditures. This is further reflected in a relation of accounting standards to R&D similar to that we reported for growth. As in the growth equation, industries with high levels of external equity finance and that use skilled labor intensively have high R&D shares in countries with a large number of accounting standards. The relation with skills is particularly pronounced when the skills measure is restricted to the proportion of the workforce with the highest levels of qualifications. This suggests that information disclosure assists in the financing of the advanced skill training that is required in R&D. Unlike growth, there is no relation of concentration of ownership to R&D, suggesting that concentrations of ownership provide the commitment that is required to encourage investment by the labor force and firms in training in basic skills but not the more mobile advanced skills.

Consistent with the theories of Dewatripont and Maskin (1995), and Huang and Xu (1998a), market systems that impose tight budget constraints are associated with higher growth in industries that are dependent on market sources of finance and investments in skills training. One interpretation of the finding that R&D levels are high relative to industry and country means in countries with high accounting standards in equity-dependent and skill-intensive industries is the superiority of hard budget constraints for promoting R&D when there is high technological uncertainty, as suggested by Huang and Xu. It is plausible that equity-dependent and high-skill-intensive industries are those in which technological development is characterized by high uncertainty. Concentrations of ownership are associated with growth in industries requiring investments in less advanced skills training.

We repeat the analysis of the relation of growth to interactive country and industry variables on a set of four countries that were at an earlier stage of development as measured by GDP per capita in 1970 than the 14 used in the aforementioned analysis. It records that the influence of concentration of ownership and banking structures is quite different from that found in developed countries. High levels of concentration of ownership are associated with *lower* rates of growth of industries that are dependent on external equity finance and skills in low GDP countries. Consistent with Huang and Xu (1998a), the potential soft budget constraints associated with high concentrations of owners therefore act to the disadvantage of these industries in countries in their early stages of development. In addition, consistent with Gerschenkron's (1962) and Huang and Xu's (1998b) theses on the role of banks in initial stages of development, there is evidence of higher rates of growth of bank-dependent industries in the bank-oriented developing but not developed countries.

Finally, we examine the influence of legal structures on industry growth rates and investment. A positive influence of investor protection is found in both the growth and R&D regressions. In the case of growth, it is associated with skill-intensive industries and in the case of R&D with equity-financed industries. This supports the view that investor protection reinforces the effects of financial and corporate structures by promoting growth in external-financed and skill-intensive industries through R&D expenditures. There is also some evidence that creditor protection promotes capital expenditure in skill-intensive industries.

Consistent with the theories of Section 4, support has therefore been found for an influence of the structure of financial, corporate, and legal systems on the composition of industrial activity. Market-oriented financial systems are associated with high growth of external-equity-financed and skill-intensive industries. The effect comes through investment in R&D rather than fixed capital expenditures. High concentrations of ownership are also associated with high growth of these industries in developed countries but low growth of these industries in developing countries. Furthermore, their influence does not come via R&D even in developed countries. This suggests that, as predicted by Huang and Xu (1998a), concentrations of ownership are associated with the growth of relatively low-risk activities.

## VI. Conclusions

This essay has provided an overview of the emerging literature on the influence of financial, corporate, and legal systems on economic performance in different countries. There has been considerable discussion over a long period of time of the influence of financial systems on economic performance. Nevertheless, as noted in Section 2, international comparisons of financial and corporate systems in developed countries fail to reveal clear effects of financial or corporate structures on economic performance. On the basis of this, one might conclude, as Allen and Gale do in this book, that no financial or governance system performs particularly well in controlling agency problems and that solutions have to be sought elsewhere, in, for example, product market competition.[3]

But the studies reported in the third section paint a rather different picture. There, empirical analyses pointed consistently to an important role for financial development in economic performance. There is a clear relation between economic growth across countries and the development of both banking systems and securities markets.

In the fourth section, we described the emerging theoretical literature on the relation between financial and corporate systems and types of economic activity. Market-oriented financial systems and those with dispersed ownership are expected to be associated with high-risk R&D type activities where the imposition of tight budget constraints are important. Bank-oriented systems and those with concentrated ownership should be associated with longer term investment of a more imitative nature, where commitments to other stakeholders are required.

In Section 5 we reported the first empirical evidence in support of these theoretical propositions. There is clear evidence of an association between different financial and corporate systems and *types* of economic activity. Market-oriented systems are associated with high growth of external-equity-dependent and high-skill industries, and this effect is associated with R&D effort. High concentrations of ownership are also associated with high growth of these industries in developed but not developing countries, and the effect is not associated with R&D.

While empirical analyses of the relation between financial and corporate systems and types of economic activity are at a preliminary stage, if they are supported by further evidence then they have important policy implications. In particular, they imply that there is not necessarily a dominant financial and corporate system that is appropriate to all economies or all industries within an economy. What is right for a devel-

---

[3] In a recent test of the impact of product market competition, financial pressure (measured by a firm's burden of interest payments) and concentrated ownership at firm level on total factor productivity (TFP) growth for a sample of British firms, Nickell, Nicolitsas, and Dryden (1997) found that all three variables were individually significant with the expected positive sign and that the interaction of competition with ownership concentration was also significant, indicating that ownership concentration and competition were substitutes.

WENDY CARLIN AND COLIN MAYER

oped economy may be quite inappropriate for a developing one. What is suited to an innovative R&D intensive economy may be ill-suited to a more imitative one. There may be important trade-offs in matching systems with the industrial bases of countries and their stages of economic development and regulatory and legal policies toward financial and corporate systems need to be sensitive to these potential impacts on corporate activities.

## References

Allen, F. (1993). "Stock Markets and Resource Allocation." In C. Mayer and X. Vives (Eds.), *Capital Markets and Financial Intermediation*. Cambridge: Cambridge University Press.

Becht, M., and A. Roell. (1999). "Blockholdings in Europe: An International Comparison." *European Economic Review*, 43: 1049–56.

Burkhart, M., D. Gromb, and F. Panunzi. (1996). "Large Shareholder Monitoring and the Value of the Firm." *Quarterly Journal of Economics*, 112: 693–728.

Carlin, W., and C. Mayer. (1999). "Finance, Investment and Growth." CEPR Discussion Paper, No. 2233.

Caves, R., and M. Uekusa. (1976). *Industrial Organization in Japan*. Washington, D.C.: Brookings Institution.

Clapham, J. H. (1936). *The Economic Development of France and Germany, 1815–1914*. Cambridge: Cambridge University Press.

Demirguc-Kunt, A., and V. Maksimovic. (1998). "Law, Finance and Firm Growth." *Journal of Finance*, 53: 2107–37.

(1999). "Institutions, Financial Markets and Firm Debt Maturity." *Journal of Financial Economics*, 54: 295–336.

Dewatripont, M., and E. Maskin. (1995). "Credit Efficiency in Centralized and Decentralized Economies." *Review of Economic Studies*, 62: 541–55.

Edwards, J., and K. Fischer. (1994). *Banks, Finance and Investment in Germany*. Cambridge: Cambridge University Press.

Edwards, J., and S. Ogilvie. (1996). "Universal Banks and German Industrialization: A Reappraisal." *Economic History Review*, 49: 427–46.

Fohlin, C. (1998). "Financial System Structure and Industrialization: Reassessing the German Experience before World War I." Social Science Working Paper No. 1028. Division of the Humanities and Social Sciences, California Institute of Technology.

Franks, J., and C. Mayer. (1998a). "Ownership and Control in Europe." In P. Newman (Ed.), *New Palgrave Dictionary of Economics and the Law*. London: Macmillan.

(1998b). "Ownership and Control of German Corporations." London Business School.

Gerschenkron, A. (1962). *Economic Backwardness in Historical Perspective*. Cambridge, Mass.: Harvard University Press.

Goldsmith, R. (1969). *Financial Structure and Development*. New Haven, Conn.: Yale University Press.

Hoshi, T., A. Kashyap, and D. Scharfstein. (1990). "The Role of Banks in Reducing the Costs of Financial Distress in Japan." *Journal of Financial Economics*, 27: 67–88.

Huang, H., and C. Xu. (1998a). "Financing Mechanisms and R&D Investment." Mimeo, London School of Economics.

(1998b). "Institutions, Innovations and Growth." Mimeo, London School of Economics.

Jefferys, J. (1938). "Trends in Business Organization in Great Britain since 1856." Unpublished PhD. dissertation, University of London.

Kaplan, S. (1994). "Top Executive Rewards and Firm Performance: A Comparison of Japan and the United States." *Journal of Political Economy*, 102: 510–46.

Kennedy, W. (1987). *Industrial Structure, Capital Markets and the Origins of British Economic Decline*. Cambridge: Cambridge University Press.

King, R., and R. Levine. (1993a). "Financial Intermediation and Economic Development." In C. Mayer and X. Vives (Eds.), *Capital Markets and Financial Intermediation*. Cambridge: Cambridge University Press.

(1993b). "Finance and Growth: Schumpeter Might Be Right." *Quarterly Journal of Economics*, 108: 717–37.

(1993c). "Finance, Entrepreneurship and Growth: Theory and Evidence." *Journal of Monetary Economics*, 32: 513–42.

La Porta, R., F. López-de-Silanes, and A. Shleifer. (1998). "Corporate Ownership around the World." Mimeo, Harvard University.

La Porta, R., F. López-de-Silanes, A. Shleifer, and R. Vishny. (1997). "Legal Determinants of External Finance." *Journal of Finance*, 52: 1131–50.

(1998). "Agency Problems and Dividend Policies around the World." Mimeo, Harvard University.

Levine, R. (1997). "Financial Development and Economic Growth: Views and Agenda." *Journal of Economic Literature*, 35: 688–726.

Levine, R., and S. Zervos. (1998). "Stock Markets, Banks, and Economic Growth." *American Economic Review*, 88: 537–58.

Lucas, R. (1988). "On the Mechanics of Economic Development." *Journal of Monetary Economics*, 22: 3–42.

Nakatani, I. (1984). "The Role of Financial Corporate Groupings." In M. Aoki (Ed.), *Economic Analysis of the Japanese Firm*. New York: North Holland.

Nickell, S., D. Nicolitsas, and N. Dryden. (1997). "What Makes Firms Perform Well?" *European Economic Review*, 41: 783–96.

Rajan, R., and L. Zingales. (1998). "Financial Dependence and Growth." *American Economic Review*, 88: 559–86.

Schumpeter, J. (1912, 1931). *Theory of Economic Development*. Cambridge, Mass.: Harvard University Press.

Shleifer, A., and R. Vishny. (1986). "Large Shareholders and Corporate Control." *Journal of Political Economy*, 94: 461–88.

Shleifer, A., and R. Vishny. (1997). "Review of the Literature on Corporate Governance." *Journal of Finance*, 52: 737–83.

Veblen, T. (1919). "Captains of Finance and the Engineers." *Dial*, June.

Weinstein, D., and Y. Yafeh. (1998). "On the Costs of a Bank Centred Financial System: Evidence from the Changing Main Bank Relationships in Japan." *Journal of Finance*, 53: 635–72.

## Discussion

### Comment on Carlin and Mayer, "How Do Financial Systems Affect Economic Performance?"

*A. Marco Becht*

Carlin and Mayer provide a comprehensive and insightful overview "of the emerging literature on the influence of financial, corporate, and legal systems on economic performance in different countries." They conclude that the available empirical evidence suggests "that there is a clear relation between economic growth across countries and the development of both banking systems and securities markets." The authors put special emphasis on a particular part of this literature, which investigates the link "between financial and corporate systems and types of economic activity." In particular, they highlight the method and findings of Carlin and Mayer (1999), a recent empirical contribution that establishes a link between these three elements.

Following the structure of the essay, my comments have two parts. First, I make some observations on the "emerging" empirical literature that investigates the effect of "financial, corporate, and legal systems on economic performance in different countries." Second, I comment on related aspects of Carlin and Mayer (1999).

Carlin and Mayer show that until recently, the literature in the United States was primarily concerned with the working and effects of the market for corporate control, executive remuneration, and the trade-off between dispersed and concentrated ownership. Everywhere else, the literature was primarily concerned with the role of banks and their effect on economic performance. Comparative studies were the exception, for example Kaplan's work on the link between board turnover and performance in the United States, Japan, and Germany and executive remuneration in the United States and Japan.

Why is this literature, after 10 and more years of research, still "emerging"? An important factor has been the lack of financial and nonfinancial disclosure outside the United States and the United Kingdom. In continental Europe, the ownership of cash-flow rights and individual executive compensation are generally not disclosed (Becht 1997). Despite the efforts of international standards bodies, accounting data is still far from being comparable across countries. Nonfinancial disclosure, for example of control rights, is still a novelty in continental Europe and many other parts of the world.

As Carlin and Mayer show, this situation is changing. The right- and left-hand side variables generated by disclosure enforced by the U.S. Securities and Exchange Commission (SEC), which has benefited U.S. research since 1934, are slowly becoming available in Europe and in other parts of the world. The International Monetary Fund (IMF) and World Bank transparency initiatives that were launched in response to the Asian crisis are accelerating this trend. The new studies of corporate control Carlin and Mayer survey are direct results of these developments. For example, the data on the control of listed companies that was collected by the European Corporate Governance Network (ECGN) (1997) is disclosed as a result of the European Union's Large Holdings Directive (88/627/EEC). Other recent studies, like Claessens, Djankov, and Larry (1999) for Asia and La Porta, López-de-Silanes, and Shleifer (1999) for "the World" benefit from similar disclosure rules.

The improvements in the availability of such data for listed companies will lead to a greater understanding of the relationship between the performance of listed companies, corporate law, securities market regulation, and corporate governance. There is a danger, however, that a disproportionate amount of empirical research on listed companies will distract attention from issues like "The Costs of Rejecting Universal Banking" (Calomiris 1995) or the cost of failing to develop private equity.

A second problem that makes the literature surveyed by Carlin and Mayer "emerging," is endogeneity. Does the financial system cause differences in economic performance, or does economic performance drive the evolution of the financial system? Again, more panel data will help to separate cause from effect. In addition, quantitative economic history can provide valuable insights. These studies look at exogenous breaks that lead to major shifts in the financial system and investigate their effect on economic performance. For example, Ramirez (1997) finds "that corporate financing was adversely affected by the imposition of the Glass–Steagall Act." He compares investment before and after the implementation of the Act. Benston (1973) investigated the effect of the 1934 Act's disclosure policy on returns. Before the Act, corporations did not have to disclose sales figures. After the Act they did. Benston found that the mandatory disclosure of sales figures did not benefit investors.[1] However, the historical break approach only provides a partial solution. Dramatic legal and regulatory reforms are often the direct result of financial crisis, that is, endogenous.

In the second part of their essay, Carlin and Mayer present their own contribution to the recent macroeconometric literature that links financial systems to performance. No doubt Carlin and Mayer (1999) is an important contribution to this literature. Indeed, against the background of the developments surveyed by Carlin and Mayer in this book, it was the logical step to take to move this literature forward.

On the performance side, the authors use industry level data obtained from a comprehensive OECD database. On the right-hand side Carlin and Mayer (1999) use some of the corporate governance and legal systems information collected by La Porta et al. (1999, 1998), the equity-finance-dependence data of Rajan and Zingales (1998), and the skills data of Oulton (1996). This is supplemented by own data collection efforts, in particular with respect to bank finance.

In econometric terms, the essay correlates three dependent variables (growth 1970–95, fixed capital formation 1970–95, R&D 1970–95) with a set of industry effects and country effects. In an extension, the analysis is repeated by splitting the sample of 27 industries and 20 OECD countries into low and high GDP per capita groups.

The paper focuses on four relationships: (1) bank–firm relationships and growth, fixed capital formation, and R&D; (2) the development of securities markets; (3) ownership concentration and the resolution of agency conflicts; (4) the legal system and its influence on the operation of financial systems and markets.

The authors find a strong relationship between market systems and legal protection and legal protection of investors and growth of equity-financed and skill-intensive industries. The control variables can explain R&D variation, but not fixed capital formation. Finally, the differences between high and low GDP groups are large.

I will focus my comments on the industry variables and how their choice might affect the robustness of the results. Finally, I will return to the exogeneity issue and take a closer look at the legal origin instrument the authors use. As they point out, these tests are crucial if we want to determine whether the industry and country effects cause the observed performance, or vice versa.

Carlin and Mayer (1999) employ industry effects to capture dependence on securities markets, dependence on bank finance, and depen-

---

[1] Benston's study was criticized by Friend and Westerfield (1975).

dence on skills. The dependence on optimal or technologically endowed industry characteristics is not known. Hence, the measurement of "dependence" poses a problem. Rajan and Zingales (1998) argue that the United States is the country with the most developed financial markets and U.S. industry financially the least constrained in the world. They employ the relative importance of market finance across U.S. industries to measure market finance dependence of industries throughout the world. Carlin and Mayer (1999) extend this method. They use the skill dependence of German industry and the bank finance dependence of Japanese industry to measure the dependence of industries in other countries on these factors. I am slightly worried about this extension of the "Rajan and Zingales method."

The German training system is industry dependent. Some industries employ, almost exclusively, workers and craftsmen from restricted professions. High levels of skill formation often reflect the rents of such professions, not the "technological" need for skills of the industry. For example, consider German shipbuilding, the industry with the highest skill dependence in Carlin and Mayer (1999). Is shipbuilding the most skill-intensive industry in the world or has the skill intensity of German shipbuilding led to its decline? Perhaps we see a booming ship industry in Japan, not because it is a high-skill industry that has a negative dependence on bank finance, but because Japanese shipbuilders managed to produce high-quality ships with lower skill, which has allowed it to pay back its bank loans. Equally, is tobacco an industry that has negative equity dependence and a high dependence on bank loans and skills, or do the figures reflect a different standing of the tobacco industry in the United States and Japan?

My final comment reflects on the legal origin instrument that is used in the exogeneity tests. These rely on the argument of La Porta et al. (1998) "that legal and regulatory factors (such as creditor or shareholder rights and the origin of legal systems) are more fundamental" than other characteristics of countries (Carlin and Mayer 1999, p. 9). This view is controversial. One, how exogenous is legal origin? At least in the German case it is not. The corporate law of 1884 was the result of crisis, not of colonization. Two, why does legal origin correlate so well with various measures of investor protection today? At least for the United States, this is surprising. "The Transformation of Wall Street" (Seligman 1995) occurred in the 1930s and was, again, the result of crisis. Proxy voting, for example, was not available at the legal origin.[2] Indeed, many scholars argue that

---

[2] As Loss (1988, p. 449) observes, "Corporate practice has come a long way from the common law's nonrecognition of the proxy device."

legal and regulatory systems evolve as a result of crises, extreme cases of bad economic performance, not the other way round.

The German stock corporation act of 18 July 1884, the German legal origin, was the result of a perceived crisis. It followed a substantial increase in the number of stock corporations, fraud, and a bankruptcy wave. Between 1871 and 1873, in Prussia alone 843 corporations were founded; 257 went bankrupt within the year. A corporate law reform was discussed in the Prussian chamber of deputies as early as February 1873. One was worried about health of the railways. Extensive consultations between ministries and a commission of experts followed in 1876 (Schubert 1985, p. 1).

The law of 1884 put its faith into strengthening the two-tier board system. Supervisory board functions were separated from management functions and the supervisory board was made accountable to shareholders. In contrast, litigation and other statutory shareholder rights were considered less important. On the contrary, it was felt that direct action by shareholders would be disruptive, costly and discourage competent managers from undertaking projects (Hommelhoff 1985, p. 97). The annotations to the law include a detailed study of the corporate law of Austria, Hungary, Switzerland, the United Kingdom, France, Belgium, Italy, the Netherlands, and Spain. The law of 1884 was not imposed by chance.

There is no doubt that the 1933 and 1934 Acts and the SEC have played a decisive role in shaping the U.S. financial system. However, this did not happen because North America had the good fortune of being colonized by the British. Referring to the 1933 Act, it was Felix Frankfurter who decided that "the English Companies Act furnishes a model for the legislation that ought to be attempted" (Seligman 1995, p. 57).[3] In 1934, with the SEC in mind, Frankfurter wrote: "Above all we can no longer afford to do without a highly trained, disinterested governmental personnel. What this Administration has had to do is to create something like the English Civil Service overnight" (Seligman 1995, p. 61).

Although the U.S. historical evidence casts doubt on the thesis "that legal and regulatory factors are more fundamental characteristics of countries than ownership," it is perplexing that quantitative measures of investor protection today correlate so well with legal origin. Did the British export their financial system along with common law? After all, the insufferable "House of Morgan" did have roots in Peabody's London

---

[3] Seligman cites from a letter Felix Frankfurter wrote to James M. Landis on March 23, 1933. At the time, Landis was one of "Felix's boys" (also known as "Frankfurter's little hot dogs") and sat on his drafting team for the 1933 Act later on (Seligman 1995, p. 61).

operation. Are the legal variables we observe today due to an evolution from a financial system origin? Are ownership and the endowment of a market-based financial system perhaps more fundamental than legal and regulatory factors? Why was there no "New Deal" in Germany in the 1930s? For more than 100 years, the endogenous legal origin has shown a remarkable resistance to change. Clearly, the exogeneity issue will remain controversial and provide ample scope for further research.

## References

Becht, Marco. (1997). "Strong Blockholders, Weak Owners and the Need for European Mandatory Disclosure." Executive Report. In *The Separation of Ownership and Control: A Survey of 7 European Countries.* Preliminary Report to the European Commission. Volume 1. Brussels: European Corporate Governance Network; available from *http://www.ecgn.org*

Benston, George J. (1973). "Required Disclosure and the Stock Market: An Evaluation of the Securities Exchange Act of 1934." *American Economic Review*, 63 (1): 132–55.

Calomiris, Charles W. (1995). "The Costs of Rejecting Universal Banking: American Finance in the German Mirror, 1870–1914." In Naomi Lamoreaux and Daniel Raff (Eds.), *The Coordination of Economic Activity within and between Firms*, National Bureau of Economic Research, University of Chicago.

Carlin, W., and C. Mayer. (1999). "Finance, Investment and Growth," mimeo.

Claessens, Stijn, Simeon Djankov, and H. P. Larry. (1999). "Who Controls East Asian Corporations?" The World Bank, Policy Research Working Paper No. 2054, February.

ECGN. (1997). "The Separation of Ownership and Control: A Survey of 7 European Countries." Preliminary Report to the European Commission. Brussels: European Corporate Governance Network; available from *http://www.ecgn.org*

Friend, Irwin, and Randolph Westerfield. (1975). "Required Disclosure and the Stock Market: Comment." *American Economic Review* 65(3): June, pp. 467–72.

Hommelhoff, Peter. (1985). "Eigenkontrolle statt Staatskontrolle. Rechtsdogmatischer Überblick zur Aktienrechtsreform 1884." In Peter Hommelhoff and Werner Schubert (Eds.), *Hundert Jahre modernes Aktienrecht. Eine Sammlung von Texten und Quellen zur Aktienrechtsreform 1884 mit zwei Einführungen.* Berlin and New York: Walter de Gruyter.

La Porta, Rafael, Florencio López-de-Silanes, and Andrei Shleifer. (1999). "Corporate Ownership around the World." *Journal of Finance*, 54: 471–517.

La Porta, Rafael, Florencio López-de-Silanes, Andrei Shleifer, and Robert W. Vishny. (1998). "Law and Finance." *Journal of Political Economy*, 106: 1113–55.

Loss, L. (1988). *Fundamentals of Securities Regulation*. 2nd ed. Boston and Toronto: Little, Brown and Company.

Oulton, N. (1996). "Workforce Skills and Export Competitiveness." In A. L. Booth and D. J. Snower. (Eds.), *Acquiring Skills: Market Failures, Their Symptoms and Policy Responses*. Cambridge: Cambridge University Press.

Rajan, R., and L. Zingales. (1998). "Financial Dependence and Growth." *American Economic Review*, 88: 559–86.

Ramirez, Carlos D. (1997). "The Cost of Glass Steagall on Corporate Investment: Evidence from Bank, Trust Company, and Insurance Company Affiliations." Working Paper No. 97.02, Economics Department, George Mason University.

Schubert, Werner. (1985). "Die Enstehung des Aktiengesetzes vom 18. Juli 1884." In Peter Hommelhoff and Werner Schubert (Eds.), *Hundert Jahre modernes Aktienrecht. Eine Sammlung von Texten und Quellen zur Aktienrechtsreform 1884 mit zwei Einführungen*. Berlin and New York: Walter de Gruyter.

Seligman, Joel. (1995). *The Transformation of Wall Street. A History of the Securities and Exchange Commission and Modern Corporate Finance*. Boston: Northeastern University Press.

## Comment on Carlin and Mayer, "How Do Financial Systems Affect Economic Performance?"

### B. Vicente Salas

The relationship between economic growth and the development of financial markets has been a topic of research for many years. Carlin and Mayer review the most relevant empirical evidence provided by this research and relate it with recent theoretical developments on how institutions influence innovation and growth. Two main conclusions are derived from their review. First, contrary to what it may appear when only already developed countries are compared, empirical evidence is found, indeed, on the influence of financial development in the economic performance of a country, when a larger sample of countries with different levels of economic development are included in the analysis. Second, the influence of financial development in economic performance is mostly through the influence on the composition of economic activity (which tangible and intangible resources are chosen as production inputs, which sectors of activity are able to grow faster . . .) and not so much on the average growth rate of the overall economy.

Since the essay presents the state of the art in the subject, my comments will necessarily be referred to the literature reviewed rather than to the essay itself.

Although with different levels of aggregation and sample sizes, most of the empirical literature on the relationship between financial development and economic growth uses cross-sectional data in which some of the variables, dependent and explanatory, are averages over 20 years or more (for example industries' growth rates) and other variables are measured at a given point of time (for example ownership concentration in 1995 or accounting standards in 1990). One has to wonder if it is reasonable to assume that these variables have remained unchanged during a 20-year period or, to the contrary, there have been changes in them. I believe that to properly evaluate the direction of causality (if it is financial development that influences economic performance or the other way around) and to control for possible endogeneity of the explanatory variables, panel data (cross-section and time series) would be required.

In this regard, a closer relationship should be established between this literature and the research on long-term growth and real convergence among countries with different levels of economic development. For example, one would expect that country-specific effects in the models of conditional convergency can be explained, at least partially, in terms of the differences in institutional development of the countries considered in the analysis.

A second practice in this research is to use U.S. and Japanese data to evaluate to what extent industries depend more on equity finance or on bank finance, respectively, to cover their needs of external finance. The underlying assumption is that Japan has a more bank-oriented financial system and the United States has a more market-oriented system. But it could happen that there may be differences in the specialization within the industry in the two countries. For example it may happen that in the United States there are more innovation and more start-up firms than in Japan, and for such activities and firms equity is preferred to bank debt. Moreover, the stage in the product life cycle U.S. industries are in is likely to be different from that of industries elsewhere.

I wonder if one can explain cross-country industry growth from 1970 to 1995 without accounting for the expansion in foreign direct investment and its specialization by industry and country. Nor has State ownership of industrial firms and direct intervention in directing financial flows to certain "basic" economic sectors been uniform across countries along the period under study. Finally, regulation of labor markets and the protection of workers' rights has also been different from country to country. As long as there are complementarities between financial and labor markets, some of the conclusions may be affected by the omission of labor market conditions among the explanatory variables.

The literature is still unclear on how institutional design can be used to foster economic growth. The theoretical and empirical results seem to suggest that the most effective legal, financial, and corporate system in early stages of a country's economic development, is different from the effective system in later stages of such development. How and when should the transition from one system to the other be made? Is a smooth transition or a big-bang effect needed? Is it sufficient to change the legal system in terms of more protection to investors' rights to start a sequence of changes in the financial and corporate systems in the right direction? If changes of the legal system require the intervention of the political process, how might such a process interfere in the legal and economic reform? What can we expect in terms of convergence of financial and corporate systems across countries with similar levels of economic development, considering the globalization of financial and product markets?

Carlin and Mayer's essay is an excellent starting point to further pursue these issues. It is concise, clear, and full of insights on the best way to proceed in trying to discover the link between institutions and growth.

# CHAPTER 5

# Information and Governance in the Silicon Valley Model

## MASAHIKO AOKI

Casual observers regard the emergent relationships between a venture capitalist and a product-development entrepreneurial firm, as most typically observed in Silicon Valley, as nothing more than the supply of risk capital to an independent-minded entrepreneur. This chapter argues, however, that the truly unique role of venture capitalists is found in their information-mediating and governance functions, which can be understood only in the context of relationships between the "clustering" of entrepreneurial firms and (a club) of venture capitalists.

As described in Section 1 of this chapter, the venture capitalists usually retain control blocks of shares in the entrepreneurial firms and exercise a broad range of governance roles in them, unless entrepreneurs have sufficient funds of their own at the outset. This does not mean that the entrepreneurs of product-development firms play a less autonomous role in information processing. Indeed, they are far more autonomous and innovative in the production of knowledge than the traditional research and development organizations within established firms. Also, their potential products can often be substitutes, so that the competition among them is fierce. However, as Saxenian (1994) documented, there is also a substantial degree of information sharing across those entrepreneurial firms. The clustering of entrepreneurial firms in Silicon Valley does not seem to be accidental. How do these ostensibly contradictory characteristics – competition in information processing on the one hand and information sharing on the other – coexist as a coherent system, say, as the Silicon Valley model? How do we understand the unique innovative capacity of this model? What incentive impact does the apparently strong governance role of the venture capitalist have? Is there anything that the Silicon Valley model can do that cannot be duplicated in either a single firm or atomistic markets? Can the Silicon Valley model be applicable elsewhere and in industries other than the high-technology industry?

In this chapter I submit that it is not sufficient for an understanding

This essay draws on Chapter 11 of my book manuscript (1999). I am very much indebted to comments by AnnaLee Saxenian, Christopher Kingston, and Thomas Hellmann.

of these issues to look only at the property rights relationship between the venture capitalist and a single entrepreneurial firm. Instead, it is necessary to look at the multifaceted relationships of a cluster of entrepreneurial start-up firms, on the one hand, and venture capitalists (as well as leading firms in respective niche markets setting an eye on successful younger ones for acquisition), on the other. The entrepreneurial firms in Silicon Valley compete in innovation, and thus their activities are fundamentally substitutes. Therefore, their information-processing activities need to be encapsulated from each other to surpass competitors. However, different from older established integrated firms, such as an earlier IBM, which conceived ex ante a concept for possible new product systems in a centralized manner, these firms are engaged in innovation efforts in particular niche markets in a decentralized way. A new product system may therefore be formed evolutionarily by combining modular products ex post that evolve from such decentralized efforts. In order for such evolutionary selection to be possible, common standards for interfaces among modular products need to be provided to make individual product attributes compatible.

Although the standardization of interfaces is much a product of architectures defined by dominant firms in niche markets and of industry standard-setting organizations, venture capitalists also play a no less important role in mediating information necessary for endogenously forming and setting standards de facto and spreading them in emerging markets. Below, I conceptualize the information systemic aspects of the Silicon Valley model, characterized by competition in information processing among entrepreneurial firms and as information mediation by venture capitalists, as V-mediated information encapsulation. As for any model, there are unique social costs involved in the Silicon Valley model, particularly the duplication of innovation efforts and expenditures. We will examine how the aspect of venture capital financing as a governance mechanism can or cannot cope with this problem.

The plan of the chapter is as follows. The first section assembles stylized facts about relationships between venture capital and entrepreneurial firms as a basis for modeling. The second section presents a framework for comparing information systemic aspects of alternative R&D organizations and analyzes the unique innovation capability of the Silicon Valley model. The third section proceeds to the analysis of the venture capital governance as an institution for supporting such an information system. Repeated tournaments among initially funded firms for refinancing necessary for the completion of projects, and the threat of termination of financial support by the venture capitalist, are seen to provide greater incentives for the entrepreneurs than under traditional financing. The fourth section discusses the incentives of the venture capitalist and other institutional characteristics of the Silicon Valley model. Conclusions follow.

## I. Stylized Factual Background

From the purely financial point of view, venture capital funds is an intermediary.[1] It serves to intermediate in the supply of a large sum of investment funds increasingly from other financial intermediaries such as pension funds (45% in 1996), insurance companies and banks (6%), together with those from foundations and universities (20%), wealthy individuals and families (7%), corporations (18%), foreign investors (4%), and others to mostly start-up entrepreneurial firms.[2] As an intermediary, the venture capital process is unique in its legal structure. It is a system of partnership in the venture capital fund, in which there are two classes of partners: general and limited. The general partners act as organizers of the fund, accepting full personal responsibility and legal liability for fund management. Limited partners supply most of the capital but are not involved in the management and investment decisions of venture capital funds, which allows them to enjoy limited liability status as well as the advantage of avoiding double taxation.[3] General partners receive an annual fee of a few percent (2–3%) of the total capital committed and receive 15–25% of the realized capital gains for their much smaller contribution to funds. Funds are set up for a fixed period of time, say 10 years, but in many cases management companies are formed and run by general partners to provide management continuity. Thus there can exist the usual principal–agent problems between limited and general partners, which we will discuss in the end. In this chapter I do not explicitly differentiate between venture capital funds and venture capital companies, referring to both simply as venture capitalists.

Venture capitalists seek promising investment projects, while poten-

[1] For relationships between venture capitalists and entrepreneurial firms in general, see Sahlman (1990), Bygrave and Timmons (1992), Gompers and Lerner (1996), Florida and Kenney (1998).

[2] Figures in 1978 give a much different picture. In that year, individuals and families are the largest contributors to venture capital funds (32%), while pension funds' share was 15%. During the last 20 years, the so-called institutionalization of venture capital funds has proceeded.

[3] It is known that the flow of funds into this organizational arrangement was given impetus by various tax measures that took place between the late 1970s and early '80s (such as the relaxation of the so-called 'prudential rules' on the pension fund management, the reduction of capital gains tax in 1978 and 1981, deregulation of initial public offerings in 1978 and 1979, etc.).

tial entrepreneurs with planned projects but insufficient funds seek venture capital financing. There are more than 200 venture capital companies in Silicon Valley alone, but experienced venture capitalists are said to receive over 1,000 applications a year. Screening and search is not easy for either side, but suppose that a promising match is found. Unless the reputation of an entrepreneur is already known to a venture capitalist and a proposed project is judged to be certainly sound and promising, the venture capitalist initially provides only seed money to see if an entrepreneur is capable of initiating the project, while possibly extending aid to help the start-up. When a venture capitalist decides to finance a start-up, elaborate financing and employment agreements are drawn up between the venture capitalist and the entrepreneur.[4] These specify the terms of financing and the terms of employment of the entrepreneur as a senior manager (Testa 1997; Hellman 1998).

Usually, start-up financing involves consortium financing by several venture capitalists, with one of them acting as a lead financier and manager. Among experienced and mutually known venture capitalists, the position of lead manager is rotated over different projects. This arrangement serves not so much as a mechanism of risk diversification than as one of reciprocal delegation of monitoring among a group of venture capitalists. The reciprocal delegation not only may avoid the duplication of intense monitoring but also functions as a device to control possible shirking of monitoring by venture capitalists (Lerner 1994a; Fenn, Liang, and Prowse 1995).[5] If a lead venture capitalist shirks due diligence or is incompetent and more than a normal number of financed projects led by that person fail, his or her reputation will be tarnished and he or she will lose opportunities for raising additional funds and participating in potentially profitable future projects organized by others. (Up to the end of this chapter, I abstract from this reciprocal relationship among venture capitalists, and regard the relationship of an entrepreneur with venture capital funds as if it were with a single venture capitalist.)

At the time of start-up the venture capitalist commits only a fraction of the capital needed for the ultimate development of a project, with the expectation that additional financing will be made stepwise, contingent upon the smooth proceeding of the project, which may not be contractible – a process that Sahlman (1990) called "staged" capital commitment. Financing of venture capitalists normally takes the form of

---

[4] In 1997, more than 3,500 companies were newly registered in Santa Clara county, almost all if not all of them financed by venture capital.

[5] In this aspect, the consortium has characteristics similar to those of the Japanese main bank system in its heyday. See Aoki (1994).

convertible preferred stocks or subordinated debt with conversion privileges (Fenn, Liang, and Prowse 1995; Gompers and Lerner 1996). They are paid before holders of common stock in the event of project failure, so venture capitalists are protected from downside risk. Also, they retain an exit option exercisable by refusing additional financing at a critical moment when a start-up firm needs the infusion of new funds to survive. However, a typical shareholding agreement allows an entrepreneur to increase its ownership share (normally in common stock) at the expense of investors if certain performance objectives are met. Fired entrepreneurs forfeit their claims on stock that has not vested.

The venture capitalists, lead as well as nonlead, are well represented on the board of directors of the start-up firms. Lerner (1994b) reports that venture capitalists hold more than one-third of the seats on the boards of venture-backed biotechnology firms – more than the number held by management or other outside directors. In addition to attending board meetings, lead venture capitalists often visit entrepreneurs cum senior managers at the site of venture-funded firms (see also Barry et al. 1990). They provide a wide range of advice and consulting services to senior management: helping to raise additional funds; reviewing and assisting with strategic planning; recruiting financial and human resource management; introducing potential customers and suppliers; providing public relations and legal specialists. They also actively exercise conventional roles in the governance of the start-up firms, often firing the founder-managers when needed. According to panel data compiled by the Stanford Project on Emerging Companies (SPEC), which collects panel data on 100 high-technology start-up firms in Silicon Valley, the likelihood that a nonfounder will be appointed CEO in the first 20 months of a company's life is around 10%; this likelihood increases to about 40% after 40 months and to over 80% after 80 months, to say nothing of companies going out of existence and thus not included in the sample (Baron, Burton, and Hannan 1996; Hannan, Burton, and Baron 1996).

There are many business failures among entrepreneurial start-up firms.[6] Many failures crop up early, usually in the first one or two years. Frequent failures may be caused not only by overzealous competition among ambitious entrepreneurs but also because the venture capitalist itself may contribute to this. For example, William Sahlman and Howard Stevenson observed the following phenomenon in an emerging segment of the computer data storage industry in the mid-1980s. "In all, 43 start-

---

[6] Between 1990 and 1997, about 21,000 new businesses were registered in Santa Clara county. About 7,000 entrepreneurial firms are said to currently exist. See Joint Venture (1988).

ups were funded in an industry segment that could be expected in the long run to support perhaps four." Thus, "'failure' is at the very least endemic to the venture capital process, an expected commonplace event; in some cases, the process itself may even promote failure" (Gorman and Sahlman 1989, p. 238). In casual conversations in Silicon Valley, venture capitalists normally regard 3 successes out of 10 initial fundings as reasonable. We will consider in subsequent sections the social benefits and costs of the duplicated funding of development projects and high probability of failure.

If the project is successful, the relational financing terminates either with initial public offering (IPO), typically taking place 5–10 years after the start-up, or with acquisitions by other firms. Venture capitalists decide when to go to a market for IPO, and supply needed marketing expertise. In order to control possible moral hazard, the lead venture capitalist remains as a board member after IPO. Capital gains are distributed between the venture funds and the entrepreneur according to their shares at that time. Experienced venture capitalists can time the IPO to occur when market valuation of portfolio firms is particularly high, while less experienced and less reputable venture capitalists may have incentives to bring a portfolio firm to market prematurely (Lerner 1994a; Gompers 1995).

Some authors argue that the presence of active IPO markets is an essential element of the success of venture capital financing and product innovation therefrom, and that their absence may be responsible for the fact that other economies have a difficult time emulating the Silicon Valley phenomenon (e.g., Bankman and Gilson 1996). Although there may well be an element of truth in this claim, it is also important to note that recently successful start-up firms have been increasingly becoming the targets of acquisition by leading firms in the same market rather than going to IPO markets (for example, see Stanford Graduate School of Business case materials S-SM-27). These firms are often themselves grown-up entrepreneurial firms who have been successful in taking leadership in standard setting in their niche markets. They aim at acquiring successful start-up firms either to kill off potential sources of challenges to their set standards, or to further strengthen their market positions by acquiring and bundling complementary products. These are said to have influence on venture capitalists in guiding their activities, especially toward the end of venture capital financing. From the viewpoint of start-up entrepreneurs, they are said to prefer acquisition to IPO, when they have only a single innovative product line (Hellmann 1998b).

Thus the venture capitalist performs the integrated functions of ex ante monitoring (screening of proposed projects to cope with the possible adverse selection problem), ad interim monitoring, and ex post monitoring (the verification of project result and the controlling decision as to which exit strategy is to be exercised) vis-à-vis venture-funded firms. Ex ante and ad interim monitoring of an entrepreneurial project requires professional engineering competence in specialized fields, while ex post monitoring requires financial expertise. The venture capitalists meet such needs and tend to focus on companies in specific industries. Although the venture capitalists play a dominant governance role in venture-backed firms, their property rights arrangements have complex elements of joint ownership with provision of bilateral option rights: the venture capitalist's rights to exercise an exit option against the entrepreneur's interest in bad times, and the entrepreneur's right to exercise a stock option in good times. Control rights are voluntarily relinquished ex ante by the entrepreneur, particularly if he or she is liquidity constrained at the outset (Hellmann 1998a). But as the project moves successfully, he or she may regain control rights.

## II. The Information Systemic Characteristic of the Silicon Valley Model

### 2.1. Comparative R&D Organizations

The introductory section suggested that the venture capitalist is normally involved in the governance and managerial structure of the entrepreneurial start-up firm to an extent far beyond the provision of normal financing services and associated monitoring. However, for an understanding of the innovative nature of the Silicon Valley phenomenon, it is not adequate and appropriate to limit the scope of analysis merely to the bilateral relationships between the venture capitalist and an *individual* entrepreneurial firm. This may lead to a misplaced emphasis on the governing power of the venture capitalist. In order to understand the other important aspect of the venture capitalist as a catalyst of technological system innovation, we need to look at systemic relationships between the venture capitalists and a *cluster* of entrepreneurial firms as carriers of development projects.[7]

---

[7] The total number of jobs in Silicon Valley were about 1.2 million in 1996. Even if we hypothetically assume that half of these jobs are supplied by entrepreneurial firms estimated to number about 7,000, they are roughly in the same order of jobs supplied by IBM or GM at their height of employment. Thus, the comparison of a large integrated traditional firm and an individual entrepreneurial firm in Silicon Valley does not make much sense. A proper comparison ought to be between the former and a cluster of entrepreneurial firms.

Although there are some notable differences in their internal organizational structure,[8] entrepreneurial start-up firms have a common feature regarding their relationships toward product markets. Instead of creating mutually competitive, stand-alone product systems of their own, they tend to be specialized in the development of innovative product designs that may constitute useful modules in the evolving industrial frame and thereby help them carve out niche markets or gain a better bargaining position vis-à-vis larger firms aiming to integrate. The standardization of interfaces is as much a product of architectures defined by dominant firms (especially Intel and Microsoft in the current era) and of industry standard-setting organizations such as Semiconductor Equipment and Materials International (SEMI) and the Internet Engineering Task Force (IETF) as of coordination by venture capitalists. Similarly, firms like Sun are competing with products like Jini and Java to define the interface standards for emerging markets. Even the leading positions of established firms in respective niche markets may not be secure in highly uncertain and competitive technological and market environments. Rather, standards may be conceived to be evolutionarily formed and modified through the interactions of firms, large and small. This situation may impose two important information requirements on the side of entrepreneurial firms. They need to continually process and share wider information relevant to the evolving industrial frame, on one hand, and, on the other, each needs to integrate and encapsulate specific information crucial to its own module-product design to stay competitive.

To capture the information-mediating role of venture capitalists in this nonhierarchical structure of product development and contrast it with R&D organization of traditional firms, let us first introduce a simple conceptual framework for comparative R&D organizations. Imagine a generic R&D system simply composed of the management, denoted as M, and two product design teams, denoted as $T_i$ ($i = a,b$). The management is engaged in such tasks as development strategy, the allocation of R&D funds, and so forth, while the teams are engaged in the design of

---

[8] The "internal" characteristics of the individual firms clustered in Silicon Valley are *not* uniform. By analyzing the SPEC panel data mentioned above, Baron et al. identified three types of organizational means of controlling and coordinating work used in their sample cluster of emergent entrepreneurial firms (Hannan et al., 1996, pp. 512–13): "peer control and cultural control" where the employees have extensive control over the means by which work gets done but little control over strategic directions, projects to be pursued, etc.; "professional control" based on the delegation to professionals of the right in both the means and strategic directions; and "managerial control" embedded in formal procedures and rules with supervisory monitoring.

Table 5.1. *Comparative Information Systemic Characteristics of R&D Organizations*

| Organization | (E-s) Systemic (Technological and Industrial) Environment | (E-e) Systemic-engineering Environment | (E-i) Team-specific Engineering Environment |
|---|---|---|---|
| Hierarchical R&D organization | Manager's task | System engineer's task | Design team's task |
| Interactive R&D organization | Information assimilation through feedbacks from project teams to management | Information-sharing among project teams | Individual project team's task |
| V-mediated information encapsulation | Venture capital-mediated quasi-information assimilation | Information encapsulation among entrepreneurial firms | |

products, each of which is to constitute a component (say, a monitor, a hard drive, etc.) of an integral technological system (say, a laptop computer). The organizational environments are segmented as shown in the first row of Table 5.1. Namely, there is a systemic segment, E-s, say the availability of total R&D funds, emergent industrial standards, that simultaneously affects the organizational returns to decision choices by M as well as the T's. Next, there are the segments of environments that affect the organizational returns to new product design by $T_i$'s, say engineering environments, which can be further divided into three subsets: E-e, common to both projects, and E-a and E-b, idiosyncratic to respective projects. Various segments of organizational environments can be processed and associated decisions are made by M and $T_i$'s in various manners to be specified momentarily.

The product design involves the choice of "design attributes," such as depth versus breadth, digital versus analogue, cable versus wireless transmission, and so on. Design attributes may or may not be strongly connected between the two component projects. The farther intended designs are from existing standards, the costlier their development may be. In that sense the two component projects are competitive in the use of R&D resources. If the design attributes are strongly connected so that their designs of two component projects need to be coordinated in the same direction in spite of possible resource costs, then we say that "design projects of teams are complementary" (if not, "they are substitutes").[9] With the aid of Table 5.1 we now present three stylized organizational models differentiated by ways in which the monitoring of the evolving systemic environment, as well as the information processing of engineering environments, are structured among organizational constituent units.

*(i) Hierarchical R&D Organization.* In this organization, M is the research manager of an integrated firm and $T_i$'s are its internal project teams. Between them the intermediate agent IM, say the system engineer, is inserted between M and $T_i$'s. M is specialized in monitoring the state of the systemic environment, E-s. Based on observations of these conditions, M decides on R&D expenditures and basic system development concept and its decision choice is communicated to IM. IM performs system analysis and basic design within the budget and other constraints imposed by M by processing the systemic engineering environment, E-e. Then it hands over its design choice to $T_a$ and $T_b$. These component product design teams then resolve problems that arise in their respective design-specific engineering environments, E-i ($i = a,b$). This organization may be thought of as reflecting the essential aspects of the R&D organization of the traditional, large hierarchical firm, sometimes referred to as the "waterfall" model (Klein and Rosenberg 1986; Aoki and Rosenberg 1989). It may also be considered as corresponding to what Hannan et al. (1996) called the "factory model," which they rarely find implemented among the emergent entrepreneurial Silicon Valley firms they study.

---

[9] Suppose that the design attributes of $T_a$ and $T_b$, $y_a$ and $y_b$, can be linearly aligned and their values are normalized in such a way that their existing standard values are set to zero. Assuming that the farther from the standard values the design attributes need to be set, the more costly it is, the value that the organization can create may be represented by the following quadratic value function:

$$V = V_* + \gamma_s x + (\gamma_s + \gamma_e + \gamma_a)\gamma_a + (\gamma_s + \gamma_e + \gamma_a)\gamma_b \\ - Ax^2 + Dx(y_a + y_b) - K(y_a + y_b)^2 - L(y_a - y_b)^2$$

where $x$ denotes the decision choice of the research organization manager, M. The effects of attribute choices on expected organizational value depend on the stochastic environmental variables $\gamma_i$, representing the $i$-th component of environments ($i = s,e,a,b$). $A > 0$ represents the constraints imposed by M's limited resources (financial or managerial) leading to diminishing financial returns to scale; $D$ ($A > D > 0$) the degree of requirements of coordination between M and $T_i$'s; $K$ the degree of organizational strain placed by competition between T's in funds allocation arising from design innovation, and $L$ the degree of attribute connectedness between the two design projects. If $K > L$ (alternatively <0), then we say that design projects between the teams are complementary (alternatively substitute). This formulation may appear at first sight to be rather too specific, but it is actually very general as a quadratic approximation of a general value function.

*(ii) Interactive R&D Organization.* In this organization as well, M is the research manager and $T_i$'s are interacting development teams. There is information sharing among them all regarding the systemic environment E-s. The two development teams collaborate on research and development affected by the systemic engineering environment E-e, while working individually on technical and engineering problems arising in their own segments of the engineering environment, E-i ($i = a,b$). Each project team thus has wide-ranging information about environments, partially shared and partially individuated, on which their respective decision choice (product design) is based. This system may be considered as corresponding to what S. Klein conceptualized as the "chain-linked model" of innovation in that feedback mechanisms are operating across different levels and units (Klein and Rosenberg 1986; Aoki and Rosenberg 1989). Information assimilation may be thought of as being realized through the feedback of information from the lower level to the higher level, as well as through information sharing and joint development effort across design project teams on the same level. This system may be considered as akin to the coordination aspect of what Hannan et al. called the "peer and cultural control model where the employees have extensive control over the means by which work gets done, etc." They found that some of the emergent Silicon Valley entrepreneurial firms internalize such a model.

*(iii) The V-mediated Information Encapsulation.* In this system, there is information sharing regarding the systemic environment among M and the $T_i$'s, as in the interactive R&D organization. The difference is that in this case there is no information sharing between $T_a$ and $T_b$ regarding the engineering environments including systemic ones. Development designs are completely encapsulated within each of them and their new product design is based on individuated, differentiated knowledge derived from independent development effort. Such a model may be internalized within the firm, with each project team having strong autonomy in information processing and product design. However, I submit that this model captures in an embryonic form some aspects of the relationships between venture capitalists and entrepreneurial firms, as well as those among entrepreneurial firms in Silicon Valley. In this interpretation, M is the venture capitalist and $T_i$'s are independent entrepreneurial firms. There is some degree of information sharing among them all about emergent industrial systemic environments, often mediated by the venture capitalists (even if they are not carriers of information themselves, they do often mediate contacts among entrepreneurs, engineers, university researchers, et al., in the valley). The degree of information sharing

among them in this respect may be weaker in substance and amount, though, than under the interactive R&D organizations. Therefore we may refer to this aspect as quasi-information assimilation, on which we will elaborate more below. However, technological information that is necessary for product design is generated within individual firms in an integrative manner and hidden from others until the completion of product design. Thus, this system is referred to as V-mediated information encapsulation.

### 2.2. Comparative Information Systemic Performance of the V-mediated Information Encapsulation

*(i) A Basic Proposition.* We start with the case where three organizations face exactly the same organizational environments.[10] Each unit of the organizations processes information emergent in the assigned segment of the environments with some precision. For the $T_i$'s level, this implies that each project team is engaged in development effort with some level of competence.[11] Based on its own information processing results, each unit then chooses its own decision variable (e.g., funds allocation, design specifications, etc.) according to a certain rule. Given a certain distribution of information processing competence across product development project teams for each organizational type, if there is a set of decision rules for one of the above organizations which yields a higher expected organizational return than another organization, we say that the former organization is potentially *informationally more efficient* than the other for that distribution of information processing competence. In order to provide a benchmark for a dispassionate comparison, let us consider the case that the level of information processing competence by any agent about any variable is identical. Then, the following basic propositions hold:

*Proposition 1. If and only if design projects are not complementary, the V-mediated information encapsulation becomes potentially informationally more efficient than hierarchical and interactive R&D organizations.*[12]

[10] In terms of the organizational value function introduced before, it is assumed that the parameters $D$, $K$, and $L$, as well as the stochastic distributions of environmental parameters, are the same for all three organizations.

[11] The competence level of a design project team may be measured in Bayesian terms by the ratio of the prior variance of an observed environmental parameter to the variance of observation error.

[12] Assuming the organizational value function assumed in the previous footnote, this proposition may be seen as an extension of a theorem due to Cremer (1990). For the proof, see Aoki (forthcoming, ch. 11).

If design projects are complementary, then the choices of design attributes of two project teams need to be coordinated in such a way that their choices fit each other. Such coordinated choices are internalized in the hierarchical and interactive R&D organizations, because information utilized by the project teams for decisions become assimilated, apart from idiosyncratic technological information. In hierarchical organizations, common information about E-e is contained in the hierarchically transmitted message originating from the intermediate system engineer, while in the interactive organization it can be extracted as an outcome of joint development effort or information feedback. These two organizations place relatively greater weight on the common knowledge in decision making and are more likely to induce isodirectional choices in design variables. In contrast, in the V-mediated information encapsulation the observations of systemic technological information by the entrepreneurial firms are mutually hidden. Therefore, choices of decision variables by them would be less correlated in comparison to those of their counterparts.[13]

*(ii) Endogenous Reduction of Attribute Complementarity by Interface Standardization.* Attribute complementarity of design projects at the T2 level can be reduced and the compatibility of their products can be enhanced when the internal workings of individual products are modularized with simple mutual interfaces. Then ad interim coordination in design efforts across project teams becomes less imperative. Compatible interface design may be set centrally and ex ante (in the sense "before research and development") by the management of a large hierarchical R&D organization, or in some cases even by the government. But such centralized and ex ante approach may not yield a good outcome when a high degree of ex ante uncertainty is involved in developmental design. In such case, emergent information in the process of development effort may be better utilized. One possible informational advantage of the interactive R&D organizations vis-à-vis hierarchical organizations may be their flexibility in fine tuning interfaces in response to emergent information. However, in interactive R&D organizations ad interim adaptation (i.e., adaptation after development started but before design is completed) to emergent information is not in general limited to inter-

---

[13] The comparison of information efficiency between the hierarchical and interactive R&D organizations is not our immediate object. However, we can submit the following claim: If there is a large degree of disparity in the level of information processing competence among agents, it is informationally more efficient to place a more capable agent in the R&D manager. If competence levels are fairly homogenous among agents, however, interactive R&D organizations are expected to be informationally more efficient.

face design but often involves simultaneous changes in the contents of product designs of individual project teams. Thus information load in this type of organization can be high.

In the V-mediated information encapsulation, engineering information necessary for product designs are encapsulated so that the coordination of design extended to the content of products is not feasible, that is, products of $T_i$'s (entrepreneurial firms) are modularized. However, as the proposition above suggests, the information efficiency of this system can be enhanced vis-à-vis interactive R&D organizations, if the interfaces of their products are standardized. We can envision that the information assimilation role of M (venture capitalist) is precisely to mediate the systemic information concerning emergent interface standards for modular products of $T_i$'s (entrepreneurial firms) ad interim. Then, $T_i$'s can adapt to emergent standards, even sometimes involved in the formation of de facto standardization, without their content design being mutually affected. Thus, once the system of V-mediated information encapsulation and de facto interface standardization of modular-product design start to be combined, there will be a momentum to reinforce each other. The engineering environment advantageous to the V-mediated information encapsulation is endogenously generated by itself.

*Proposition 2. As the interfaces of modular products are standardized ad interim in response to emergent systemic information, the informational efficiency of the V-mediated information encapsulation is enhanced. On the other hand, the V-mediated information encapsulation helps de facto standardization of interfaces to evolve. Thus, they are mutually reinforcing.*

*(iii) The Evolutionary Nature of the Innovation Process under Information Encapsulation.* We have made a comparison of informational efficiency among alternative organizations, but the derived propositions are based on the assumption that each organization is composed of a fixed number of project teams (we assumed that there are only two teams, but the number can be any for the derived propositions to hold). However, this assumption fails to capture one essential aspect of the Silicon Valley model in comparison to hierarchical and interactive R&D organizations. An appropriate modeling should be that there are multiple competing teams (entrepreneurial firms) for each modular product design project in the Silicon Valley model.

Consider an innovation process of a large-scale, complex product system. Suppose that it can be hierarchically decomposed into several distinct steps, such as basic conceptualization, system analysis, detailed

182

design, pilot manufacturing, testing, and so on. Some steps such as design and pilot manufacturing may be further decomposed into subtask units. In such a hierarchical decomposition, once a system concept is centrally conceived and a system design is drawn accordingly, even if some revision to the system comes to be perceived as necessary afterwards because of the occurrence of unanticipated events at a later stage, it may become too costly to redo the whole process from the beginning. Then the design may have to be only partially revised on an ad hoc basis at a later stage, sometimes losing the internal coherence and consistency initially intended. If a new generation of the product system is to be designed, the whole process may have to be repeated all over again, which takes time and resources.

The interactive R&D organization can possibly cope better with emergent unexpected events by the use of frequent feedback mechanisms between different stages of product development, as well as the collaboration in problem solving between teams engaged in interrelated tasks at the same level. In this type of organization, the product system may be continually improved, or accumulated learning from unexpected events at all development stages may be utilized for the design of a new generation of the system. However, once communications channels are set up between different developmental stages and task units, it may become difficult to change the basic organizational structure of development in a radical way such as to replace a group of tasks. Accordingly innovation in the product system may tend to be only incremental.

In contrast, if the system of V-mediated information encapsulation is composed of more than one competing team for each project (that is, for each product design project, there exist many firms) at the outset, the generation of a product system may be made through the evolutionary selection of a team out of the many for each project in accordance with their emergent development outcomes. Such selection ad interim or ex post (i.e., after design processes are completed) becomes feasible because of standardization of the interfaces. Innovation in the product system can then evolve without a priori centralized design and free from forces suppressing a radical departure from existing bundling patterns of modules. It may rapidly evolve from a relatively simple prototype system into an ever-more-complex system by flexibly rebundling continually improved modular products from different entrepreneurial projects. Or, product systems may become more easily reconfigurable. An often invoked analogy to this possibility is Lego building blocks with their interlocking-cylinder faces. The number of objects that can be built with Lego is limited only by imagination (Pine 1993). The evolutionary selection under the V-mediated information encapsulation becomes particularly innovative when the prior uncertainty regarding engineering environments is particularly high or the engineering landscape is rapidly changing. Under such situations, ex ante centralized design of product system in the hierarchical R&D organization may be very risky, while incremental innovation under the interactive R&D organization may not be able to realize a breakthrough innovation nor can it catch up with the rapidly changing engineering environment.

However, the cost of such flexibility is the duplication of development efforts and expenditures supporting them. In the next section we analyze how the governance aspect of the Silicon Valley model tries to deal with this problem.

## III. Governance of Innovation by Tournament

In the previous section, it was suggested that the efficiency and innovativeness of the mechanism of V-mediated information encapsulation is enhanced when design-attribute connectedness is reduced by the standardization of interfaces among products of the industry. However, by the nature of the mechanism, a standard of interfaces cannot be set entirely hierarchically or by any other centralized mechanism such as government regulations. Although the standardization of interfaces is largely a product of architectures defined by dominant firms and of industry standard-setting organizations, even the choices of those firms and organizations cannot be entirely free from emergent innovation and practices. In order for this evolutionary mechanism of de facto standardization to work, there must in turn be a mechanism by which information regarding the evolving industrial frame is collected, transmitted, and shared across competing firms. One of the important functions of the venture capitalist suggested by the preceding argument is precisely to mediate such a communication process. Based on this insight, the present section tries to explore in a game-theoretic framework how such a mechanism can be incentive-wise implemented by the venture capitalist and entrepreneurial start-up firms.

### 3.1. The Structure of the Stage Game

As background for the model below, imagine that time consists of an infinite sequence of stage games, each of which is played over three dates between venture capitalists and entrepreneurial firms. The venture capitalists live permanently, competing with each other to nurture valuable

184

firms, while entrepreneurial firms start up at the beginning of date 1 of a stage game and exit by the end of date 3 either by going public, being acquired by other firms, or being terminated. When terminated, entrepreneurs can come back to the next stage game as new start-up firms. In this subsection, we do not explore the impacts' that the repeated nature of the game may have on venture capitalists reputations, or the risk-taking traits of would-be entrepreneurs, and we concentrate instead on the analysis of the single-stage game between one venture capitalist and multiple start-up firms, embedded in the repeated game. We take up the possible impacts of the repeated nature of the game and competition among venture capitalists in the next section.

We assume that before date 1 starts – thus outside the model – a venture capitalist, denoted by VC, has screened many developmental projects proposed by cash-constrained, would-be entrepreneurs and selected some of them for start-up funding (ex ante monitoring). For simplicity's sake, there are only two types of projects and the VC has selected two proposals for each. The start-up firms are indexed by subscript $ij$, where $i = a,b$ denoting a project, and $j = 1,2$ distinguishing entrepreneurial firms. Hereafter we use a "start-up firm" and its "entrepreneur" as interchangeable terms. The entrepreneurs are ex ante symmetric in their parametric characteristics except for the project types they are engaged in. There are three dates within each stage game: the first corresponds to the phase of individual information processing – research and development – by entrepreneurs; the second to that of communications between entrepreneurs and the VC and associated design specification by the entrepreneurs; and the third to that of refinancing selection by the VC and project completion by selected entrepreneurs. At the end of date 3, the values of the entrepreneurial firms are realized and distributed between them and the VC according to contracts to be drawn in the beginning of date 1.

At date 1, each start-up firm funded by VC is engaged in research and development effort. The choice of entrepreneurial effort level at start-up firm $ij$ is denoted by $e_{ij}$ and its cost by $c(e_{ij})$ with the usual increasing marginal cost property. The actual levels of effort implemented by the start-up firms may afterwards be inferred as we will specify later, but are not verifiable in the courts, so that they are not contractible. The development effort of entrepreneur $ij$ generates noisy one-dimensional information $\xi_{ij}$ – research results – regarding uncertain engineering environment measured with the precision $\Pi_{ij}(e_{ij})$. The higher the effort level, the higher the precision of the entrepreneur's posterior estimates regarding the environment that it faces. The fixed amount of funding provided to each entrepreneur by VC at this date covers only the cost of information processing (including wages) at this date and is not sufficient for further product development.

At the beginning of the date 2, when uncertainties regarding the environments still persist, on the basis of research results obtained in date 1, the entrepreneurs tentatively specify product design attributes, with observable interface properties and performance characteristics $y_{ij}$ from a one-dimensional set $Y_i$ $(i = a,b)$ – let us call this observable portion of the design the external design specification. Besides information obtained in date 1, each entrepreneur needs to take into consideration in his own design how industrial standards are evolving – which relates to the segment of the environment E-s. In order to obtain information regarding others' choices, entrepreneurs engage in communication through the intermediary of VC, using external design specifications of products as verifiable messages with products' internal workings hidden. The VC mediates entrepreneurial communications, combined with his own assessment of the emerging industrial frame partially set by established leading firms. The entrepreneurs successively revise their design attributes, internal and external, in response to VC's message and others' open design specifications. Communications and revisions continue until the process converges to an equilibrium value $\xi_{vc}$ measuring the environment E-s (we assume it does so within date 2). We regard this process as the process of entrepreneurs and the VC mutually improving and assimilating their estimates of the industrial environment, E-s. Suppose, for simplicity's sake, that the precision of their assimilated information is a function $\Pi_{s,vc}(.)$ of the VC's mediating effort, $e_{s,vc}$. The costs of VC's mediating and monitoring efforts are represented by $k(e_{vc})$ with the usual increasing cost property. Suppose that the precision of VC's information is observable to the entrepreneurs (but not court verifiable). At an equilibrium entrepreneur $ij$ specifies its product design attribute $y_{ij}$ as a combination of the VC-mediated assimilated information $\xi_{vc}$ and its own research results $\xi_{ij}$ with respective weights equal to $\Pi_{vc}(e_{vc})$ and $\Pi_{ij}(e_{ij})$.[14]

At the beginning of date 3, the VC estimates which combination of a product design from each type is expected to generate higher value, if the respective firms are offered to the public, or acquired by an existing firm, at the end of the date. According to this judgment, the VC selects one proposal from each type of project for implementation and allocates one unit of available funds to each of them. The VC's decision is represented by $x = (x_{a1}, x_{a2}, x_{b1}, x_{b2})$, where $x_{ij} = 1$ if the $ij$ product is selected

---

[14] See Aoki (forthcoming, chs. 5 and 11) for the rationalization of the linearity assumption.

for financing and $x_{ij} = 0$ if it is not. If $x_{ij} = 1$ then $x_{ik} = 0$ for $k \neq j$. The firms that are not selected by the VC exit.

At the end of date 3, the selected projects are completed and the VC offers the ownership of these firms to the public through markets or sold to an acquiring firm. At that time, all environmental uncertainty is resolved and the total market value, $V(x_{a1}y_{a1}, x_{a2}y_{a2}, x_{b1}y_{b1}, x_{b2}y_{b2}: E)$, is realizable, contingent on the state of environment $E$ prevailing at that time. The realized value is distributed among the VC and the entrepreneurs. Let us denote the distributive share of the value to firm-$ij$ by $a_{ij}$ and that of VC by $\alpha_{vc} = 1 - \Sigma_{ij}\alpha_{ij}$. The payoff of each firm is then $\alpha_{ij}V - c(e_{ij})$ ($i = a,b; j = 1,2$) and that of the VC is $\alpha_{vc}V - \kappa(e_{vc})$, assuming there is no discounting over dates within a stage game. The incentive of each agent is to maximize its own expected pay-off.

Summarizing, the date 1 strategies of the entrepreneurs are choices of effort levels for research. At date 2, entrepreneurs choose an open design attribute specification $y$'s based partially on results of their own research and partially on available information mediated by the VC, while the VC decides on the allocation of project implementation financing $x$'s in date 3. The VC expends effort in dates 2 and 3 for information mediation and capital market monitoring. In addition, before the beginning of the stage game, the VC and the entrepreneurs have to agree on the way in which realized values are to be distributed at the end of date 3.

The timeline of this Venture Capital Game can be summarized as shown in Table 5.2.

### 3.2. Incentive Impacts of Governance by Tournament

We have imagined that toward the end of date 2 effort expenditures have been made by the entrepreneurs as well as by venture capitalists and that the resulting information has now become available to them. At that moment, the entrepreneurs and the VC alike are interested in maximizing their expected value. It was assumed that the contribution to expected value by individual entrepreneurs becomes estimable with some noise to the VC at date 3 after observing the external attribute specifications of the proposed design. Suppose the VC chooses one entrepreneur from each project for refinancing and project implementation if and only if that project is expected to yield higher value in her judgment. That is, the VC runs a tournament among entrepreneurs and only those who win in terms of their design's expected value creation get the refinancing necessary for the completion of their proposed design in date 3. At the time that winners are selected, a share $\alpha_{ij} = \alpha_i > 0$ is vested with the winning entrepreneur ($i = 1,2$) and the unfunded entrepreneur for-

Table 5.2. *The Time Line of the Venture Capital Game*

|  | Before the game | Date 1: Development | Date 2: Design specification | Date 3: refinancing selection | End of the game |
|---|---|---|---|---|---|
| Entrepreneurs | Contract agreement: start-up financing | Development effort | Design specification | Exit or project implementation | Value realization and distribution |
| Venture capital |  |  | Information mediation | Selective final-stage financing |  |

feits any share ($\alpha_{ij} = 0$). We refer to this scheme as *VC's governance by tournament.*

As two entrepreneurial firms in the same project are assumed to be the same, if a mistake the VC may make in value estimates of entrepreneurial firms is believed to be unbiased, entrepreneurial firms in each project are expected to choose the same effort level ceteris paribus and have equal chances of being selected ex ante so that the entrepreneur's choice must satisfy the following first-order condition: its marginal expected individual benefit of additional effort is equal to its marginal cost. The marginal expected individual benefit is composed of two parts: its share times the probability of being selected for refinancing times its marginal expected value contribution *plus* its share times the marginal increase in the probability of being selected for refinancing times its expected value contribution. Let us refer to the second term as the "tournament effect." Note that the second term involves the *total*, not marginal, expected value contribution.

Let us compare this choice with the following alternative as a comparison benchmark. Suppose that the financier selects ex ante (i.e., before the date 1 begins) only *one* proposal from each type and promises each of them to be entitled to the same share $a_i$ of the value V as realized by the winning entrepreneur at the end of the stage game. Besides, the financier neither mediates information assimilation across entrepreneurs nor selects/rejects projects ad interim. He might as well sell his own share ad interim to buyers in the market who do not have any capacity to be directly involved in the governance structure. Let us call this scheme the *arm's length financing contract.* As their effort levels are not observable, the effort choice of the entrepreneur would be described simply by the marginal expected value of effort being equal to the marginal cost of effort. Comparing the two conditions, we see that, if the total value that the winning entrepreneur can produce is very large relative to the marginal effort product, then the governance by tournament can elicit higher development effort than under arm's length financing, even though his winning chance is one-half and therefore not certain as under arm's-length financing.

Let us take the balance obtained so far from the viewpoint of the VC. The VC's benefit from running a tournament is her share in the additional gains from the tournament effect. Her costs are: (1) duplicate start-up funding at date 1, and (2) intermediating and monitoring effort costs in dates 2 and 3, which would induce more confidence by the entrepreneurs in her project selection. We can prove the following (see Aoki forthcoming, ch. 11 for a proof):

*Proposition 3. If the total value created by entrepreneurial development efforts is expected to be high relative to marginal value (that is, the effort elasticity is small), then it is possible that, even for the same share allocation, the venture capitalist governance by tournament can elicit higher development efforts from entrepreneurs that can compensate venture capitalist for their duplicated start-up financing and interim monitoring costs.*[15]

There are unique social costs and benefits arising from venture capitalist governance by tournament that institutionalizes ad interim selection of projects. One cost is that of the duplication of research and development efforts by entrepreneurs that are sunk in date 1. The effort costs of entrepreneurs who do not win the tournament become deadweight losses. As just stated, there is also the loss of the initial funding to them by the VC. The net balance between the deadweight losses and the benefits from increased effort by the entrepreneurs is not clear without a further parametric specification of the model. It might well be negative. Nevertheless, even in such a case venture capital financing may be preferred to arm's-length financing by the VC as the preceding proposition indicates. If entrepreneurs are risk lovers who place a high utility on an uncertain high value obtainable as the prize of the tournament, then venture capital contracting may be preferred to arm's length contracting by entrepreneurs as well in spite of the possibility of ex post bearing of the deadweight loss. I will discuss in the following subsection how such risk-taking traits may be endogenously formed when governance by tournament is institutionalized.

---

[15] More precisely, the expectation of the entrepreneurs regarding the venture capitalist value assessment also matters. See Aoki (forthcoming, ch. 11).

As already argued, however, there is a unique social benefit from venture capitalist governance due to the possibility of ad interim selection of projects, particularly when technological uncertainty involved in project development is very high while design attribute complementarity between project types is low. So we may assert:

*Proposition 4. Venture capitalist governance by tournament generates deadweight losses of loser's research and development efforts. However, it can configure ad interim a system of product design in response to the emergent state of engineering environments and this possibility creates unique system benefits in the absence of strong attribute complementarity between modular product designs which are not possible under other types of R&D organizations.*

## IV. Further Institutional Ramifications of the Venture Capital Governance

### 4.1. Market Reputations and Club Norms of Venture Capitalists

Finally, we add a few words about the venture capitalist's incentives. In the model of the previous subsection, the venture capitalist's net payoff within a stage game is $a_{vc} E[V] - k(e_{vc})$, namely its share in realized value minus its effort cost. Assuming that the VC maximizes the payoffs only within the horizon of the current stage game, we derive the first-order condition: $a_{vc} E[dV/de_{vc}] = k'(e_{vc})$; that is, its share times the expected total value is equated with marginal cost. However, for optimality the condition ought to be: $E[dV/de_{vc}] = k'(e_{vc})$; that is, the marginal expected total value ought to be equal to the marginal cost. Evidently, undersupply of effort by the VC occurs. At this point, it becomes necessary to make explicit the repeated nature of venture capital financing, albeit vis-à-vis a different set of entrepreneurs in each stage game, and to make explicit the role of reputation and competition among multiple venture capitalists. As stated in Section 1, venture capitalists are financial intermediaries who manage venture capital funds contributed by other financiers who lack expertise in administering the system of governance by tournament. Venture capitalists compete with each other in securing those funds for the formation of successive venture capital funds over time. At the same time, they invest together as a consortium in entrepreneurial start-up firms, while reciprocating the role of lead financier. In such situations, reputation mechanisms that operate in markets for the supply of funds, as well as among venture capitalists, can play an important role. If a venture capitalist fails to deliver a high value to her own investors at the contractual end of a fund, it will have difficulty in raising future funds. If she fails to do the same for the other venture capitalists who have delegated monitoring to her, she may be ostracized from future consortiums through a club norm regulating reciprocal delegation of monitoring.[16] The benefits for venture capitalists from pursuing the value maximization of current funds are not limited to a one-time share in the current venture capital funds that they manage, but include the avoidance of losing their reputations in markets and clubs.

To see more formally the impacts of market competition and a club norm on venture capitalists' incentives, suppose that, if the realized value of a venture capital fund at the end of date 3 falls short of a threshold value V then the capacity of its manager (VC) to raise further funding or to join profitable consortiums led by other venture capitalists from the next stage game on is weakened, and consequently her earning ability is lowered by some large amount. Suppose that the venture capitalist chooses her effort level in each period to maximize her own continuation value in the face of such possibility of punishment for the underperformance. However, note that investors and other venture capitalists can observe only the realized value at the end of each period, but not her effort level. Under this situation, we can derive the following proposition.

*Proposition 5. The decision of suppliers of funds regarding partnership renewal with venture capitalists on the basis of the previous records of their capital gains realization, as well as a club norm regulating their reciprocal delegation of monitoring, can elicit higher efforts from them. But this effect is reduced if the stochastic distribution of funds' final performances is widely spread.[17]*

### 4.2. Endogenous Risk-taking Traits of Entrepreneurs

If the venture capitalists remain active over multiple-stage games, they will be able to accumulate expertise in administering governance by tournament, such as mediating information exchanges among entrepreneurs and judging the compatibility of component product designs in a systemic context, hence helping them to configure a complex system

---

[16] See Aoki (1999, ch. 4.1B) for the club norm. Major venture capitalists in Silicon Valley cluster in a small office complex located on Sand Hill Road between Stanford University and Route 280. They know each other very well and casually converse and have lunches together.

[17] For a proof, see Aoki (forthcoming, ch. 11).

in a self-organizing way. As a by-product of this process, the venture capitalists accumulate knowledge about the research and engineering competence and potential, as well as entrepreneurship, of the founders of start-up firms, partially independently of the success or failure of their particular product-design projects in a one-time tournament. The failure of an entrepreneur to complete a design project in one round of a stage game may not necessarily have been due to his or her inherent incompetence, but might have been caused by sheer bad luck, lack of fit of an inherently good design with an evolving system, a slight lag in design completion, or other factors. Therefore, the entrepreneur may be qualified to enter another tournament. Making such judgments (ex ante monitoring) is another important function of venture capitalists. The knowledge about would-be entrepreneurs obtained on site from past stage games may be helpful for selecting new competitors for a subsequent stage tournament. Thus there can be an important complementarity between ad interim monitoring and ex ante monitoring.

If, however, potentially capable entrepreneurs can have reasonable expectations of being allowed to participate in subsequent tournament rounds in spite of past failures, their risk-taking attitudes may be endogenously enhanced. Namely, even if there is a chance of losing in a tournament, one may be tempted to repeatedly mount a challenge in new tournaments in the hope of someday getting a large prize. Thus one may say that the risk-taking traits of entrepreneurs under venture capital financing are shaped by the venture capital governance that may warrant such expectations.

*Claim 1. The repeated play of the governance by tournament may endogenously shape the risk-tolerance trait of entrepreneurs, thus reducing the (private and social) costs of unsuccessful duplicated efforts.*

### 4.3. Complementarity between Venture Capital Governance and Mobile Engineers' Markets

We have assumed that the venture capitalist has the ability to select a better entrepreneurial firm from each project at date 3 of each stage game. However, the venture capitalist's expertise in judging the technological potential of entrepreneurial firms by himself or herself may actually be limited. However, such shortcomings may be compensated for by the mobility of engineers across entrepreneurial firms. Ambitious and competent engineers may be constantly looking for a "cool" technology.

If the research and development of a new entrepreneurial firm at date 1 is not generating a satisfactory outcome, it may be the engineers in that firm who can recognize this first. If other entrepreneurial firms are continually being organized to search for "cool" technology with the aid of VC financing, those engineers may then exit the slowed-down firm and move to a new firm. "The story in Silicon Valley is that people work for the Valley; they do not work for a firm" (Gilson 1997, p. 1467). Such mobility of engineers provides negative momentum to the process of research and development of the slowed-down firm and reveals its losing status in the tournament to the VC.[18] Thus we submit:

*Claim 2. The limited ad interim monitoring ability of venture capitalists to assess the progress of financing projects may be supplemented by the signal given by engineers who exit ad interim from failing projects. However, the mobility of engineers from slowed-down entrepreneurial firms to new start-up firms is aided by the repeated play of the institution of venture capital governance by tournament. Thus, the venture capital governance and the highly mobile engineers' markets are complementary.*

## V. Conclusions

In this essay, I have argued that, in order to understand the unique governance role of the venture capitalists in the Silicon Valley model, it is not sufficient to take a look only at relationships between an entrepreneurial firm and a venture capitalist. Neither is it appropriate to regard the role of the venture capitalist simply as the supplier of risk capital. Since the truly revolutionary nature of the Silicon Valley model vis-à-vis traditional hierarchical or interactive R&D organizations lies in its ability to generate innovative product systems through the evolutionary selection of modular products generated by entrepreneurial firms in niche markets, it is crucial to take a look at multifaceted relationships between the venture capitalists, on one hand, and the cluster of entrepreneurial firms, on the other. We have focused here on the information structural relationship as well as governance relationships between the two and tried to identify social benefits and costs of the Silicon Valley model. The major social benefit is, as just said, the ability to generate innovative product systems when attribute complementarity among development projects is low. The major social cost is the duplication of

---

[18] I owe this point to Thomas Hellmann.

research efforts and expenditures. This cost may be mitigated by the endogenous formation of a risk-tolerance attitude among entrepreneurs. One important insight of analysis is that the venture capital governance by tournament can elicit higher efforts from entrepreneurs only if the amount of total prize for winners is very high. Therefore, the application of the Silicon Valley model may be limited to domains in which successful developmental projects are expected to yield extremely high values in markets. There is an element of lottery.

But, at the same time, the identification of conditions for the information efficiency of information encapsulation may have broader implications for corporate organizations in general. Because of the development of communications and transportation technology, even mature products (e.g., desktop computers, automobiles) are increasingly decomposed into modules, of which production and procurement become less integrated in comparison to traditional hierarchical firms (as represented by traditional American firms of a decade ago) or interactive firms (as represented by Japanese firms). This tendency renders compact modular organizations (either in the form of independent firms or subsidiaries) increasingly more efficient and viable. Various innovations in corporate governance appear to be evolving even in existing firms, somewhat emulating the Silicon Valley model, such as governing subsidiaries with flexible coupling and decoupling, less operational intervention, but with tournament-like financial discipline. But this subject matter is beyond the scope of this essay.

## References

Aoki, M. (1994). "Monitoring Characteristics of the Main Bank System: Analytical and Developmental View." In M. Aoki and H. Patrick (Eds.), *Japanese Main Bank System*. Oxford: Oxford University Press, pp. 109–41.

(Forthcoming). Toward a Comparative Institutional Analysis. Book manuscript, Stanford University Press.

Aoki, M., and N. Rosenberg. (1989). "The Japanese Firm as an Innovating Institution." In T. Shiraishi and Shigeto Tsuru (Eds.), *Economic Institutions in a Dynamic Society*. New York: Macmillan, pp. 137–54.

Bankman, J., and R. J. Gilson. (1996). "Venture Capital and the Structure of Capital Markets: Banks versus Stock Markets?" *Journal of Financial Economics*, 51: 289–303.

Baron, J. N., M. D. Burton, and M. T. Hannan. (1966). "The Road Taken: Origins and Evolution of Employment Systems in Emerging Companies." *Industrial and Corporate Change*, 5: 239–75.

Barry, C. B., C. J. Muscarella, J. W. Peavy III, and M. R. Vetsyapens. (1990). "The

Role of Venture Capital in the Creation of Public Companies." *Journal of Financial Economics*, 27: 447–71.

Bygrave, W. D., and J. A. Timmons. (1992). *Venture Capital at the Crossroads.* Boston: Harvard Business School Press.

Cremer, J. (1990). "Common Knowledge and the Co-ordination of Economic Activities." In M. Aoki, B. Gustafsson, and O. E. Williamson (Eds.), *The Firm as a Nexus of Treaties.* London: Sage Publications, pp. 53–76.

Fenn, G. W., N. Liang, and S. Prowse. (1995). "The Economics of the Private Equity Market." Staff Study, n. 168, Board of Governors of the Federal Reserve System.

Florida, R., and M. Kenney. (Forthcoming). *Financiers of Innovation: Venture Capital, Technological Change, and Industrial Development.* Princeton, N.J.: Princeton University Press.

Gilson, R. (1997). "The Future of Corporate Governance in the United States." *University of Richmond Law Review*, 31: 1459–72.

Gompers, P. (1995). "Optimal Investment, Monitoring, and the Staging of Venture Capital." *Journal of Finance*, 50: 231–48.

Gompers, P., and J. Lerner. (1996). "The Use of Covenants: An Empirical Analysis of Venture Partnership Agreements." *Journal of Law and Economics*, 39(2): 463–698.

Gorman, M., and W. A. Sahlman. (1989). "What Do Venture Capitalists Do?" *Journal of Business Venturing*, 4: 231–48.

Hannan, M. T., M. D. Burton, and J. N. Baron. (1996). "Inertia and Change in the Early Years: Employment Relations in Young, High-Technology Firms." *Industrial and Corporate Change*, 5: 503–36.

Hellmann, T. (1998a). "The Allocation of Control Rights in Venture Capital Contracts." *Rand Journal of Economics*, 29: 57–76.

(1998b). "Teaching Note for Symantec Corporation (S-SM-27)." Stanford Business School. Joint Venture. *1988 Index of Silicon Valley.* Palo Alto, Calif.

Klein, S., and N. Rosenberg. (1986). "An Overview of Innovation." In R. Landau and N. Rosenberg (Eds.), *The Positive Sum Strategy.* National Academy Press.

Lerner, J. (1994a). "The Syndication of Venture Capital Investments." *Financial Management*, 23: 16–27.

(1994b). "Venture Capitalists and the Oversight of Private Firms." Working Paper, Harvard University.

Pine, B. J. (1993). *Mass Customization: The New Frontier in Business Competition.* Boston: Harvard Business School Press.

Sahlman, W. A. (1990). "The Structure and Governance of Venture Capitalist Organizations." *Journal of Financial Economics*, 27: 473–521.

Saxenian, A. (1994). *Regional Advantage: Culture and Competition in Silicon Valley and Route 128.* Cambridge, Mass.: Harvard University Press.

Testa, R. (1997). "The Legal Process of Venture Capital Investments." In *Pratt's Guide to Venture Capital Sources.* Wellesley Hills, Mass.: Venture Economics.

## Discussion

### Comments on Aoki, "Information and Governance in the Silicon Valley Model"

*Miguel A. García-Cestona*

This is a quite interesting and innovative essay whose reading I strongly recommend. Masahiko Aoki offers us several new ideas and a number of terms concerning corporate governance, innovation, and organization, together with an evolutionary approach to organizations based on information.

Two are, in my opinion, his most important contributions in this work: First, he presents alternative mechanisms to the market for corporate control. His previous work on Punctuated Contingent Governance and his V-mediated Information Encapsulation are two frameworks where an intermediary, different from the market, is able to control in an optimal way. Second, he points out that the development of new, complex technological systems can be evolutionary rather than preconceived, and some types of governance may prove to be more fitted than the market in such contexts. That is, it is becoming more infrequently the case that a large firm is able to impose a standard, or an industry frame, on the remaining companies. Interactions among different companies are then needed, and this paves the way to the study of organizational coordination.

As can be seen, this is quite an ambitious paper and the reader has to accept sometimes the price of an extra load of new terminology. Nevertheless, important issues are at stake and the author does help us to improve our understanding of them.

Let me outline the remaining comments: I deal first with the motivation and results of the essay. Next, I take on some stylized features of the Silicon Valley model to illustrate Aoki's evolutionary idea and point out what I believe are some limitations of this approach.

### 1. Motivation, Framework, and Results

Even though there is no agreement in the economic literature about a definition of the term *corporate governance* (CG), many authors have in mind a framework with managers and shareholders. The former may behave in an opportunistic way, while the latter try to design measures to control the managers, either directly or through a third party able to control. Markets for corporate control have usually played this ex post control, or third-party role. Aoki adopts here a new approach, trying to combine CG issues and internal organization of the firm. In particular, he wants to show that under certain scenarios there could exist a third party, an ex post monitor as he puts it, different from the market for corporate control and able to perform that task. That is, markets are not necessarily the ultimate monitors. Furthermore, this intermediary might be a bank, a holding firm or a regulatory agency, as in his Punctuated Contingent Governance, but it could also be a venture capitalist as it is later developed in the analysis of the Silicon Valley.

To justify these alternative ways, the author relies on an informational approach, with coordination aspects coming from the internal organization of the firm. The question becomes to determine how should we assign or distribute the information process activities when agents have limited capabilities to process information. Three generic modes are described in the paper: (1) hierarchical decomposition, (2) information assimilation and information sharing, and (3) information encapsulation. Moreover, R&D organizations are presented as nested forms of these generic modes, and doing so, we can identify some common forms or R&D organizations in Figure 5.1. Those are

(i)   Hierarchical R&D organization
(ii)  Interactive R&D organization and
(iii) Venture capital-mediated information encapsulation

After such description, the question that arises is why do we have different forms of organizing an information system? The author conducts an interesting comparison of informational efficiency among alternative organizations. In this comment, I will only focus on his third, more innovative, mode: the idea of information encapsulation, IE, and his V-mediated mode.

Why do we need this IE? Certainly, we don't need it in every scenario; a functional hierarchy can do a better job under certain conditions. But we deal now with organizations and individuals who are boundedly rational, and where well-educated, well-formed employees (human capital, if you prefer), become crucial. If we add, furthermore, contexts that make use of information technologies, experience important advances in communications and where uncertainty is quite present, then coordination modes will emerge as important tools.

Moreover, Aoki speaks in his essay of an environment composed of common and idiosyncratic aspects. When we consider evolutionary approaches in new, complex technological systems or information technologies, the lack of a standard becomes a big problem. As I have understood this essay, we have a situation where the important goal is to reach a good agreement on the industry standard and here, IE can prove to be quite a useful answer to this coordination problem, in spite of the additional cost of duplicated efforts. The presence of modules allows firms to quickly replace parts of the process without redesigning the whole process. This is important for situations where the standard is not yet clearly defined. Interactive R&D organizations require wide exchanges of information and the creation of communication channels that cannot be freely and quickly reestablished if fundamental changes are demanded.

As was pointed out earlier, another important contribution of the essay refers to the better understanding of evolutionary approaches. IE presents advantages in coping with uncertainty and with an increasingly complex technological environment and the description of the Silicon Valley context will help to clarify this point.

## 2. The Silicon Valley Model: Some Stylized Features and Comments

I proceed now to describe some features of the V-mediation mode and my comments in the context of the organizational coordination framework.

2.1. Aoki points out that this is *not a one-to-one relation*: in the model we have a cluster of entrepreneurs (firms) dealing with a venture capitalist, who makes them compete in a tournament. At the beginning, they are all wondering about the industry standards, trying different approaches, and falling into duplications before choosing a winner of the tournament. Thus, there is information assimilation concerning the external specifications, a search for standards, and encapsulation at the operative level.

This is an interesting approach and helps us to see the idea of innovation and encapsulation. Nevertheless, I believe further analysis is needed on the side of venture capitalists (VC). The competition among them must be formulated too or we will be missing some important elements if we only work with a representative VC. This loss becomes more important when different VCs have different knowledge and they play an active role in the success of the projects.

In fact, the author talks of a consortium of VCs and the corresponding reputation mechanisms. Reputation certainly helps, but I think there are still some concerns when the standard might be fixed not by a single VC but by *different* VCs competing among themselves. If so, how do we deal with this? How does the consortium itself work? Is there competition among different consortiums of VCs? The existing literature on the main-bank system may help at this point, but it also tells us that it is not easy to formulate such an approach.

*2.2. Stage funding* is also an important feature. In this manner, control or property rights are allocated to the fund providers who can then stop the project. After saying that, the question is what does prevent another VC from taking the loser and competing at that point? Or related to the previous feature, how is a VC's bargaining power taken under control?

Empirical studies seem to agree on a 3 to 10 ratio to keep the VC system working in the United States – that is, 3 successful projects out of 10. One important issue would be to check if American VCs tend to specialize: one wonders if this 3 to 10 ratio refers to projects involved in the same or very similar areas, whose results can reinforce each other and where the tournament approach can be implemented. This does not seem to be the case in Europe, where the VCs are involved in different sectors and where comparable ratios could reach a 7 or 8 to 10 figure. Furthermore, the tournament approach implies the choice of a winner: could it be that the choice is made in function of other parts of the system? Can we always be sure that encapsulation works and the best alternative is always selected? What happens if some other project is equally good? What happens with other successful projects left in the process?

Finally, the presence of venture capitalists does not seem to be enough for a V-mediated Information Encapsulation mode to work and it would be interesting to understand why. For example, venture capital firms are also quite important in the biotechnology industry, but encapsulation does not seem to play a role there.

To wrap up these comments, this is an interesting essay, dealing with important issues in an innovative way. In general, we lack good explanations for evolutionary approaches and I think the notions of Information Encapsulation and the V-mediated form become useful tools to understand some industries where the standards are evolving. Besides, this essay also provides a view of the informational role of the venture capitalist and future work on the topic will make use of this framework.

CHAPTER 6

# The Governance of the New Enterprise

## RAGHURAM G. RAJAN AND LUIGI ZINGALES

The publication of "The Modern Corporation and Private Property" in 1932 by Adolph Berle and Gardiner Means set the terms of the modern debate on corporate governance. Berle and Means focused on the separation of ownership and control in large corporations where multiple layers of salaried managers coordinated production and distribution. What is perhaps less well recognized about their work is that the large public corporation had only recently become the dominant way of organizing production in the United States (see Chandler 1977). The book was therefore prescient in that it recognized this way of organizing the enterprise would be lasting, and hence it was important to study how they would be governed.

At that time, the archetypical public firm was General Motors. The enduring fascination with this firm has been, in part, because of its size and the industry it is in, and, in part, because it was the focus of two of the best known managerial books, Alfred Sloan's *My Years with General Motors* and Peter Drucker's *The Concept of the Corporation*.

GM was, and in large part still is, a vertically integrated firm, which owned and controlled a large amount of highly specialized inanimate assets, ranging from plant and machinery to world-famous brand names. In the past, as we will argue, these assets were very hard to replicate and were primarily what made the firm unique. The human capital of employees was, in large part, tied to these assets and immobile. Thus ownership of unique inanimate assets was the primary source of power in the corporation. Moreover, since ownership rights were delegated to the top management by dispersed shareholders, there was a tremendous concentration of both power and the rents generated from production, at the top of the organizational hierarchy of the vertically integrated organization.

It should come as no surprise that the corporate governance debate developed as it did. The entity being governed, the firm, was stable and well defined, with its boundaries represented by the ownership of unique assets. The fundamental issue in corporate governance was how the

We benefited from the comments of Carmen Matutes, J. Enric Ricart, and Xavier Vives.

surplus that accumulated at the top of the organizational pyramid could be taken away from the sticky fingers of top management and given to the rightful owners, the dispersed shareholders. We say "rightful" because, after all, top management came into the surplus largely because shareholders delegated to them rights over the firm's unique assets, which were the primary source of the surplus.

The nature of the firm in the United States in particular, and the world in general, is changing. Large conglomerates have been broken up and their units have been spun off as stand-alone companies. Vertically integrated manufacturers have relinquished direct control of their suppliers and moved toward looser forms of collaboration. A steel manufacturer like Nucor, for instance, has abandoned the tradition of backward integration typical of its industry and outsourced the entire supply of raw material (Holmstrom and Roberts 1998). Even GM is changing its internal structure, having recently proposed to spin off its major parts supplier, Delphi.

But perhaps the most significant change has been to human capital. Recent changes in the nature of organizations, the extent and requirements of markets, and the availability of financing have made specialized human capital much more important, and also much more mobile. But human capital is inalienable, and power over it has to be obtained through mechanisms other than ownership. As the importance of human capital has grown, power has moved away from the top and is much more widely dispersed through the firm.

The changing nature of the corporation forces us to reexamine much of what we take for granted in corporate governance. What precisely is the entity that is being governed? How does the governance system obtain power over it, and what determines the division of power between various stakeholders? And is the objective of allocating power only to enhance the returns of outside investors? The study of governance today has to go beyond the Berle and Means framework of simply determining who owns and whether the true owners can exercise their rights adequately.

This essay will take a small step toward what is no doubt an extremely (perhaps overly) ambitious goal. We will first sketch a framework that describes how transactions within the firm differ from transactions within the market. When this framework is applied to the prototypical firm of Berle and Means's time, it suggests why the focus of governance was initially on how to strengthen the rights of outside owners over management. Corporations, however, have changed tremendously. We provide some examples of how the new corporation differs from those in existence at the time of Berle and Means. Perhaps the most important difference is the increased importance of human capital relative to inanimate assets. We then argue that given the changed nature of the firm, the focus of corporate governance must shift to studying mechanisms that give the firm the power to provide incentives to human capital. We conclude with examples of the kind of subjects that should now be the legitimate focus of study in corporate governance.

## I. How Firms Differ from Markets

In the early 1930s, a young British economist, Ronald Coase, visited a number of major U.S. companies, including GM, in an attempt to understand the essence of the modern business enterprise. Coase (1937) concluded, in a seminal article, that the distinguishing feature of the firm was its suppression of the price mechanism that prevailed in the marketplace, in favor of the allocation of resources through power or authority. To understand why this could make transactions conducted in the firm more efficient than transactions conducted outside, we have to understand first what we mean by power, where it comes from, and how it affects the efficiency of production.[1]

### 1.1. The Economic Definition of Power

"Power" is a term that is widely used in very different contexts with completely different meanings. So it is useful to define our use of the term. Economists say someone in an organization has more bargaining power if they can get more of the surplus produced by the organization (net of their costs). There are three important ways in which an individual obtains bargaining power over the organization's surplus. The first comes from how tough a negotiator the individual is. For example, a patient negotiator can get more, as can a negotiator who is willing to carry out crazy threats. Since this power is individual specific, it is generally of little help in understanding theories of institutions.[2] Power can also come from how the rules of bargaining are structured. The first mover could have an advantage, as could one who gets to make the last take-it-or-leave-it offer. Since we will describe situations where bargaining takes place

---

[1] Space considerations will prevent us from doing justice to the rich literature in theory of the firm, starting from classics like Alchian and Demsetz (1972), Klein, Crawford, and Alchian (1978), Williamson (1985) and extending to more recent contributions like Aghion and Tirole (1997), Baker, Gibbons, and Murphy (1997), Gertner (1998), and Holmstrom (1997).

[2] We say "generally" because one could construct theories where the institution selects out the toughest or weakest bargainer for certain positions, and this enhances overall efficiency.

repeatedly over a long period of time, it is hard to ascribe a sustained advantage to one party as a result of how the rules are structured.[3]

Finally, an individual can derive power from the valuable resources she brings to the production process (and, hence, the resources she can threaten to withhold). It is this source of power that sociologists (and, more recently, institutional economists) have emphasized, and will be what we focus on.[4] Thus power refers to an individual's control over valuable resources. But one has to be careful here. One pays a newsagent to deliver a paper every morning. The fact that he does so does not signify that one has power over him, since this is a fair market exchange effected through a contract. So we will refer to power as the control over valuable resources over and above that determined through explicit contract in a competitive market. Some examples are in order.

### An Example: Ownership as a Source of Power

Historically, a major source of power has been that conferred by legal mechanisms enforced by law – what we call de jure sources of power. This may seem strange especially as we have just argued that power should refer to the rights of control over resources that are not specified in voluntary contracts. The apparent inconsistency is resolved when we recognize that contracts are typically incomplete and do not specify rights and duties in all contingencies. The law, however, through some legal mechanisms, offers parties control rights in eventualities that are not covered through contract – what Grossman and Hart (1986) felicitously term the "residual rights of control." For example, guardianship of a child confers on the guardian a substantial amount of decision-making power over the child's future, even though none of this is laid out in an explicit ex ante contract.

Perhaps the most powerful de jure mechanism offered by the law is ownership. The law allows individuals to own physical assets and intangible assets such as brand names. Not only can the owner contract as she pleases with the organization over the asset, but also ownership gives her the right to specify how the asset is used in situations not covered by contracts. It is this control that gives the owner power in any negotiations over the use of the asset.[5]

---

[3] There are exceptions. For example, an intermediary has a natural advantage because he can initiate bargaining with either side that he intermediates between.

[4] See Emerson (1962), Pfeffer (1981), and Hart (1995).

[5] There are other de jure mechanisms. For example, when an organization incorporates as a corporation, it obtains certain rights over its employees that an ordinary organization would not have. Specifically, the corporate opportunity doctrine restricts the ability of managers to personally take advantage of opportunities that come to them while they are agents for the firm.

So, for example, a worker who owns a van can contract with the organization on how it is to be used. And if a holiday, not specified in the original contract, intervenes, she can decide to allow the organization to use the van, or she can drive away on a picnic. If the van is valuable to the production process and cannot be easily substituted, her residual rights of control give her power.[6]

Of course, the owner's power depends on how great her residual right of control is (i.e., how many important contingencies were left unspecified in the original contract) and how unique the resource is, that is, how costly it is to replace the van.

### 1.2. Why Does the Allocation of Power Matter?

Why does the allocation of power matter? If agents could write all possible state-contingent contracts at no cost and ensure that these contracts are not renegotiated, then the allocation of power does not matter. In such a world all relevant decisions would be made ex ante, and the allocation of power will have distributional consequences but no efficiency consequences.[7] In other words, once every contingency can be anticipated and contracted up front, and the legal system can fully enforce contracts, there is little room for the exercise of power.

In practice, however, contracts are not fully contingent and the law is not enforced perfectly, so organizations have to negotiate about rights and duties all the time rather than simply adhere to a contract. Power affects outcomes in these negotiations.

There are at least three reasons why the allocation of power affects efficiency. First, the more power an agent has, the larger the amount of surplus she gets, which, in turn, affects her incentives and thus her decisions. This effect on incentives can be of two types. When an agent has power, she becomes confident that she will get a substantial share of the surplus from a relationship with the organization, even though she knows contracts do not protect her adequately. This is the "average" effect of power, and it may induce an otherwise reluctant agent to enter a relationship.[8] Power can also increase with the specialized investment the agent makes (or the effort she exerts), and this will increase her incentive to invest. This is the "marginal" effect. Since specialized investment can improve the functioning of the organization, the appropriate alloca-

---

[6] See Grossman and Hart (1986) for the seminal paper on ownership and power.
[7] See Zingales (1998). For an opposite view see Tirole (1998).
[8] See Klein et al. (1978) or, more recently, Rotemberg (1994).

tion of power can enhance the organization's efficiency.[9] Ownership may be one way of allocating power to agents so that it has beneficial average and marginal effects.[10]

Second, the allocation of power affects the feasible set of punishments that are imposed on an agent who does not behave in a way that enhances firm value. While the owner of an essential asset cannot be excluded from the organization even if her human capital is not valuable to the organization, a nonowner can (and will) be excluded from participation if somebody else is the owner. Since the nonowner can be punished more easily, and the threat of punishment to the organization can enhance the nonowner's incentives to specialize, the allocation of ownership, and hence, power, has a clear effect on the organization's productive value.[11]

Third, power may itself be necessary to prevent inefficient jockeying for power. In large organizations, for instance, there are some tasks that confer a disproportionate amount of power on the people who undertake them.[12] There is an excessive desire to specialize in those tasks and too little incentive to specialize in other important tasks that generate less power.[13] An analogous situation is movie casting, where every actor would like to play the main character, and nobody the bit roles. Yet the movie will not work without good performances by supporting actors. As in a movie, this allocation problem is not resolved by prices (in fact the main character is generally paid more than the others), but by fiat. By allocating roles, the movie director prevents an improper allocation of talents. Similarly, in a firm, top management uses its power to allocate

---

[9] Specific investment can be with respect to the firm's assets (the employee learns to use a specialized lathe or write in a specialized software language). Alternatively, it can be with respect to other employees (the secretary learns to work with his boss).

[10] The latter effect is emphasized in Grossman and Hart (1986) and Hart and Moore (1990). In the absence of contracts, each agent's share of the ex post surplus depends upon her outside option. Whenever the value of the owned asset increases with the owner's investment, ownership increases the outside option of the owner, increasing her incentive to invest. Rajan and Zingales (1998a) argue that the marginal effects of ownership could well be reversed, and reduce the incentive to invest (see later).

[11] This effect is not present in Grossman and Hart (1986) or Hart and Moore (1990) where ownership only offers the threat of exclusion, but no one is actually excluded in equilibrium. See Rajan and Zingales (1998a) for an example of when ex post exclusion actually takes place, and the appropriate allocation of ownership can enhance ex ante incentives.

[12] This is again true only in a world of incomplete contracts, because otherwise the rewards from undertaking different tasks could be more closely aligned with their costs.

[13] This is related to, but different from, the inefficiency generated by rent seeking (Milgrom and Roberts, 1990). For other applications, see Hirshleifer (1995), Rajan and Zingales (1998c), Rajan, Servaes, and Zingales (1998), and Skaperdas (1992).

tasks so that the specialized investments by employees are coordinated toward the common good.[14]

## II. The Traditional Corporation in the Time of Berle and Means

Until the middle of the 19th century, the U.S. (and world) economy was mostly composed of small, manager-owned businesses that rarely had more than a hundred employees. It is only with the advent of the second industrial revolution that a new organizational form emerged: what Chandler (1977) calls the *modern business enterprise* (MBE). By the end of the 1920s MBEs dominated most sectors of the U.S. economy.

It was the realization of the dramatic possibilities in this form of organization that spurred Berle and Means's analysis. Thus, it is important to review the main characteristics of the MBE and how they affected the debate on corporate governance.

As Chandler (1990) argues, the primary advantage of the MBE was its scale and scope. The MBE had the cost economies from size and the extensive brand image from mass advertising to pose formidable competition to new entrants. As a result, competition in the final output market was limited.

A related characteristic of the MBE was the great extent to which it was vertically integrated. Many of these firms were set up when their industry was young, and few suppliers or customers of intermediate goods existed. Presumably, these could not be persuaded to set up because all they could see for the foreseeable future was a monopolist buyer or supplier. Whatever the reason, firms had to integrate both upstream and downstream to ensure the right level of throughput (see Chandler 1977).

One consequence was that most of the transactions involved in the production process took place within the firm. The few transactions that took place between the firm and the outside were largely at arm's length (as between the firm and the final consumer). Thus the realm of transactions governed by power rather than prices tended to coincide with the legal boundaries of the corporation. Hence, the MBE is often referred to as the modern corporation (which, not coincidentally, is half the title of Berle and Means's book).

Another consequence was that each industry came to be dominated

---

[14] Rajan and Zingales (1998a,b) refer to this role of power as control over access.

by a few, vertically integrated giants, with few independent suppliers in intermediate markets. Interestingly, once the pattern of limited competition in intermediate markets was established, it was probably very hard to break out of it. The vertically integrated firm would typically have its own distinctive standards. Any supplier of intermediate products would have to produce a very specialized product with only one likely buyer – not a prospect that would elicit much investment!

The absence of competition in the intermediate markets led to several organizational consequences. The absence of market signals or competitive pressures at the intermediate levels created the potential for organizational slack. This had to be controlled via a rigid command-and-control system. Such a system was feasible because the scarcity of competitors, and the absence of industry-wide standards, together implied a thin outside labor market, able to use (and pay for) the skills that employees acquired on the job. Through its control of the firm's assets, the headquarters effectively controlled the main source of employment open to their specialized employees. This gave top management enormous power and led to an accumulation of organizational surplus at the top. This was so much so that once the command-and-control system of the MBE was in place, the main problem became one of how to guarantee enough power to employees who specialized, so as to motivate their specific investments.

In large part, organizations achieved this by creating steep organizational hierarchies, where top management communicated with lower management only through intermediate managers in the hierarchy. Not only was this organizational pyramid necessary to coordinate the enormous organizations, but also intermediate positions in the hierarchy accumulated some power because they were the channels through which top management communicated with, and controlled, the mass of lower level employees. In other words, the steep hierarchy was a way for top management to cede some power to intermediate management by giving them control over some resources (the lower level employees). Higher positions in the hierarchy were associated with higher rents and were a reward for employees who dedicated themselves to the organization (for a model along these lines, see Rajan and Zingales 1998b).

But in general, given the limited alternative opportunities for specialized human capital and the difficulty of reproducing the mass of inanimate assets these corporations had created, the critical resource was inanimate assets, to which the human capital of employees was, willy-nilly, tied. As a result, the legal claims over assets became the most important source of power.

The last defining characteristic of the MBE was the emergence of salaried managers and absentee owners. The economies of scale and scope, which provided to the MBE its major comparative advantage, made the firm too large to have ownership rest only in the hands of management. Outside investors were needed to finance assets of such size and to bear the risk associated with such large ownership stakes.[15] At the same time, the command-and-control system depended heavily on the specific assets owned by the corporation. Outside owners could delegate control to salaried managers, because the outside owners retained the threat of withdrawing the assets and making management (and operations) impossible if the top managers were not pliable. Hence, Berle and Means (1932) were primarily concerned about the problems that arose when the outside owner was too dispersed to exercise control over top management, and not about whether they had any tools to control managers with.

Summarizing, there are three main features of the MBE that shaped the ensuing debate on corporate governance. First, the MBE was well defined by the ownership of assets. The *legal* boundaries of the corporation could be drawn around these assets and also coincided with its *economic* boundaries. Moreover, these boundaries did not change unless ownership changed. Since the boundaries were well defined, the main issue in corporate governance was how the surplus generated within these boundaries was to be allocated, and not on how to preserve and protect the boundaries.

Second, the MBE typically required more investment and more risk taking than within the capacity of the management. Moreover, outsiders could obtain power by virtue of their ownership of the crucial assets. As a result, the MBE came to be owned by outsiders.

Finally, the concentration of power at the top of the organizational pyramid, together with the separation between ownership and control, made the agency problem between top managers and shareholders *the* corporate governance problem.[16] Whether managerial compensation is aligned with shareholder wealth maximization, whether boards are independent, whether Poison Pills are in the interests of shareholders – these are the kinds of questions that have dominated the corporate governance debate in recent years. But while these issues are being debated, the firm itself has changed dramatically from Chandler's MBE.

---

[15] These investors could have taken debt rather than equity claims. For a discussion of why they might have chosen the latter, see Rajan and Zingales (1998a).

[16] Consistent with this approach, Shleifer and Vishny (1997) define corporate governance as having to do with "the ways in which suppliers of finance to corporations assure themselves of getting a return on their investment."

## III. Changes and Cause of Changes

There are powerful forces at play that are changing the nature of the firm. These forces have had two important, and intimately related, effects: they have increased the importance of human capital relative to inanimate assets, and they have led to the breakup of the vertically integrated firms. In this section we describe the forces, using the example of the financial sector where these changes are especially clear-cut.

### 3.1. An Example: The Financial Sector

The financial sector is one area where the relative importance of human capital has increased tremendously. For instance, Rebecca Demsetz of the New York Federal Reserve finds that the share of employment of low-skilled workers in banks declined from an average of 60.4 percent in the period 1983–6 to 52.5 percent in the period 1993–5. Correspondingly, there is a move away from workers without college degrees toward workers with college degrees. While Demsetz finds an economy-wide trend in the increasing employment shares of highly skilled workers, she finds the effects particularly pronounced in banking.[17]

Why is this happening? One possible explanation is simply the increased automation in banking (or, in the jargon, "skill-biased technological change"). But there is another explanation that may complement this. To a large extent, the banks' primary asset used to be the ability to raise money from captive depositors and channel credit to customers who had little choice. Outside owners could own this asset by virtue of their ownership of the bank's charter. And top management's control of this asset gave them authority over loan officers. While the credit evaluation skills of the loan officer mattered, they were of secondary importance to the funds that the bank placed in her hands to lend. Without the funds, the officer had little value. And regulatory restrictions on competition meant there were not many banks competing in the same region to which she could transfer her skills if the bank let her go.

Technological change, especially the improvement in communications technology, and institutional change, such as the advent of credit rating agencies, have loosened the link between depositors and the local bank. And markets have become better able to track and evaluate the performance of firms directly, without recourse to an institutional intermediary. Competition from markets and other institutions has meant that the ability to channel funding is no longer the critical asset it once was. As

---

[17] Also see Machin and Van Reenen (1998).

a result, the importance of the loan officer has changed. Rather than simply keeping her hand on the spigot controlling the flow of funds, she has to create new ideas for structured financing for firms that will attract their attention in an increasingly competitive and crowded market. Innovative and customized deals are the source of profits now rather than the old plain-vanilla loan, which is now a commodity. The loan officer's human capital, both in terms of her product and industry knowledge, and her client relationships, has become an important source of value to the commercial bank.

But this raises enormous problems of external and internal governance. It is no longer clear who owns one of the most critical assets, the client relationship (and it is clear that the loan officer, and not the bank's owners, owns her human capital). Banks that have attempted to force their officers to share their relationships with other parts of the bank so that more products can be "cross-sold," have often faced subtle sabotage. The more savvy banks have first sat down with their own loan officers to negotiate about who owns the relationship.[18] These negotiations would never have been necessary in the past, when the ownership of the bank charter (and hence the access to critical funds) gave top managers substantial authority over lower managers, and outsiders authority over management.

The growing importance of human capital at the expense of other, more tangible, assets makes it hard to keep the vertically integrated firm intact because it weakens the command-and-control system that emanated from the ownership of inanimate assets. Consider another example. Salomon Brothers' bond trading group in the late 1980s and early 1990s consisted of extremely talented traders and "rocket scientists" (Ph.D.'s who used mathematical models to uncover mispricing of financial assets that could be profited from) who made enormous sums of money for Salomon. But there was not much that Salomon gave them other than its capital and name. As we have argued above, capital became easily available elsewhere, so Salomon became less and less able to control the group, and had to fork out enormous salaries and bonuses just to keep the group happy.

And in 1991, a misguided attempt to corner the Treasury bill auction by a member of the group led to an enormous loss of capital and name to Salomon. Even though John Meriwether, the head of the group, was fired, this had little long-run punitive effect. Over time, a number of talented traders, responsible for 87 percent of Salomon's profits between 1990 and 1993, left Salomon to join him in a new venture, Long Term

---

[18] We thank Mark Knez for this example.

Capital Management.[19] For good reason, this became known as Salomon North. The bonds of human capital proved much stronger than the bonds of ownership, a fact that even Salomon's CEO did not realize.[20] So what exactly were the boundaries of Salomon?

From a legal standpoint, the bond-trading group was an integral part of Salomon. Certainly, the public thought so and penalized Salomon for its actions. But if we take the standpoint that the boundary of the firm is the point up to which top management has the ability to exercise power (rather than persuade only through monetary rewards), the group was not an integral part of Salomon. It merely rented space, Salomon's name, and capital, and turned over some share of its profits as rent. The reduced importance of inanimate assets like capital, relative to the traders' human capital, led first to Salomon's implicit loss of control, and eventually to its explicit loss of control over the group.

## 3.2. More Generally . . .

More generally, the changes in the financial sector are mirrored in almost every industry, and in many rich countries. A recent study by Machin and Van Reenen (1998) finds that the relative demand for skilled workers has increased in all seven OECD countries investigated.[21] This is partly because technology has changed to require more skilled labor. But technological change does not occur in a vacuum, and undoubtedly the changes in industrial organization and organizational structure have had no small effect.

Vertically integrated organizations that enjoy rents because their assets, brand names, or even government charters give them an unassailable position in the industry are becoming creatures of the past. Improvements in financial markets have made it easier to finance large investments, so capital intensity is no longer a source of protection against competition. Cross-border trade has expanded market size tremendously, and firms that were once oligopolists with a tremendous first-mover advantage in their own small domestic markets now fight it out in a larger, competitive, world market. Communication costs have

[19] See *Institutional Investor*, November 1996, p. 62. The saga of LTCM is making headlines even as this paper is being written.

[20] *Instutional Investor* (November 1996, p. 62) reports a conversation between Derek Maughan, the CEO of Salomon, and Rosenfeld from Lazard Freres. Maughan asked Rosenfeld what his worst nightmare for Salomon was. "That the arb [arbitrageur] people would all leave now that Meriwether was'nt coming back," Rosenfeld said. According to Rosenfeld, Maughan shot back: "No way. Those guys are all tied to Salomon."

[21] The seven countries are the United States, Denmark, France, Germany, Japan, Sweden, and the United Kingdom.

fallen dramatically. Old brand names need constant reinvestment so as to maintain their salience in an increasingly noisy world. At the same time, new names, if sufficiently distinctive, can quickly carve out a niche. In the past, the Yahoos of today's marketplace would have spent years in obscurity, earning their stripes. These changes have increased competition at all levels. But increased competition at the intermediate goods level, in particular, has coincided with the breakdown of the traditional vertically integrated firm.

It is hard to tease out what caused what since almost everything has happened together in a short span of time. But here is a reasoned conjecture. As markets became more open, vertically integrated firms in the United States faced competition from firms that were differently organized. For example, firms (say from Japan) that have a tradition of outsourcing at the intermediate level, developed a few independent local (U.S.) suppliers for their U.S. factories. The suppliers were willing to make large investments because the Japanese firms had a reputation for fair treatment of suppliers in Japan. The presence of viable, competitive, independent, intermediate goods producers placed strong constraints on the ability of top management in the vertically integrated hierarchy of the U.S. firms to exercise command and control. For one, employees at intermediate levels in their own firms had alternative sources of employment, so the vertically integrated firm had much less power over them. An employee who thought headquarters was too heavyhanded would simply quit. Thus control at a distance became much more difficult.

Moreover, internal units could benchmark their performance against the outside. Units in the vertically integrated firm that performed well now realized the bottlenecks created by poorly performing units. Clearly, they were upset if their performance and compensation was held hostage to the performance of the worst-performing unit. But such forced cross-subsidy is an unavoidable outcome if the vertically integrated firm does not source outside. Again, upset managers could easily leave.

Finally, a vertically integrated firm that did not produce at the optimum level at each stage faced much stiffer competition from less integrated competitors, who could buy from the best. In summary, the opening of a competitive market for intermediate goods reduced the ability of the vertically integrated firm to control its remote units, while at the same time making transparent the cross-subsidies implicit in the system. This put pressure on the firm to break up and also forced whatever remained integrated to standardize intermediate products so that it could benefit from competitive suppliers. The break-up of integrated firms, combined with the lower barriers to and costs of entry, further increased competition at all levels, accentuating the forces at play.

An immediate consequence is that the firm's human capital, as represented by its employees, has become much more important. First, as competition has increased, physical assets have become less unique and employees have many more outside options. This is reflected in the economy-wide diminished expected length of tenure in any single job. Second, a firm has to be distinctive in terms of its costs or quality to make money in the competitive marketplace. This has increased the importance of innovation, not just as represented by R&D but also reflected in process innovation and quality improvement. Innovation comes from human capital, not from inanimate assets. So at the same time as employees have been unshackled by the competitive market, they have also become more important to firms.

The growing prominence of corporations where physical assets are unimportant relative to human assets raises a number of new issues of governance. Where do outsiders get authority, especially because human capital is not ownable? What determines the boundary of the firm? Where does top management get authority over subordinates?

## IV. Power in a Human Capital Organization

We argued earlier that power comes from control over valuable resources. However, the law does not allow a person to be bought or sold without her consent (except to a limited extent in sports). Furthermore, even if an agent sells her labor, she cannot sell it irrevocably for a long period. Thus the individual cannot pledge the residual control rights over her human capital to someone else for any significant length of time through contract.

Control over valuable human capital would seem then to be a greater source of power than control over physical assets since almost all control rights over it are residual, that is, not allocable through contract.[22] But it poses new challenges. Since de jure mechanisms are of little direct use in offering residual rights over human capital, how does a firm obtain control over a unit that is composed entirely of human capital when the law does not help in this matter?

[22] We say almost because employment contracts do give an employer some rights. For instance, as Masten (1988) argues, there is a legal difference between an employment contract and a contract with a contractor. The employee is liable for the process by which work is done – e.g., he agrees to show up at work every day, work a certain number of hours, and obey reasonable orders. Of course, nothing ensures that the work is done with enthusiasm or efficiency. By contrast, the contractor is held responsible for output but not for the process by which he does it, unless contractually specified.

## 4.1. Complementarities

The answer lies in building links between the person or unit that the firm seeks to have power over, and the firm. Not any link will do; what is needed are links that cause persons or units to be better off voluntarily following the firm's commands rather than going their own way. Economists call such a link "complementarity." More precisely, a complementarity is said to exist when the unit and the firm can together create more value than they can going their own separate ways. Once the complementarity exists, the unit may obey orders from the firm for fear that disobedience would jeopardize the joint value they can create together. More generally, while ownership legally links an inanimate asset to a firm, complementarities economically link some person or unit that cannot be owned to the firm.

One form of building complementarities is through specialization. It is useful to distinguish at this point between technical specialization and firm-specific specialization. Technical specialization is specialization to the technology necessary for production in an industry. For example, a machinist in the aircraft industry may work with a special kind of lathe, and his skills may be valuable only for the high-precision needs of the aircraft industry. An individual or unit that is technically specialized is tied to the industry but not to a specific firm unless the industry is a monopoly. Firm-specific specialization is specialization to the idiosyncratic needs of the firm. For example, a supplier may invest so that his software can communicate with the firm's special order processing computer. This sort of specialization ties the individual or unit to a specific firm.

Berle and Means's (and Chandler's) vertically integrated firm existed in what was, at best, an oligopolistic industry. Employees were tied to the firm largely because they were technically specialized. Their incentive to specialize much more was limited because there was a very limited market for their skills.

The advent of competition destroyed technical specialization as a source of complementarity since employees could do as well by joining competitors as by staying with the firm. Paradoxically, this has increased the extent to which employees acquire technical skills since these are now rewarded in the marketplace.

The enterprise in today's competitive marketplace cannot rely on their employees' technical specialization to acquire power over them. The firm has to get employees or units to make firm-specific investments. But this leads to a problem – why would employees or units choose to specialize to the firm when they know that this will make them dependent on the firm? Moreover, why would they do so when they can focus on acquiring more marketable technical skills that are rewarded in the industry?

### 4.2. Control over Access

The solution for the modern enterprise seems to be to create a situation where employees or units know that their rewards will be greater if they make firm-specific investments. The enterprise does this by giving key employees or units privileged *access* to the enterprise or its critical resources, so that they have power if they specialize (see Rajan and Zingales 1998a). Some examples will make the point clearer.

A brokerage firm usually gives brokers leads to new clientele. This is a form of access. At the time of receiving leads, a new broker's human capital is not particularly valuable to the firm. But over time, he develops the leads into solid relationships with clients. Now the broker's human capital is very valuable because it is the crucial link between the firm and its clients. Thus by giving a newcomer access to leads, the brokerage effectively allocates valuable residual rights or power to him.

But this allocation is not unconditional. If the broker does not invest in the leads and develop them into fruitful relationships, his human capital does not become valuable. The leads can easily be taken away and given to others. Thus the power that comes from privileged access is contingent on the agent specializing.[23]

The selective allocation of access to key firm resources is what we call a de facto mechanism to allocate power. If the brokerage provides enough unique value to clients, the broker is of little value without the firm to back him. By investing in building relationships to clients, the broker builds complementarities between himself and the brokerage, giving it some power over him. But he also has power over the brokerage because he "owns" the clients. Thus the broker and brokerage achieve a more even balance of power than do employee and corporation in Chandler's vertically integrated MBE.

What is new and interesting is that the brokerage has to commit to give up power in order to get power. In exchange for committing to share some of the surplus with the broker, it obtains his loyalty, which gives the brokerage power in its interactions with other players. We will explain this in greater detail shortly.

We have discussed controlled access as means of allocating power to

[23] Unlike ownership, which directly bestows residual rights on the owner, access combined with specialization does not create any new rights, but simply enhances the value of the chosen individual's preexisting rights over her human capital. The net effect is, however, similar: access can be used to bestow power on individual members.

employees. It could also explain the new forms of customer–supplier relationships that are supplanting the old vertically integrated firm. For example, Toyota has a system where two independent suppliers are offered privileged access to Toyota's technical specifications, and its latest innovations including, on occasion, the research findings of the competing supplier.[24] On their part, suppliers are required to invest to meet Toyota's needs. Suppliers who specialize thus acquire a certain degree of market power ex post because they are only one of two capable suppliers. But Toyota does not promise them a fixed share of its business forever. Instead, it shifts quotas among the suppliers in proportion to how efficient they are.

By restricting access to only two suppliers, Toyota gives them the possibility of acquiring power. But the amount of power they actually get depends on how much they invest. In effect, Toyota creates a form of managed competition, whereby it levels the playing field every so often by sharing all the innovations among the suppliers. As suggested by Rajan and Zingales (1998a), a policy of creating limited competition between suppliers, and leveling the playing field every so often, can spur much more specialized investment by suppliers than if the supplier were part of the same vertically integrated firm and confident of receiving the firm's business.

### 4.3. Why Is Access Valuable?

We have cheated a little. We have argued in both examples above that employees or units can be given incentives to make specialized investments that bind them to the enterprise if they are given privileged access. But what makes access worth having?

Certainly, the brokerage could possess some inanimate assets such as a reputation that are a source of surplus, and that is what the new broker desires to attach himself to. Similarly for Toyota's suppliers. But inanimate assets need not be the source of economic surplus that makes access valuable. Instead, the web of past specific investment that creates complementarities between different agents may itself be what is valuable and worth gaining access to. Moreover, by directing these specific investments appropriately, it is possible for an individual or group to place itself at the center and gain some of the command-and-control

[24] This is similar to the customer–supplier relationship typical of technology firms operating in the Silicon Valley. While all firms develop a very close relationship with a limited number of customers/suppliers with which they share crucial information, they also make sure that no customer or supplier accounts for more than 20% of the business, to maintain and foster competition (Saxenian 1996). See also Aoki (1998).

powers that otherwise emanated only from the ownership of critical inanimate assets.

To see this, let us reexamine Salomon's bond trading group. We argued earlier that Salomon had little power over the group. But the group itself may have been a tightly bound unit, connected to each other through specialized investment and responding to the commands of its head. There are a number of reasons why the head of a bond-trading group (the Meriwether equivalent) may have substantial control over its members. For one, he is the focus of the group's outside image and is the source of their capital. More important, the head would have coordinated task allocations (i.e., controlled access) so that each member of the group is likely to be specialized to some aspect of bond trading. One understands how to uncover bonds that seem underpriced, another knows the institutional details and tax laws that may sometimes create an illusion of underpricing, while a third has the ability to negotiate for their purchase at a reasonable price. Since each member of the group is specialized in a narrow aspect of bond trading, individually their skills are not very valuable, but collectively they have immense value. And since the head of the group provides the coordination function to all these specialized skills, he becomes indispensable to the group, and effectively obtains control rights. A new member would value access tremendously and accept the head's task assignments unquestioningly, knowing that the rest of the group is attached to the head, and the group collectively is a well-oiled unit generating tremendous surplus. In a sense, by giving limited access to a group member, the head gives her some power over surplus. But once she is specialized, the head obtains her loyalty, and the collective loyalty of specialized members enables him to command the group, including even unspecialized members.[25]

## 4.4. Distinctive Characteristics of the New Enterprise

When the ownership of inanimate assets is no longer the primary source of power, mutual dependencies and specialization between various units of the enterprise are what make it distinctive, and allow power to govern transactions. Since ownership is relatively unimportant, and human capital is not tied to inanimate assets, the legal definition of the firm, which centers around ownership of the inanimate assets, is not very helpful. Instead, the unit of economic organization, which we call "the enterprise," has less distinctive boundaries. Something is more a part of

[25] See Rajan and Zingales (1998b) for a more detailed model. The head commits to sharing surplus and thereby obtains control over access.

the enterprise when it has greater complementarities with the rest of the enterprise. So Salomon's bond trading group is not really part of the Salomon enterprise, though each individual trader is a member of the bond trading enterprise. Toyota's suppliers are members of the Toyota enterprise even though they are separately incorporated. On the other hand, GM's suppliers, who have traditionally been placed in competition with each other without any privileged access, are not part of the GM enterprise.

Certainly, there will be great reluctance to abandon the idea that a firm's boundaries are determined by the common ownership of assets. There are still a large number of old corporations (though far fewer of the young ones) for which this is the best description of their boundaries. Moreover, this definition is very convenient for jurisprudence for it makes issues such as antitrust easy to comprehend and act on. But the definition is becoming more and more anachronistic and will someday have to be abandoned for something like our definition, which is less clear-cut but more realistic.

Another change is that the surplus in the modern enterprise is no longer concentrated at the top. Since the enterprise gets power over a unit only because it commits to share surplus with the unit, the surplus is shared much more evenly through the enterprise. This democratization of rents expands the job of governance beyond simply watching the top managers.

Finally, unlike in the vertically integrated firm, the enterprise need not be commonly owned. Since no single unit requires enormous investment there is no need to have a large number of investors. Thus ownership and operational control in the enterprise can be much more closely associated than in the past.

### 4.5. Mergers and Acquisitions

We have argued that large vertically integrated firms are harder to control today, which is why some of them are breaking apart. But what explains the tremendous increase in merger activity in developed economies in the last few years? Is it evidence against our arguments?

A sizable fraction of the mergers are horizontal mergers. As we have discussed, firms are losing power because of various changes in the marketplace. Horizontal mergers are an old-fashioned way of regaining power, specifically, market power. This has the benefit of strengthening a firm's hold over its employees and recovering some of the command and control that has been slipping away. A horizontal merger therefore postpones the necessity of reconfiguring the governance system to adapt to changes. Of course, there are other rationales for horizontal mergers that have to do with other forces sweeping industries. For example, they permit easier capacity reduction in a declining industry (see Mitchell and Mulherin 1996).

But there are some industries where a number of vertical mergers have taken place. For example, in the media industry, giants like Time Warner or Disney now control everything from content creation to distribution, while earlier they accounted for only one portion of the value chain, movie production. Why is this?

The changes we have described before have not always pushed in the direction of deintegration. For example, in this industry they have had the effect of changing the nature of the critical asset, and thus enhancing its value. A movie is not simply meant to entertain. Instead, a movie is often the media event with which a brand name is launched – and under this umbrella, toys, books, videos, CDs, and clothing are sold. As with all modern brand names, its impact on the public consciousness is for a very limited duration. But during this period, it is very valuable, and substantial investments have to be made through the value chain to enhance it. For example, a movie may have to be shown longer than directly profitable in order to enhance merchandise sales, or merchandise may be sold more aggressively to boost a forthcoming movie.

The critical asset now is the brand name not the movie, and the extent to which it becomes important depends on investments made by each part of the value chain. So rather than one part of the value chain owning the asset and distorting the incentives of the other parts of the value chain to invest, it makes more sense for the brand name to be centrally owned by headquarters. While the entire value chain belongs to the same firm, each part gains power through specific investments, giving it the incentive to make it (in much the way of multiple suppliers having greater incentive to invest since none has a monopoly). Conversely, since the brand name is critical to each part, headquarters has control over the value chain.

Finally, it may be somewhat Panglossian to assume that all the mergers we see add to efficiency. For example, commercial banks have spent huge amounts of money trying to become universal banks offering the entire spectrum of financial services. A number of banks (most recently, Barclays) have withdrawn from such an effort after realizing that they simply do not have the ability to control such an operation effectively. Others (for example, Deutsche Bank) persist despite past failures. Only the future can tell which strategy is more efficient, but our theory offers some ways to form priors.

## V. Consequences for Enterprise Governance

The main objective of corporate governance was traditionally identified with the maximization of shareholder's value. In a world where the boundaries of the enterprise were well defined and the primary concern was reducing the agency cost at the vertex of the organization, this was translated to imply that the duty of directors was to monitor top management and limit its rents.[26]

The major changes in the nature of firms we have described thus far, however, call for a radical rethinking of the objectives and methods of governance. Applying the old approach to the new type of firms can be extremely costly, as illustrated by the saga of Saatchi & Saatchi.

### 5.1. Old Governance of the New Enterprise: Saatchi & Saatchi

In 1994, following several years of lackluster performance, U.S. fund managers, who controlled 30 percent of the shares, opposed the award of a generous option package to Maurice Saatchi, the charismatic chairman of Saatchi & Saatchi. Together with his brother Charles, Maurice had founded the company in the early 1970s and built it up through mergers into the largest advertising agency in the world.

The opposition of the fund managers led to the departure of Maurice Saatchi and was quickly followed by the resignation of several key senior executives. These executives, together with the Saatchi brothers, started a rival agency (M&C Saatchi), which in a short period of time captured some of the most important accounts of the original Saatchi & Saatchi, including British Airways, Mars, Dixons, and Gallaher. Interestingly, one of the executives who left wrote in his resignation letter: "I am not leaving the company. The company has left me."[27] The original firm, which later changed its name to Cordiant, was grievously damaged.

In hindsight, the mistake the U.S. fund managers made was to treat Saatchi & Saatchi as a traditional company, with clear boundaries defined by its assets. Because they had ownership (thanks to their 30 percent holding of the votes), they may have thought they controlled the firm. Instead, much of the firm broke off as they attempted to exercise their traditional ownership rights.

In this new environment, corporate governance becomes a more complex task. To begin with, maximization of shareholders' value is not

---

[26] See for instance Hermalin and Weisbach (1998).
[27] Valerie Grove, "Maurice Saatchi finds his voice" *Times* Newspapers Limited, January 5, 1996.

necessarily the right objective. The theoretical justification for this objective was derived from the "nexus of contracts" view of the firm.[28] According to Fama and Jensen (1983), each party belonging to the nexus has contractual claims on the surplus with predetermined payoffs. The exceptions are shareholders, who accept a residual payoff because they have a comparative advantage in diversifying risk. Maximization of shareholders' value, then, necessarily leads to maximization of the value of the enterprise. But in a world of incomplete contracts and multiple sources of power, the contractual protection provided to the parties in the nexus of contracts is necessarily incomplete. As a result, almost all parties can be, at some time or the other, residual claimants. Maximization of shareholders' value does not necessarily lead to maximization of enterprise value.

Second, even if we were to accept this traditional objective, the way it should be pursued by directors is very different. In what follows, we attempt to outline how the duties of a corporate director might change with changes in the enterprise.

### 5.2. Protecting the Integrity of the Enterprise

A completely new task that directors are, and will be facing, as a result of the changes in the nature of the firm is to protect its integrity. When most of the value of a firm was embedded in assets that could be owned, its boundaries were fixed and there was nothing directors could, or were required to, do to guard them. But now most of the value comes from assets that cannot be easily appropriated, like information or human capital. This raises a new challenge.

As the Saatchi & Saatchi example indicates, directors' actions can affect the boundaries of the firm. It may be too late to intervene when surplus is being divided because directors may have little power to mold the firm despite having ownership. Instead, intervention should come earlier as the enterprise is being put together. It is at this stage that directors should intervene to make sure that customers, suppliers, or employees are not given the opportunity to accumulate too much power, which would allow them to expropriate a large fraction of the value of the enterprise.

For example, banks are linking up with Internet firms to provide better services to customers. A major source of concern is how much access the

---

[28] The "nexus of contracts" view of the firm essentially suggests that all parties enter into fixed contracts with the one party who becomes both the residual claimant and the possessor of control rights. Given that he has the residual claim, this party has the incentive to improve value.

external providers will have to the banks' customers. Since customer relationships are a major (perhaps *the* major) resource the banks possess, losing them to the provider might hurt the bank and thus its shareholders more than any agency problem at the top. Similarly, before attempting to fire Maurice Saatchi, Saatchi & Saatchi directors should have anticipated the problem and ensured that the company was not too dependent upon the Saatchi brothers. The exercise of governance is no longer simply a matter of casting a vote but also may involve a long prior period of organizational design.

In a sense, organizational design is a major service the venture capitalist provides a fledgling firm. At the early stages of the development of an enterprise, when the structure of the firm is still amorphous, it is all too easy for the founder to insinuate herself into every relationship. While this may make the small firm function well, it makes it harder for it to grow beyond the capacities of the founder. Also, outside financing becomes hard because the founder controls so much power. One of the roles of the venture capitalist is to make sure that the management of the firm is professionalized so that it is not too dependent upon the entrepreneur or any specific professional manager. In this way, they make the firm easier to finance, initially by themselves, and eventually by dispersed outsiders.

We have focused thus far on issues of organizational design. The new enterprise also may be run very differently. For example, it changes the need, and the tools available, for motivating employees. We conclude with the example of stock options to show how the theory may explain operational changes in the enterprise.

### 5.3. Motivating the Employees

As the control rights associated with the common ownership of a large body of assets have diminished, there has been less need to hold these assets together. As fewer assets are owned together, it has become much easier to use ownership to motivate employees, in part because employees can have a larger stake, and in part because the share price corresponds more closely to factors in their control. Thus while the control rights associated with ownership may have diminished, the role of ownership in providing motivation may have increased.

A case in point are the new knowledge-based high-technology companies, where employees are not merely automata in charge of operating valuable assets but valuable assets themselves, operating with commodity-like physical assets. Reflecting these views, we have heard a founder of a small start-up company say that his biggest concern was to provide the right future reward for key employees, not for the financiers. In fact, employees – in his own words – "do not invest a fraction of their portfolio, they invest their life." Employees need to be motivated or – to borrow a popular term from the managerial literature – "empowered." At the same time, the firm has to ensure that it retains some ability to govern the empowered.

One clever solution to this problem is the award of long-term stock options, which vest over a long period of time. Stock options ensure a share of the rents to the crucial employees. At the same time they do not give them voting power (at least until the time they are exercised), eliminating potential sources of conflicts (see Hansmann 1996 and Rajan and Zingales 1998a). Delayed vesting also diffuses the threat of departure of key employees.[29]

This highlights a new important trend in corporate governance: the generalized award of stock options to employees. While there exists a large literature, both theoretical and empirical, on the role played by stock options to reward top executives, the use of stock options to reward lower level employees has received little attention, in spite of the magnitude of the phenomenon.[30]

There are many other changes in the nature of the governance of the new enterprise that deserve further study. We do not have the space here to examine these. But hopefully we have convinced the reader that the nature of the enterprise has changed, and there is a need to reinvestigate the issue of governance.

## VI. Conclusions

The terms of the modern debate on corporate governance were set in the 1930s, influenced in large part by changes in the nature of the firm that occurred in the previous fifty years. In those days the dominant model was a vertically integrated firm, controlling a large set of unique assets through a rigid command-and-control system. As a consequence, corporate governance mainly focused on the agency problem at the vertex of the organizational pyramid.

Since then the nature of the enterprise has changed greatly: human capital has replaced physical capital as the main source of value and vertically integrated firms have given way to more competition in the intermediate product markets. We argue that these changes require also a

---

[29] On this see also Rodriguez-Palenzuela (1997).

[30] For example, in 1997 Microsoft awarded $400 million (10% of the earnings) in stock options to employees.

change in the focus of the corporate governance debate. We should spend less time discussing how to strengthen the rights of dispersed owners and more time on mechanisms to control and retain human capital. We sketch some ways in which this new approach could fundamentally change the role corporate directors should play. As the new enterprise becomes more dominant on the corporate landscape, these issues should be studied in greater detail.

### References

Aghion, P., and J. Tirole. (1997). "Formal and Real Authority in Organizations." *Journal of Political Economy*, CV: 1–27.

Alchian, A., and H. Demsetz. (1972). "Production, Information Costs and Economic Organization." *American Economic Review*, 777–805.

Aoki, M. (1998). "The Corporate Governance of Venture Capital: Silicon Valley." Mimeo, Stanford University.

Baker, G., R. Gibbons, and K. J. Murphy. (1997). "Implicit Contracts and the Theory of the Firm." Working Paper, Harvard Business School.

Berle, A., and G. Means. (1932). *The Modern Corporation and Private Property*. New York: World.

Blair, M. M. (1995). *Ownership and Control*. Washington D.C.: Brookings Institution.

Chandler, Alfred. (1977). *The Visible Hand*. Cambridge, Mass.: Belknap Press. (1990). *Scale and Scope*. Cambridge, Mass.: Belknap Press.

Coase, R. (1937). "The Nature of the Firm." *Economica*, 4: 386–405.

Demsetz, R. (1996). "The Re-Tooling of the Banking Industry: Evidence from the Labor Force." Working Paper, Federal Reserve Bank of New York.

Drucker, Peter F. (1946). *Concept of the Corporation*. New York: John Day Company.

Emerson, R. (1962). "Power Dependence Relations." *American Sociological Review*, 27: 31–41.

Fama, E., and M. Jensen. (1983). "Separation of Ownership and Control." *Journal of Law and Economics*, 26 (June): 301–25.

Gertner, R. (1998). "Coordination, Dispute Resolution, and the Scope of the Firm." Working Paper, University of Chicago.

Grossman, S., and O. Hart. (1986). "The Costs and the Benefits of Ownership: A Theory of Vertical and Lateral Integration." *Journal of Political Economy*, 94: 691–719.

Hansmann, H. (1996). *The Ownership of Enterprise*. Cambridge, Mass.: Belknap, Harvard.

Hart, O. (1995). *Firms, Contracts, and Financial Structure*. New York: Oxford University Press.

Hart, O., and J. Moore. (1990). "Property Rights and the Nature of the Firm." *Journal of Political Economy*, 98: 1119–58.

Hermalin, B., and M. Weisbach. (1998). "Endogenously Chosen Boards of Directors and Their Monitoring of the CEO." *American Economic Review*, 88: 96–118.

Hirshleifer, J. (1995). "Anarchy and Its Breakdown." *Journal of Political Economy*, 103: 26–52.

Holmstrom, Bengt. (1997). "The Firm as a Subeconomy." Mimeo, Massachusetts Institute of Technology.

Holmstrom, Bengt, and J. Roberts. (1998). "The Boundaries of the Firm Revisited." *Journal of Economic Perspectives*, 12: 73–94.

Jensen, M. C., and W. Meckling. (1976). "Theory of the Firm: Managerial Behavior, Agency Costs and Capital Structure." *Journal of Financial Economics*, 3: 305–60.

Klein, B., Crawford, and A. Alchian. (1978). "Vertical Integration, Appropriable Rents and the Competitive Contracting Process." *Journal of Law and Economics*, 21: 297–326.

Machin, Stephen, and John Van Reenen. (1998). "Technology and Changes in Skill Structure: Evidence from Seven OECD Countries." *Quarterly Journal of Economics*, 113, 4: 1215–44.

Masten, Scott. (1988). "A Legal Basis for the Firm." *Journal of Law, Economics and Organization*, 4: 181–98.

Milgrom, P., and J. Roberts. (1990). "Bargaining Costs, Influence Costs, and the Organization of Economic Activity." In J. Alt and K. Shepsle (Eds.), *Perspectives on Positive Political Economy*. Cambridge: Cambridge University Press.

Mitchell, M., and H. Mulherin. (1996). "The Impact of Industry Shocks on Takeover and Restructuring Activity." *Journal of Financial Economics*, 41(2): 193–229.

Pfeffer, J. (1981). *Power in Organizations*. Marshfield, Mass.: Pitman Publishing, Inc.

Rajan, R., and L. Zingales. (1998a). "Power in a Theory of the Firm." *Quarterly Journal of Economics*, CXIII: 387–432.

 (1998b). "The Firm as a Dedicated Hierarchy: A Theory of the Origins and Growth of Firms." Working paper, University of Chicago, http://gsblgz.uchicago.edu.

 (1998c). "The Tyranny of the Inefficient: An Inquiry into the Adverse Consequences of Power Struggles." Working paper, University of Chicago, http://gsblgz.uchicago.edu.

Rajan, R., H. Servaes, and L. Zingales. (1998). "The Cost of Diversity: Diversification Discount and Inefficient Investment." Working paper, NBER, http://gsblgz.uchicago.edu.

Rodriguez-Palenzuela, D. (1997). "Endogenous Spillovers and the Theory of the Firm." Mimeo Universität Pompeu Fabra.

Rotemberg, J. (1994). "Power in Profit-Maximizing Organizations." *Journal of Economics and Management Strategy* 2: 163–98.

Saxenian, A. (1996). *Regional Advantage*. Cambridge Mass.: Harvard University Press.

Skaperdas, Stergios. (1992). "Cooperation, Conflict, and Power in the Absence of Property Rights." *American Economic Review*, 82: 720–39.

Shleifer, A., and R. Vishny. (1997). "A Survey of Corporate Governance." *Journal of Finance*, 52: 737–83.

Sloan, A. (1963). *My Years with General Motors*. Garden City, N.Y.: Doubleday.

Tirole, J. (1998). Corporate Governance, mimeo.

Williamson, O. (1985). *The Economic Institutions of Capitalism*. New York: The Free Press.

Zingales, L. (1998). "Corporate Governance." *The New Palgrave Dictionary of Economics and the Law*.

## Discussion

*Comments on Rajan and Zingales, "The Governance of the New Enterprise"*

### A. Carmen Matutes

This essay presents an interesting approach to the governance of new corporations. The essay is thought provoking and a pleasure to read.

In a nutshell the message of the essay is as follows. The new corporation is no longer a collection of physical assets. Rather, human capital as well as ties to customers and suppliers have become the main asset. Valuable resources generate power, but human capital cannot be appropriated by third parties because of antislavery laws. By inducing specialization to the group, the head of the group gets power. In exchange, individuals have access to the group's valuable resources, the complementarities created by the group. Why should shareholders be in control? They are not: they are neither the residual claimants, nor do they have the ability to exercise ownership rights (except in theory).

The question arises as to how insiders become powerful. The essay distinguishes between alternative definitions of power. In particular, it opposes to "how tough a negotiator one is" as a possible definition the alternative of "how many valuable resources she brings to the group." A different view of bargaining power, possibly more market oriented, would instead replace these questions by "how tough a negotiator one can be" or "how specific to the firm and well known to outsiders are the resources that the potential employee can bring," respectively. However, answering the question as to how tough a negotiator one can be requires addressing the issue of how valuable one is to the firm and to outsiders, and how much do outsiders know about it. That is, the two questions are essentially the same and the answer to either determines the equilibrium contract that will prevail in the market. Admittedly, the contract need not be complete. Still, it will reflect the parties' opportunities.

In my view the essay could be clearer about what the specific relationship is between power within the firm and the market for human capital. In particular, we are told that by inducing specialization to the group the leader can appropriate rents associated with the human capital of the members of the group. But if the members specialize, it must be optimal for them to do so. The authors suggest that it is indeed optimal to specialize and thus obtain "access." What this means is that the head must commit (implicitly) to share the surplus. That is, the head must give at least as much surplus (power) as the worker gets outside and thus the head must limit her own power. If so, what does it mean that power equals control over and above that determined through a competitive market? In other words, once the group is formed and if properly led, due to complementarities, the head may become very powerful, but ex ante, before the group is formed the leader must have some exogenous power or members of the group must not have other opportunities (i.e., be powerless) and hence the argument is somewhat circular, or else team members are bounded rational. More generally, if human capital has become the essential asset, it is important to understand better how the contracts between the firm and these special workers are determined and how they interact with power acquisition within the firm. Clearly, the role of market transparency cannot be overemphasized in this sense,[1] yet information issues have been left aside in this essay.[2]

Regarding empirical implications, the essay predicts that stock should be quite general. This is also consistent with different strands of the literature on (implicit) labor contracts.[3] A more novel implication of the essay is the prediction that as human capital becomes more important one should expect flatter hierarchies. That is, as most employees become more powerful, those on top of hierarchies become relatively less powerful. It would be interesting to know whether firms such as consulting, business, or law firms have traditionally had flatter hierarchies than other less human-capital–intensive businesses. Likewise evidence about the changing role of shareholders as the corporation has switched emphasis from physical assets to human capital would enhance the value

---

[1] See in particular, Burguet, Caminal, and Matutes (1999), who explore the impact of the information leakage to outsiders about the quality of the worker on equilibrium contracts, quits, and layoffs.

[2] This is so perhaps because the role of information within the corporation has already been analyzed extensively. See for instance, Holmstrom and Tirole (1987).

[3] See, for instance, Akerlof and Katz (1989) or Hashimoto (1981).

of the essay. Generally speaking, developing and specially testing empirically the implications of the essay would be a very welcome contribution.

The authors are right to emphasize that control in the new corporation is not a by-product of ownership, and I find this essay a particularly interesting and promising attempt to explore new avenues.

### References

Akerlof, G., and M. Katz. (1989). "Workers' Trust Funds, and the Logic of Wage Profiles." *Quarterly Journal of Economics*, 104: 525–36.

Burguet, R., R. Caminal, and C. Matutes. (1999). "Golden Cages and Gloomy Freedom: Optimal Switching Costs in Labour Contracting." CEPR, Discussion Paper No. 2070.

Hashimoto, M. (1981). "Firm Specific Human Capital as a Shared Investment," *American Economic Review*, 71: 475–82.

Holmstrom, B., and J. Tirole. (1987). "The Theory of the Firm." In R. Schmslensee and R. Willig (Eds.), *The Handbook of Industrial Organization*. Amsterdam: North-Holland.

## Comments on Rajan and Zingales, "The Governance of the New Enterprise"

*B. Joan E. Ricart*

The essay we have in hand is a very interesting and suggestive piece of work dealing with an important and relevant issue: What is the theory of the firm for the new corporation? This work is a continuation of previous papers by the same authors, most of them in working paper form, developed from the seminal paper recently published in the *Quarterly Journal of Economics*.

The starting point of the argument of the essay is the pervasive relevance of human capital in organizations. If the key assets of a firm are tangible assets with possibilities of developing scale and scope advantage, property of these assets, together with long-term contracts, gives owners both the residual rights to control (power, in the terminology of the essay) and allows them to appropriate the returns from these assets. But in most firms, the relevant assets are intangible assets mostly associated with human capital. How then can "the owner" develop power in businesses where knowledge and privileged relationships are the key assets for competitive advantage?

The essay develops two mechanisms to get power, defined as residual rights of control:

(1) The "de jure" mechanism, when the law allocates residual rights over some resources to a given party, as it does with ownership. However, this mechanism is limited in presence of human capital.

(2) The "de facto" mechanism, based on the ability to control access to the group when individual specialized knowledge is enhanced by this access. In this way, specialization creates dependence, making individual rights more valuable but also creating new residual rights and providing, as a consequence, a mechanism to appropriate rents from human capital.

In a nutshell, the owner of a valuable resource has power, whether the resource is intrinsically valuable or made valuable through a process of specialization. He may have effective control over human capital of others because their human capital is either specialized to his own or specialized to an asset he owns. The specialization creates new control rights and therefore new power.

This argument, previously developed in other papers, is enlightening and illustrates a process by which cospecialization creates residual rights of control. However, it is based in the same philosophy of the classical theory of the firm associated to tangible assets; that is, it is essentially a theory of value appropriation, instead of value creation, an argument we will further develop later on. First, let's see some of the implications of the theory being proposed in this essay.

The new corporation has three distinctive characteristics: (1) The legal boundary as defined by ownership of physical assets is not a very helpful definition. (2) The surplus of the firm is not concentrated at the top but there is a democratization of rents. (3) Vertically integrated forms need not be commonly owned.

Such radical differences in firm characteristics have to have *important implications for the governance of the new corporation*: Using Saatchi & Saatchi as an example, the authors conclude about two main roles that should be incorporated in the debate on corporate governance: (1) The protection of the integrity of the enterprise when the key assets are things like information or human capital. (2) The motivation of employees by different means like stock options because it is the network of employees, the main source of access power into the firm.

In general, one can conclude that the authors develop an interesting theory and apply it to study the relevant question of governance of the new corporation, trying to show the different implications in contrast to other theories of the firm. However, arguments used in the applications are still incomplete, showing that this essay is still *preliminary* and more work is needed to develop the complete arguments and to select the

230

important implications. So said, and as a way to conclude these short comments on the essay, I would like to go back to my previous claim that this theory is another economic theory of value appropriation and I believe that the important managerial problem is *value creation*. In a similar way that Grossman and Hart showed to us that *ownership* matters for the right incentives to invest in specialized assets, this theory shows us that *access* may play a role similar to ownership and, therefore, it affects investment decision in specialized human capital. As ownership, access is a power instrument to appropriate rents. Obviously rent appropriation is fundamental because it provides incentives to invest. However, it is able to explain only the development of "co-specialized" human capital and it does not explain the value of *innovation*.

Many of the examples in the essay use privileged relationships as the intangible assets being considered. These are human capital assets people "own." However, today the problem of value creation is the development of organizational capabilities that allows new forms of combination of human capital and provides the right vision so that, through creativity and innovation, new value is being created. It is the combination of specialized knowledge in the context of an organization that creates innovation value. And this combination ability is based on capabilities that are socially complex, path dependent, and difficult to imitate, and, as a consequence, the basis for sustainable competitive advantage. Then value is created.

This context for creative combination of knowledge requires empowering, teamwork, employability contract, shared ownership, and so on, explaining governance forms that this essay tries to explain based in alternative arguments. And more important, there is an intrinsic contradiction between economic theories of value appropriation such as the one presented here, and institutional frameworks for innovation by knowledge combination, where the concepts of trust, social networks, shared vision, and similar organizational issues substitute the minimizing transaction cost implicit in value appropriation theories. Some relevant references in this direction are Ghoshal and Moran (1996), Nahapiet and Ghoshal (1998), and Tsai and Ghoshal (1998). It would be nice to work in the direction of trying to reconcile both views of the world.

No doubt of the greatest interest for academics and practitioners is the development of new theories of the firm or the combination of them to develop a more general theory of management. Furthermore, it is extremely necessary to have such theory be used as the basis for a theory of corporate governance sensible to a stakeholder's view as a collaborative system. This is a very important issue for the future of effective governance of new and old corporations.

## References

Ghoshal, S., and P. Moran. (1996). "Bad for Practice: A Critique of Transaction Cost Theory." *Academy of Management Review*, 21: 13–47.

Nahapiet, J., and S. Ghoshal. (1998). "Social Capital, Intellectual Capital and the Organizational Advantage." *Academy of Management Review*, 23: 242–66.

Tsai, W., and S. Ghoshal. (1998). "Social Capital and Value Creation: The Role of Intrafirm Networks." *Academy of Management Journal*, 41: 464–76.

# Index

adverse selection, 64, 101

agency costs: of free cash flow, 118–22; of internal finance, 114

agency theory: in approach to corporate governance, 4–9, 62, 76, 85–6; costs of free cash flow, 118–22; shareholders and managers in, 23

Aggarwal, Rajesh, 92

Aghion, P., 11–12, 60

Alchian, Armen A., 56

Allen, Franklin, 64, 85–8, 143, 147, 149

Aoki, M., 14, 46

Austria: corporate ownership concentration, 142

Baker, George P., 91

banking systems: hausbank system in Germany, 46–7, 77, 103; main bank system in Germany, 104–8; United Kingdom, 50, 140

Baron, J. N., 176n8, 179

Baums, T., 126–7

bearer shares, 97, 102

Becht, M., 142

Benston, George, 161–2

Berger, Philip, 74

Berle, A. A., 1, 23, 76, 201, 209, 215

Bhagat, Sanjai, 37

Billett, Matthew T., 93

Black, Bernard, 37

board of directors: in corporate governance, 6–7; Japanese corporate governance system, 24; shareholders' control through, 26–8, 37–8; staggering election of, 42. *See also* supervisory boards

Bolton, Patrick, 44, 96

Burkart, Mike, 41, 44, 64

Burton, M. D., 179

Carlin, W., 13, 152, 154–5, 160, 162–3

cash flows: differences in firm and sector, 115–16; rights of shareholders, 142, 161; as signal related to investment, 116–17. *See also* free cash flow theory

CG. *See* corporate governance

Chandler, Alfred, 207

Charkham, Jonathan, 47

Clapham, J. H., 140

Coase, Ronald H., 62, 203

Codetermination Act, Germany, 28

compensation: dependent on share price, 38–9; executive, 38–9, 91–2

competition: as control mechanism, 61–2; discipline effect on management, 56–61, 90–3; in firm's evolution, 65–7; in market for corporate control, 41–2; for markets, 67–76, 88; between nonprofit and for-profit organizations, 53–6; within product cycle, 74–6, 86; in product markets to discipline managers, 56–61; between profit-maximizing and nonprofit firms, 53–6; role of, 10–11; in role of takeover in product markets, 67–76; substitutibility between corporate governance and, 11

complementarities: building through specialization, 215; defined, 215

contracts: complete, 96, 98; contracts view of the firm, 222; corporate governance as branch of contract theory, 96; incomplete, 89, 96, 98, 206n12; protection of outside shareholders, 125

control, corporate: in absence of outside financing, 112–15; active and passive, 6; competition as mechanism for, 61–2; in corporate governance, 6; effect of ownership concentration on, 142–4; market for corporate, 9, 23–4, 40–8, 110–12; in new-style firms, 14–15; relation to banks in selected countries, 126–8; trading control for financing or credit, 100–12

corporate governance: agency approach and alternative, 4–9, 62–5, 76; in Berle/Means-type organization, 1, 23, 76, 201, 209, 215; codetermination in Germany, 28–9; competition in evolutionary, 65–7; complete-contracts analysis, 96; creditors, 8–9, 48–9;

233